THE HUNTER PRESS
ATLANTA

THE
DISPOSABLE
MALE

SEX, LOVE AND MONEY
YOUR WORLD THROUGH DARWIN'S EYES

MICHAEL GILBERT

**THE
HUNTER
PRESS**

Cover illustration by Gary Overacre
Cover design by Robin Kemkes
Interior design by Sherry Roberts

Manufactured in the United States of America

10 9 8 7 6 1 2 3 4 5

Publisher's Cataloging-in-Publication
(*Provided by Quality Books, Inc.*)

Gilbert, Michael, 1943-
  The disposable male : sex, love and money : your
world through Darwin's eyes / Michael Gilbert.

  p. cm.
  Includes index.
  LCCN 2006920246
  ISBN 0-9776552-3-7

  1. Evolutionary psychology. 2. Evolution (Biology)
3. Sex role. 4. Man-woman relationships.   I. Title.

BF698.95.G55 2006   155.7
                   QBI06-600036

For information about bulk purchases, please contact:
www.thehunterpress.com

TABLE OF CONTENTS

INTRODUCTION

THE BIG PICTURE

THE EVERYDAY MALE IS IN TROUBLE. IT SEEMS THAT MANHOOD NO longer requires preparation. Boys stumble without a map onto the pathways to masculinity, forced to learn by their own devices the essential traits and qualities of authentic manliness. Without a clear sense of purpose, young men are hardly motivated or encouraged to support their partner and family, much less serve their community. Men's ancient and defining roles as resource provider and defender have been down-sized and outsourced. Declared obsolete and cast adrift, the modern hunter is searching for a new job description.

Meanwhile, women have been propelled into unfamiliar territory, encouraged or forced to support themselves and build careers in today's long stretch between puberty, marriage, and beyond. The contemporary woman has become a hunter as well as a gatherer. Barely one in three American women held a paying job in 1950; almost three-quarters do now. And there's not much relief when a husband and children are added to the equation: two-thirds of women with children under six now hold down a job compared to less than 20 percent half a century ago. For many of these sleep-deprived women, forced to assume the triple role of wife, mother, and employee, "you can have it all" has turned into a cruel joke. "You have to *do* it all" is the not-so-funny punch line.

Despite all the changes over the last two generations—or perhaps because of them—young women often report that they are struggling to cope in a man's world while many young men believe women get all the breaks. As a result, America is turning into a culture of severely diminished men without distinctive roles and responsibilities, and over-burdened women trying to balance too many agendas. In the process, masculinity has become a disease, femininity has become a burden.

According to recent surveys, young adults of both sexes now experience unprecedented confusion around gender roles and mating behavior. As today's "twixters" move into their prime reproductive years, often graduating from broken homes, they enter a lengthy, unsettled breakup culture of "no rings, no strings," according to a Rutgers University study on the state of marriage. Modern romance, if that's the word, seems reduced to a kind of use-and-discard universe of coarse sexual barter. The ageless and intimate masculine-feminine union turns ever more edgy and fragile. "Trust no one" has become today's social mantra. To many observers, contemporary mating has begun to look like a battleground of broken dreams. Minor skirmishes and countless little hurts and bruises add up to a crude, transient social culture.

The intimate bond between men and women, the primacy of reproduction, and the lifelong commitment to wedlock are going the way of the dinosaur. Increasingly isolated, we are opting for freedom over permanence and marrying later, if we marry at all. We are living alone or living together without formal ties and becoming single parents in record-breaking numbers.

In the anonymous cosmopolitan landscapes in which most of us now live, families and clan are often scattered and kinship ties broken. Statistics chronicling the disintegration of the family are as familiar as they are distressing. From preparing meals to housing the elderly, family functions have been outsourced or subcontracted. Three out of four young adults tell pollsters they are less family-oriented than their parents. Our friendships also feel more temporary and mercenary even as trusted family, kin, and community supports erode. In the big metropolis, we are hardly accountable to anyone anymore.

Not coincidentally, polls regularly support the notion that American society is increasingly abrasive and selfish. Reports of anxiousness and depression in the general population reached epidemic levels even before 9/11. Although the ordinary citizen earns nearly three times the income of his or her counterpart at the end of World War II—and lives in more than twice the household space—levels of clinical depression are, depending on how you define it, three to ten times greater in just two generations.

A blue chip national commission charged with studying youth

preparedness concluded, "Never before has one generation of American children been less healthy, less cared for, or less prepared for life than their parents were at the same age." The American Psychological Association now rates the everyday levels of anxiety among children aged nine to seventeen as exceeding the scores of psychiatric patients just two generations ago.

Assessing these enormous social upheavals calls for a perspective both wide and deep. Yet seldom are we able to pause on the treadmill of twenty-first century life to consider where we've come from, to ponder our current predicament, or to explore the root causes of modern sexual confusion and social disarray. Perhaps what is missing is a panoramic sense of history, the bigger picture. For instance, the embattled institution of wedlock may be just a few thousand years old, but the intimate pair bond between the sexes that drives it is a partnership anchored in ancient origins, bearing a long and colorful legacy. That it has survived this long is no accident.

Bewitched, Bothered, and Bewildered

For as far back as history records and the natural sciences can trace, men and women have shared common goals even if they often had opposing agendas. Dependent upon each other, the sexes' unique tasks and specialties have been etched out and deepened over the ages by necessity, chance, and circumstance. During humanity's recent leap from an eternity as primitive foragers to today's city sophisticates, the hard-wired and complementary feminine and masculine energies so essential to our success have been obscured and devalued, weighed down with a paralyzing modern ambiguity. Men and women have gone from nature's perfect partners to uneasy, cosmopolitan competitors.

Yet despite humanity's stunning dash from hunter-gatherer societies to the edgy frontiers of cyberspace and today's information overload, our biological core and our basic instincts, built up over eons, have hardly changed. While men and women today imagine that they are thoroughly modern, that they have been liberated from nature's primitive yoke, our current motivations, aptitudes, and capacities have in fact been laboriously molded and massaged into place over millions of years.

The Disposable Male puts forward the view that the individual and collective detachment from our natural heritage is the primary culprit behind the marginalization of men, the overburdening of women, and the failings of modern relationships. Today's social disarray and many of the everyday anxieties of our time result from being out of touch with our natural inheritance—our innate biology and evolutionary anchors. Estranged from our earthly foundations, nature has become something we visit on the weekend. Primitive creatures adrift in a sea of modern abstraction, we have lost our natural compass.

When we examine today's social problems and the challenges of contemporary life through the lens of our natural history, we begin to discover an important, perhaps unintended, modern predicament: we are not getting the best from men and we are asking too much of women. Except in the upper-most alpha male perches, boys and men are being systematically neutered, disparaged, and displaced. Masculinity is being bleached out.

As it fades away, we are exposed to a backlash—unhealthy parodies of male overcompensation and destructive acting out. Down in the ranks, men find themselves bewitched by the presence of women in their traditional domains, bothered by the itch of enduring hormones, and bewildered by a lack of clear roles and a definitive purpose.

How does modern masculinity look through the eyes of evolution? Why are men sexually oriented and driven toward resource acquisition while most women seek committed relationships? Why do women tend to build supportive social networks while men compete for power and status? Can ordinary men and women use evolutionary viewpoints to improve their lives and their relationships? We can. And we can use this deeper perspective to understand so much more—from flirtation to fidelity, childrearing, and family matters, as well as modern workplace behavior.

In the pages ahead we zero in on these universal subjects of intense personal concern—who we find attractive, why we fall in love, how we feel about blood ties and why we go to work every day. We explore the source of today's intimate dilemmas by unearthing the secrets of sex, love, and the human motivations buried within our natural history. By retracing the story of the sexual bond from its archaic roots to the tattooed kids with tongue-studs at the local coffeehouse, we will discover how ancient primal forces continue to influence the psychology and behavior of twenty-first century men and women and explore what they can teach us about achieving harmony in today's troubled intimate relations.

An evolutionary point of view holds the promise of alleviating many of the anxieties and confusions weighing down today's young men and women. By summoning the deep-seated, still vibrant forces that continue to shape our modern thinking, we can develop a better understanding of our own nature, dreams, and desires. Reconciling our evolutionary heritage with the realities of modern life can also help us reinforce the health of our families, stabilize our communities, and make sense of the chaotic world around us. Most of all, reclaiming our natural inheritance can help us improve our intimate relationships and launch a lifelong adventure of self-discovery.

On the Origins of My Thesis

The Disposable Male was born out of the author's dilemma. I am an adult survivor of a happy, traditional home. It never occurred to me that my parents were anything but equal. They were a pair, a unit, a rock-solid kind of partnership, and we were a united family making our way together in the world. My parents each had different functions; they displayed unique qualities and handled their children in distinctive ways. Not better or worse qualities, not more important or less important ways. Just different ones.

As the broad cultural and political eruptions of the 1960s and 1970s played out through the waning decades of the century, my personal confusions emerged, triggered by the new effervescent social philosophies working their way into society. Some of the implications of the unisex thinking of that time seemed well-intentioned, appealing directly to my sense of fairness.

Options and access for women as well as men? Equal pay for equal work? Hard to fault these concepts. Sexual "freedom" for women? No argument from the guys. A concept called "gender" emerged—a feature that was somehow different than my sex. Then it got even more complicated. I was informed that male and female are cultural inventions, that the differences between the sexes don't go much beyond some minor, if amusing, peculiarities in their plumbing systems.

There lingered seeds of doubt, however. Beyond the lure of mirror-like symmetry being proposed for the sexes, ancient imprints and lively hormones kept seeping out to claim my attention. Were all the powerful male-female urges and energies we all experience confined only to the lock-and-key mechanics of sex? After we uncouple from these fervent biological clutches, do men and women return simply to neutered, programmable modules? Is it just when we come together in intimate embrace that men become masculine and women turn feminine?

Holding two conflicting beliefs is a form of cognitive dissonance. The same pay for the same work made obvious sense, but I knew just enough about natural history and biology to understand that, when it came to the big stuff, if men and women were doing exactly the same thing, we would be a rarity in the animal kingdom. Although men and women share many tasks, nurturing children and rounding up resources summon specialized skills in nearly every species.

Aside from all the big gender "equality" notions that were gaining acceptance, "sameness" didn't seem to be working in everyday life either. Boys get rowdy and turn everything they can into a gun or a projectile. Girls persist in playing house and making nice. Despite all the determined attempts to balance our educational institutions, a majority of young men continue to gravitate toward technical, action-oriented interests and jobs, while many young women opt for more stable, relationship-oriented careers. When it comes to dating, women still usually wait for men to make the first move, confirming the durable adage that while men propose, women dispose.

Now it's one thing to walk around confused and conflicted about the little things in life, but the discord around sex and gender impacted a lot of issues I held near and dear—things like sexual intimacy, love, marriage, and family. So much of the hope and joy I looked forward to in my adult life, the ache I felt for a partner, for my other half, seemed to depend on working through this confusion. A voice of curiosity and agitation had awakened inside me concerning these crucial matters. I resolved to make sense of my confusion.

Nature's Point of View

Fortunately, my determination to reconcile the conflicting messages between the culture and what I was feeling inside coincided with an awakening of research and a trickle of publications in the 1970s heralding some exciting new ideas in the behavioral sciences. Books appeared on aggression and men in groups; bestsellers described a world of naked apes; still others delved into our African origins or explored the territorial imperatives of animals. Science was drawing closer connections between nature, evolution, and human behavior—the strands of sociobiology brought together so eloquently by Harvard's Edward O. Wilson in *On Human Nature*.

By the 1980s, selfish genes were in the news, and an explosion of research and survey findings pushed evolutionary principles into the social sciences. By the last decade of the century, classical anthropology, psychology, the study of history, and even modern literature were drinking from evolution's deep well. Concepts proposing that all living creatures are designed by nature through a process of natural selection emerged from more than a century of troubled incubation.

Today we are bombarded by scientific research about the origins of human behavior and how our species is a link in a chain of nature stretching back millions of years. News dispatches regularly attest to the connection between many of the things we do and feel and the ancestral influences and deep biological drives that continue to power so much of our personal agenda. Explanations of how evolutionary forces and our natural history have contoured the modern minds of men and women are featured widely in mainstream commentaries, essays, and news reports. The sequencing of the human genome and the promise and perils of genetic engineering have further ignited public curiosity and debate.

As my quest unfolded, exploring the ground under sex, relationship, and family meant devouring an ever-growing body of provocative and relevant data. Even more compelling than the sheer volume of information pouring forth from many sources was the fact that an increasing number of discoveries in the behavioral sciences had begun to point in similar directions. A distinctive, useful way of filtering the world around me came into focus, a matrix to help me navigate my own personal universe.

Absorbing a steady stream of books and research, I could, for instance, sense the ageless rites of entry into manhood and mentoring that are behind what's left of male initiation in athletics or religious ceremony. The dexterity and efficiency of archaic gatherers began to alight before my eyes in the balance and grace of ballerinas on stage. Ancient territorial instincts showed up in everything from "king of the hill" games that boys play to the way grown men maneuver for a bigger sales territory or a corner office. For all the world, the older men ahead of me at the office began to look like ancient tribal elders as they huddled in strategy sessions and sent young warriors out to battle for the big sale.

After years of pursuing and digesting a nature-based approach to life, I had begun to sense the primal agendas that still operate between women and men. I had acquired a distinct and novel way of looking at the pivotal issues of love, life, and the pursuit of happiness. I had uncovered a powerful new perspective. With the help of this growing evolutionary mind-set, confusion gave way to clarity. How do our important drives, relationships, and the rest of modern living look through the lens of evolution? The book before you grew out of this odyssey and seeks to answer these crucial questions.

As it happens, as many as half of all Americans and nine-out-of-ten Western Europeans accept the general idea that humans have evolved over millions of years. Still, for many of us, the actual workings of evolution and the related genetic mechanisms remain shrouded in mystery. In the popular literature, the motivational tomes and "how-to" relationship books barely hint at the deeper forces operating in men and women. On the other hand, weighty, plodding efforts to explain evolution by well-meaning scholars—volumes about disentangling the genome, the life and times of Charles Darwin, the genetic origins of our minds—can be a challenge for busy people.

This book is written by and for the inquisitive layperson. It is designed for people who want to know more than which planet the sexes come from, but who aren't ready to take on Darwin's *On the Origins of Species* over the weekend. *The Disposable Male* pulls together what the latest scientific research has to tell us about masculinity, femininity, sex, love, and mating and shows how to apply an evolutionary perspective to our personal problems, to our everyday challenges, and the broader social issues now confronting us.

In the service of scientific integrity, preparations for the book morphed from a determined personal adventure into a considerable enterprise which draws on a wide range of the natural and social sciences, from anthropology to comparative biology and genetics. More than four years in the writing, it engaged a team of researchers to ensure its accuracy and completeness. More than four hundred books were scoured, together with countless research reports and articles. The result, I hope, is an all-in-one, user-friendly guidebook to our private thoughts and feelings, and a way to reconcile the ancient promise of personal intimacy with our modern, techno-driven lives.

Although the book draws upon several main sources, first and foremost it is guided by what modern science has directly observed about human mating and the family ties that surround it. The part hormones play in lust and love, for example, and why we persistently demonstrate a preference for certain qualities in an intimate partner, a friend, or a colleague. A second, promising avenue of inquiry into nature's continuing influence is the study of other primates and living creatures. Our connection to these animals accounts for our avid interest in watching zoo primates and those fascinating nature programs on TV.

A third approach is to look for what the world's many cultures have in common. (Like me, you may be surprised to learn that more than a thousand have been systematically studied.) Lastly, in our exploration of masculinity and femininity, we consider our own bodies. How did they assume their design? Where do our instincts and self-regulating systems come from? How does sexual identity affect our outlook on life? Our bodies, it turns out, are living specimens which can help us explain our evolutionary history and our contemporary drives.

You're Invited

In addition to generating novel and thought-provoking perceptions, the nature-based thinking proposed in these pages—what this book calls an evolutionary lens—may help us better understand why we feel the way we already do. For some readers, the revelations in the text provides the scientific explanation to support their existing intuitions and beliefs. For others, this evolutionary perspective offers a new angle for looking at the most important things in life. Either way, you are invited on an adventure of self-discovery as we connect the vital elements of our natural history to the bewildering issues of modern life.

In developing this outlook on contemporary living, there are some fundamental notions to keep in mind about "natural." For one thing, natural does not necessarily mean good, or even better. Earthquakes and famine are natural. So are aggression, jealousy, and viral epidemics. Nature is neither good nor bad, fair nor kind. Among the worthy and comforting things that nature *does* bequeath us, however, is an overall equality between the sexes, a premise that forms one of the philosophical foundations of this book. But "equal to" does not mean "the same as." And whether we realize it or not, this truth has long set our hearts dancing and our minds aglow.

Drawn to the intimate partnership by our common personal goals, surely it is the things that are different about men and women that excite us. When these useful, often delectable distinctions between the sexes are drawn in these pages, they should be construed as averages and general patterns in a broad population. Men, on average, are five-and-a-half inches taller than women. Yet tall women take great strides among us, and short men thrive everywhere in our midst. (However, one of the things this book explains is why they rarely wind up with each other.)

When we consult the growing data banks of information about the ancestral forces that have forged our bodies and helped assemble our minds, we also run the risk of getting lost in science's statistical maze. Exploring issues common to all people may cause us to lose sight of what is relevant and unique about *each* person. Natural history may suggest some directions in our lives, but it does not dictate our destination. Evolution is a process, not a conclusion. Natural intuition is an anchor, not a noose. As much as genes have to say about some aspects of our makeup, they are most often joined in an intricate embrace with our environment.

Every parent likes to think that his or her child is special. Every parent is right. No two of us are the same. Despite our powerful shared aptitudes, motives, and fears, we are each the radiant product of a particular point of conception. Every one of us boasts a customized version of the human genome. This makes us all unique genetic experiments. And, if the contemporary fashion for personal self-fulfillment is not an entitlement, pursuing it is surely our right, even our obligation. Under a canopy of countless human possibilities in a complex world, we still live our lives one person, one family, and one neighborhood at a time. Humans may be 99.9 percent the same, but that one part in a thousand makes all the difference.

The Program

Consider yourself warned. This is volatile territory. Along the way to building an evolutionary point-of-view, some cherished beliefs may be challenged. From abortion, adultery, and homosexuality to race, rape, and the role of religion, evolutionary perspectives offer unique insights into a wide range of contemporary human behavior. By the time we're finished, you may even come to view those laptop-toting, cell phone-chatting commuters as loin-clothed hunters carrying modern versions of bows and arrows. But even if you do not see the shadows of ancient tribal warfare looming at the local football stadium, this book will have succeeded if it simply arms you with another distinctive way of looking at relationships and the world around you.

Adopting an evolutionary frame of mind can be a practical, wide-ranging tool. Evolutionary dynamics expose the motives behind the reproductive agendas of women and men, and offer us valuable hints about why we find some people so appealing. Primal explanations can help us understand the continuing edginess of masculine competition and the power of male bonding, and why females tend to build strong social networks and inclusive circles.

Regaining a sense of our evolutionary past can reveal the genetic glue that binds us to our family, kin, and ethnic origins. An evolutionary lens offers us a way to anticipate, even predict, many kinds of behavior. With this nature-based focus as our guide, we can learn to accept human frailty, come to terms with the animal side of our nature, celebrate our scintillating sexual differences, and gain a deeper sense of life's important passages.

The Disposable Male is organized chronologically. Beginning with the Big Bang, we make our way out of Earth's primordial depths where life began and, in no time, get off our knees and walk into ancient history with the hominids. We need to know what happened back in the ancient forests and savannas because that's where our human operating systems and instinctive drives were honed over the eons. But do not despair about excessive downtime in these primordial swamps; we probe the research on sexual fantasies before we are out of the book's first section.

In the second section, we trace the rise of humanity and seek the method behind modern mating. We sift through the evidence about sexual attraction and lay bare the connections between physical allure and nature's demands for efficiency and health. This exploration brings us face-to-face with the Trickster called Love. Our pursuit of intimacy's roots touches on such matters as why men all over the world try so hard to control women and why less than half the world's people get to choose their own mates. We delve into the reasons so many men go for visuals and pornography while women are so attracted to romance novels.

Our natural history is also drawn on to explain such not so trivial things as what high heels can signal and why a man's ability to cut a check has tickled women since long before there were banks. Moving through more recent epochs, when our ancestors separated into distinctive cultures, the second section closes by chronicling how masculine innovation and technologies have transported us in a double-click from hunter-gatherer epochs to the World Wide Web.

In the book's third section, "The World Today," we use the evolutionary lens we've developed to assess modern life directly, to explore the forces behind the disintegration of the family and the rise of modern cultures of selfishness, before turning to the troubled relations between the sexes. Using the perspective framed during our ascent through natural and recorded history, we first cast an evolutionary eye on the predicaments confronting today's women. Then we focus on men, assessing how their modern circumstances in labor and love stack up against the ancestral male heritage.

In the last section, we look at what the future holds for relations between the sexes. From the disparagement of boys and the damaging myths about everyday male power to the increasing burdens placed on women and the coarseness of modern mating, it is an ever faster-paced future filled with disturbing challenges and tantalizing hope.

Fortunes to Be Made

Happily (for both of us) this is not a textbook. As we begin the trek through natural history to modern times, we keep a lid on the science and leap across billions of years. Along the way, we encounter some intriguing characters, track mythic hunters and gatherers, and go right to the center of some challenging modern dilemmas.

While we're on the subject of intriguing characters, we eavesdrop on my amiable investment advisor whose voice and e-mail laments are woven throughout the text. These fragments from his recorded messages would normally be as valuable as last week's closing market prices, but on these pages, his tribulations may seem relevant, if not revelatory. Troubled by modern romance like many of us, he's just out there looking for love—the kind of engaging friend who likes to send goofy cartoons and the latest e-mail joke. As we turn occasionally to his romantic and workaday trials, we have an opportunity to see if the machinery of evolution is still at work in the contemporary man.

Just how my friend and the rest of us came to populate the earth can be explained by natural processes that were set loose long ago. Given enough time and promising habitats, it seemed likely that some exotic animals would eventually emerge on the planet. Tested and shaped by nature's challenging environments, these creatures might develop exceptional levels of intelligence. Perhaps, then, in a boisterous lurch for self-knowledge, they might someday begin to figure out the mystery of how they got here. The evolution of life, the struggle for survival, and the sexual embrace that propelled it would no doubt fuel a magnificent epic.

But that's our story, and we're getting ahead of it.

BEEP

"You there? Pick up.

"I'm dying a slow death here. Haven't moved a block in half-an-hour. I'm choking on exhaust fumes. This is soul-destroying traffic.

"Meanwhile, the market's tanking. Nobody calls back anymore.

"Another day in paradise.

"Oh, about the new girlfriend? I know I said she was unbelievable, that this time was different. Boy, when the chemistry first kicks in it's a rush, isn't it? Just you and her. The invincible team. Nothing can touch you!

"Well . . . we broke up over the weekend.

"Will you look at this clown blocking the intersection? He's on his cell phone, working his hand-held, a mocha on the dashboard, and he's navigating with a GPS.

"Excuse me, dude? YOU WANNA KNOW WHERE YOU ARE? YOU'RE STUCK! THAT'S WHERE YOU ARE!

"Like me.

"Some day I'll be brave enough to open the window when I shout at guys.

"Anyway, it's getting old this running around, drumming up business. And now I get to start over with the clubs again. Checking out the action. Lining up new women.

"This, and the traffic, could drive a guy to road rage. Maybe even marriage.

"Hello! A break in traffic.

"Can't wait to get to the office, slip through the metal detector, and make sure my spyware is working so I can open the mail and get to work.

"After all, there are mountains to climb, fortunes to be made for my beloved clients. Like you.

"Seriously, don't worry about me and the breakup. I'm an incorrigible optimist. I'll be out there on the hunt again just as soon as the ache kicks in.

"Later."

In the Beginning

1

IMPERIAL NATURE

Eternal Forces Shape All Living Things

WHEN ANCIENT MAPMAKERS PUZZLED OVER WHAT LAY BEYOND THEIR uncharted world, they inscribed the words: "Here There Be Dragons." The omnipotent force behind the Big Bang, the cosmic explosion that gave birth to the universe remains anyone's guess. Every civilization has fashioned its own creation story to unravel this most basic mystery, addressing a universal desire to make sense of the world and our place in it. If we were to sift through these epic tales, surveying cultures far and wide, we might not stumble upon dragons, but we would surely discover a vast pantheon of gods and goddesses.

In search of a suitably impressive origin for the Big Bang, our attentions might well focus upon the majestic Greek god Zeus, known to the Romans as Jupiter. Though he displayed awesome power and commanded breathtaking authority, Zeus revealed a fondness (some called it a weakness) for mortal women. Supposedly, he often descended to our realm to pursue earthly pleasures with those who attracted his attention. Back atop Mount Olympus he was fond of hurling thunderbolts when angry, yet another of his human quirks. The colossal lightning dagger he thrust into space almost fourteen billion years ago to get things started must have been impressive indeed because the explosion is not over. The universe continues to expand.

The Big Bang was an eruption of unimaginable force, a thundering exclamation of raw, brute energy. Launching the elements of creation in every direction from a single point of origin, the convulsive spasms at the dawn of the universe sent flashes of radiant light against the dark emptiness. It was hot—ten billion degrees hot. Fashioning time and space into a four-dimensional matrix, this cosmic tremor is the source of all the energy and matter in our universe.

From the thrust of the first explosive discharge sprang many more reverberations as billowing black clouds of fragmented matter and gossamer webs of embryonic galaxies gave shape to the universe. Across billions of light years, the embers we know as stars streamed outward, vibrant sparks from the convulsions at the genesis of space and time. As the seminal Big Bang explosion flamed out, it produced a hiss like a whispering seashell, an echo of creation scientists can still hear.

Among the 100 billion galaxies that formed in our universe was an auspicious constellation called the Milky Way. At the farther reaches of this spiraling web, among billions of other stars, a solar system emerged with ten big planets orbiting around a confident sun. And there, the third rock from the center, was a pristine blue and white jewel calmly spinning against a sea of dark space.

Earth.

Our planet took shape about 4.5 billion years ago as its heavier elements gravitated to the core and the lighter ones floated toward the crust. Ignited by immense lightning flashes, crashing thunderclaps, and volcanic eruptions, wild climatic tempests charged the earth's atmosphere into a cauldron of creation and destruction. During these lush incubational epochs, as our planet simmered under a radiant sun, a potent stream of asteroids hurtled through the cosmos like galactic spears, penetrating the earth's atmosphere, seeding the globe with the building blocks of life.

Within a pregnant, primordial sea nearly seven hundred million years later a miracle occurred. As the earth's surface cooled and began to take shape, chemistry transformed heat and light into biology. Life appeared as microscopic, single-cell membranes. Clinging perilously to existence, as tenuous as soap bubbles, living organisms took hold. From these puny beginnings, a mighty procession was set in motion.

Over the eons that followed, the polarities of fire and ice, light and shadow, volatility and serenity would envelop the planet and forge our natural world. Just where this uncharted adventure would lead no one could predict. But one thing was certain. There would be dragons aplenty along the way.

The Job Is to Survive

First and foremost, there is nature. It is everywhere and in everything, commanding the majestic heights and squalid depths, governing our universe with an all-encompassing and absolute force. For the longest time, when our ancestors hugged fearfully to its bosom, they engaged the natural world in mystery and awe. They took what they needed and lived by nature's commands. But the human odyssey has come a long way from the forests and savannas. These days, diverted by the distractions of modern life, nature rarely summons our immediate attention.

Until we are reminded who's boss. Shattering earthquakes, sweeping tsunamis, and violent hurricanes topple our feeble structures and drown our cities; famine claims whole tribes; killer flu pandemics and plagues rise up to smite king and peasant alike. During these tempests and trials, the Earth shudders and great cities are buried. Nature dissolves our brazen sandcastles in fits of regal temper. We are put in our place. Beautiful beyond measure, destructive beyond our capacity to resist, sweeping all before it, nature answers to no one. Nature is imperial.

As much havoc as it creates, nature propels life with even greater power. The deep will to survive is the underlying theme of all life. Plants cling to existence against the harshest conditions; animals struggle to survive in the face of crippling ailments; humans mount heroic battles to endure against tremendous odds. The will to survive is a dazzling testimony to the power of the primal command: life of almost any kind is better than no life at all.

Survival is our first and most powerful instinct. It is deeply encoded in our genetic and biological core, compelling us even without thinking, making us self-centered, calculating, and determined to persist. But sooner or later, all living creatures expire. Yielding to age they perish. To "survive" beyond our own lifetime, we must regenerate ourselves and reproduce. You are able to read these words because every one of your ancestors survived long enough to do just that—reproduce—if nothing else.

Sex is the engine of evolution. Appropriately enough, it has a torrid history. The saga begins a long time ago when the tumultuous forces shaping our Earth propelled the first gene-carrying packages into existence.

The Primordial Soup

Long after the Big Bang, when things eventually settled down on planet Earth, water—the elixir of life—seeped into the atmosphere along with hydrogen and nitrogen. Baked, boiled, radiated, and electrified by staggering bolts of lightning, these elements brewed a cauldron of filmy air in a solar inferno. In due course, the molecular building blocks of more complex life took hold.

As miraculous and baffling as this spontaneous event may seem, scientists can readily recreate this moment in their labs. Shooting sparks of electricity through a beaker containing the earth's original elementary gases produces the same chemical foundations of planetary life. Getting hot and bothered has been the driving force of creation ever since.

Bacteria were among the first forms of life. Though we are inclined to think of them as nasty little things without redeeming value, their ability to act as the foundation of more complex organisms has transformed the Earth from a barren and hostile globe to a vibrant and glorious domain. Modern life forms like us still can't survive without them.

The original kinds of bacteria were tiny, single-cell organisms. Battered by the ferocious elements, they cooked under a searing sun and were bombarded by intense radiation. Resilient little critters, they persevered, unicellular dots hanging on for dear life. That's all there was on Earth for two billion years.

Eventually, the single-cell molecules cavorting in the primal broth somehow arranged themselves in sequences. These networks of molecules then achieved a simple but quite miraculous capacity: they began to reproduce. They copied themselves and split in two. In the hop, skip, and jump of another billion years, these microscopic bits also managed to encase themselves in an outer "skin." Evolving cells, sealed in delicate membranes that separated them from their soupy environment, achieved a separate identity.

In time, these simple cells developed elementary methods of connecting with each other. They swapped notes, blending and becoming absorbed into one another mostly through bizarre acts of genetic fusion and cannibalism. Relinquishing their cellular independence, two distinct genetic parcels would occasionally merge and become one. This wasn't quite sex as we've come to know it, but you need to start somewhere.

Strength, it turns out, was achieved in unity. The little bags of merged bacterial cells began to expand and diversify internally. Less vulnerable than simple, single-cell entities to radiation and other climactic enemies, these tiny bacterial alliances kept getting better at surviving in the primordial soup. Mixing and matching their fortified genetic elements for eons, they built up reservoirs of biochemical information and triumphed over weaker organisms.

Like a division of soldiers fighting for a common cause, these increasingly complex, multicellular organisms also profited from internal specialization. Some cells, or parts of the organism, could focus on propulsion, some processed and discarded nutrients, while still others concentrated on defense. Better able to protect themselves, these more elaborate entities hung around longer and replicated more, transferring their expanding code of life from one generation to the next. From these humble beginnings, complicated things like plants and animals would soon become possible. (Well, relatively soon.)

We are used to thinking about time in the context of our own lives. Seventy or eighty years seem an eternity when that's how long we live. Usually, we organize our lives in months, weeks, and days—sometimes in minutes or seconds. To get a sense of evolutionary spans, however, we need to stretch our sense of time.

Imagine, for example, that we are measuring the epochs since the Earth first formed all the way to the present-day on a twelve-hour clock—at noon the Earth is newly born; midnight represents today. Life first appeared on Earth at about 2:30 P.M., or 3.5 billion years ago. A sense of perspective is suggested by the fact that the first dinosaurs showed up at thirty-five minutes before midnight. Our first hominid ancestors put in an appearance just thirty-nine seconds ago.

Errors and Omissions

In the same way that computers duplicate a digital file, when genes copy themselves to the next generation, they do it with astonishing accuracy. Errors are rare, less frequent than a single typo in the duplication of this book. But mistakes happen. The reproduced gene has too much or too little of something, or the order is messed up. These mistakes are called mutations.

Mutations have neither design nor intention. They're just mistakes. Most of the time, they are as insignificant as a typo. Usually, mutations get buried when the organism in which they appear dies, or they get passed along to the next generation as weightless baggage. Sometimes the mistake is so damaging it causes the creature or its offspring to die before the error can be passed on.

The important point about mutations, however, is that there are opportunities in a mistake, sometimes big ones, because these random genetic aberrations may cause a useful new trait to emerge. They open the door to innovation. The critical thing about a mutation is whether or not it conveys some kind of benefit to the organism. If it does, the plot, as they say, thickens.

A beneficial mutation may improve an animal's prospects of survival, which means being around long enough to procreate more often. Eventually, greater numbers of the evolved model are in circulation as larger proportions of the species carry the mutated gene. Over time—usually a very long time—the mutations build on one another and start to accumulate.

Imagine you are a largish creature hanging around a few million years ago, a cross between a horse and a giraffe. Your ancestors have been happily grazing in a field of grass, shrubs, and trees for generations, but lately the pastures have been tapped out and you're getting hungry. In search of food, you decide to head south, while others of your group head north, and still others stay put to tough it out. It so happens that the foliage down south is more abundant in tall plants and trees. A long neck would come in handy and any of your descendents with this mutation will win the lottery. To make a long story short, the extra neck length will allow them to feed higher on the trees; the mutation is helping, making things more efficient and life easier. Their progeny live longer and mate more often.

Like the compound interest that rockets your credit card balance skyward, useful mutations build on one another. Time-lapse photography would reveal a neck gradually getting longer, perhaps jumping ahead once in awhile. This process of accumulating mutations continues until longer necks are no longer an advantage. Descendents get so stretched out they can't hold up their heads, or they become vulnerable to attack. Or the foliage doesn't grow that high. At which point longer-neck mutations are no longer a benefit and may become a burden.

In the meantime, in the other direction, up north, where there were no trees or tall growth, shorter-neck genes worked best. Descendents of the common ancestor who picked up shorter-neck genes prospered and multiplied there. Across thousands of generations, necks got shorter and thicker, and their owners became good at eating things closer to the ground.

Over a near eternity, the original animal, the one that did not head off in either direction, may have survived in the played-out fields because so many others left; or it may have disappeared altogether. Down south giraffes evolved; up north, horses. Even if their common ancestor survived, neither the giraffe nor the horse could breed with it, or with each other. Evolved from a common, probably extinct ancestor, two distinct new species grace the world.

Nature Loves a Winner

These elementary workings of adaptation and natural selection are the forces that have shaped our bodies and our minds over a near eternity. Animals may look like they are brilliantly designed for their place in nature, but that is because, over time, they have been designed *by* nature. Advantageous mutations help plants or animals adapt more efficiently to their surroundings, promoting survival and greater reproductive success. Eventually the new and improved attribute becomes a standard feature. Of course, new species are not necessarily better ones. A horse is no better than a giraffe. Close to the ground, horses make a living on grass, while giraffes subsist on trees. We know that they are successful because they are both still around.

While many of us grasp the general concept of evolution, even the idea of a gradual lengthening of necks, the development of complex body organs is more difficult to comprehend. Consider the eye, the source of most of our sensory data. Surely this elaborate instrument did not just pop into existence one day. Hey, look everybody, I can see! Like all the complicated parts of highly evolved creatures, vision started out as a simple organ and evolved in increments. Perhaps a long-distant ancestor developed a flimsy membrane on its face, photosensitive spots thin enough for light to penetrate, allowing the creature to sense a change in its environment.

Let's say this creature is a lowly cockroach scurrying across your kitchen floor. This cunning, adaptable insect—which appeared before we did and will almost certainly succeed us—jerks to attention as you switch on the light and briefly freezes in expectation. When the light comes on, it senses a change, and its cautionary instincts tell it to scurry under something. The simple capacity to detect a difference in its environment has conferred a powerful benefit. The beetle without this mutation, caught in the open, meets an untimely death. Beneath the dishwasher, the slightly more evolved roach survives to propagate and pass on the thin membrane gene, the one that says "something's not right" when the lighting changes.

From such modest beginnings, over a maddeningly long period of time, are such heroic organs as eyes developed. Many subsequent random mutations in the new and improved line of cockroach may lead nowhere but, given enough time, the mutations will accumulate, the sensitive membrane getting thinner, drawing in more light. Eventually, as the species evolves, a simple skin depression may appear, tiny receptor cells emerge as the sockets form into spherical enclosures suggesting the direction of light and shadow. In time, a jelly-like surface, a crude lens, and optic nerve structure develop.

Many blind alleys ensue, so to speak, but over millions of years, in tiny shadings with the occasional lurch, something that looks a lot like an eye can materialize. In addition to sensing when the light changes, the evolving cockroach begins to make out shapes such as a smorgasbord of crumbs on the floor or your house cat bent on torture. Improbable as it may seem, eyes have evolved, over a near-endless span of time, separately within many different animal lineages and can be seen today, in the various intermediate stages, in animals everywhere in nature.

In the same way, explanations can be provided for all the many complicated aspects of nature—from intricate internal body organs to the development of mechanically sophisticated features such as a primate's elbow, an elephant's snout, a bird's wings, or a dolphin's rudders. From an insect's eye to the thorns that protect a rose, nature selects mutations that help an organism better adapt to its environment, survive, and propagate.

Scientists have documented this process using fossil records, the skeletal blueprints of our evolution etched in stone. Despite some gaps, the fossils display gradual alterations that, strung together like frames of a movie, tell the story of natural selection. Researchers can also recreate these basic evolutionary mechanics in their labs and on their computers, using microscopic organisms that reproduce faster than a kiss. In a matter of days, they evolve and become different creatures.

Evolutionary dynamics also can be observed in a variety of living creatures. A classic example involves a tiny river minnow that, for some longstanding benefit, developed bright red markings. When a new predator fish was introduced, the glistening dots gave the minnows presence away, in effect saying "come eat me." The minnows with fewer bright markings survived and propagated. Their descendants came to dominate the species. When the predators were removed, the original benefit of bright red markings resurfaced. The few remaining minnows with these dots survived longer, bred more, and came once again to dominate the species, a vivid demonstration of natural selection at work.

The fragile molecular adventure that began in the primeval seas consumed a staggering two billion years, or more than five hours on our twelve-hour clock, simply to develop from a single cell into multicellular complexity. But in time, through the workings of evolution, these primitive bacteria evolved underwater into plant-like and animal forerunners. Beneath the churning seas that covered most of the globe, the evolutionary procession reached a promising threshold. Only a spark was needed to set it off.

Superguppy Makes Land

Half a billion years ago, the planet was still in the throes of immense ecological strains as powerful earthquakes severed huge land masses and continents floated apart like buoyant islands. Mountains erupted, thrusting their peaks skyward, triggering massive avalanches. Climactic shifts were violent and extreme, and atmospheric conditions swung wildly. Nature wreaked havoc on a barely imaginable scale. In this fiery cauldron, the spark that ignited a major evolutionary breakthrough occurred in the ocean depths.

The Cambrian Explosion, roughly 550 million years ago, triggered a great leap in the quantity and complexity of underwater life. A biological Big Bang, it ushered in an astonishing range of seaborne creatures, launching an early pantheon of animal life and a dizzying array of evolutionary possibilities. Virtually every animal on the planet today owes its origins to this event, and, although scientists are not sure what caused it, the diversity and complexity of the world's inventory of living creatures were transformed from a few primitive organisms to a wild cornucopia in just thirty-five million years, an evolutionary moment.

The Earth's oceans began to teem with life, but the path onto land was delayed by various catastrophic convulsions, looming disasters, and genetic dead-ends. The march to terra firma consumed 175 million years following the Cambrian Explosion and was finally made possible by green algae, a hardy plant—valued even today for its nutritional content—which colonized the swamp areas at the seas' edges. This provided the food source for the first-ever amphibian. Let's call it Superguppy.

Like so many pivotal stages in the rise of complex organisms, this moment would have looked feeble and a bit curious had anyone actually been around to see it. Superguppy (more likely some ugly insect, but there are literary requirements to consider) was but a puny entry in the sweepstakes of evolution. No doubt the product of some land-accommodating mutations, this tottering little creature somehow developed the capacity to breathe for a few minutes out of water, allowing it to nibble on the lush plant life that grew wild on the shoreline.

There were probably many of these sea-to-land attempts and countless fumbling trials and errors until Superguppy got a grip. But with that obstacle overcome, the abundance of edible groundbreaking plants opened the animal floodgates. All sorts of creatures emerged to explore the rich arboreal world on the land—insects, worms, soft-body invertebrates, dragonflies, and scorpions to name a few. With no predators around and roughage flopping everywhere, it must have seemed a paradise compared to the crowded seas below.

There was something else about Superguppy, something important. Superguppy came in two versions. Carrying mix-and-match reproductive blending to a new level of efficiency, nature had triggered a specialty, a biological arrangement among Superguppy's ancestors called meiosis. We know, and love it, as sex. It eventually came to mean an egg supplier and a sperm provider, but it probably started in an ancient species when something began to poke out a little and something else got a little dented, making things fit together better. More importantly, sexual specialization turned out to be a fast and efficient way to diversify and fortify the gene pool. The one with the sperm we came to call male; the one with the egg, female. It was the big new thing.

To get a genetic sense of what the sexual equation came to mean, picture a near endless wall of slot machines in a colossal Vegas casino. When a human male and female mate successfully, each pulls down about thirty thousand slots at the same time. A big part of whoever shows up nine months later depends on how all the lemons and cherries line up during that one steamy encounter since each egg and sperm tadpole carries a one-time-only mixture of the partners' genes. With so many possible combinations, every new infant is a unique genetic experiment. Could be the blueprint for an Einstein . . . or Forest Gump. But it's about fourteen trillion to one that it lands somewhere in between.

Nearly every cell in our body, every drop of blood, every strand of hair, every egg and tiny sperm contains the complete instruction manual for how to build and operate a human being. This data is packaged within twenty-three chapters, or pairs of chromosomes, one each from Mom and Dad. These coiled-up strands of DNA—each chromosomal chapter—contain paragraph-long bits of instruction called genes, the things that get tossed around each time sex results in conception.

Even after scientists unveiled the human genome, they did not know how many genes we have. Shocked by the low first tally of less than thirty thousand (hardly more than the lowly earthworm), by 2006 they were guessing that, when finally determined, it will be between twenty-eight thousand and sixty thousand although these may include some super gene clusters. Whatever their number, genes, in turn, cook up things called proteins, which are the real workhorses in our body, producing energy, sending out directions, switching things on and off, getting rid of waste, and generally orchestrating our development from embryo to elder.

When it comes to mating, there are a lot of potential partners out there. And once you find one, there is almost no end to the ways that the gene components might pair up. While not all traits are passed on, coming together one night may mean a daughter with Dad's chin, Mom's stubbornness, his potential for diabetes, and her dazzling IQ. Conceived the next morning, their bouncing baby boy may inherit Mom's quirky smile, Dad's athletic legs, her susceptibility to depression, and his penchant for alcohol.

What survives into the next generation is not the parents, of course, but a cross-section of their genes, a process that continues from generation to generation. Genes are the things that endure. They are the units of survival. Plants and animals come and go, but so long as they replicate, a subset of their genes lives on. Some of our genetic instruction modules have made it through numerous generations and have been around for a long time. The ones that regulate most of our basic body functions are probably millions of years old.

Richard Dawkins, author of *The Selfish Gene*, draws attention to the durability of genes and the fragility of their carriers by describing people as "packaging for genes." As it happens, however, some of these gene packages look and work better than others and therein lies part of our tale. But, good looking or not, the packaging slips away in the end. Genes—remixed, repackaged, renewed, and maybe improved—march forward. The bad news about all this is that, like nature, genes are largely indifferent to our individual plight. The good news is they know they're not going anywhere without us.

The Long and the Short of It

Superguppy and the early trailblazing amphibians of both sexes trudged between the sea and the land for a long time. Venturing farther from their watery breeding grounds with each mutational expansion in breathing capacity and mobility, they nevertheless remained chained to the sea. This oceanic origin helps explain the water sac around human embryos and why the fluids in our body are so similar to seawater. Water feels so comfortable because it is our ancient home.

Humble as they were, what's important here is that living creatures had reached land. Boasting tiny lungs and fins that would ultimately morph into limbs, the amphibians were able to shuffle around on land and breathe oxygen from the air. By about three hundred million years ago, reptiles had evolved from these primitive creatures, earning a big spot in evolution's hall of fame because they were able to fully escape the water. This crucial breakthrough arrived with a seemingly simple development: the eggshell, which transformed ocean-based animals into land nomads. Reptiles were the first species to live entirely on land, and a few, such as turtles, tortoises, and crocodiles, are still with us.

Liberated from the water's edge and no longer dependent on direct solar warming, the world's evolving menagerie gained a chance to explore vast new geographic horizons. Dazzling habitats awaited them as nature turned toward shaping the creatures on land. Given enough time, the possibilities seemed endless. With half a billion years on your hands, there is time for plenty of evolutionary dead-ends and near-eternities with nothing much going on. There is also time for microscopic mutations to accumulate and turn small, simple things into some impressive machinery. Like dinosaurs.

Yet bigger is not always better. In fact, as the dinosaurs would discover, it can kill you. Dinosaurs had big bodies and small brains, but despite this unfortunate combination, they were the stars of reptilian evolution for forty-five million years. Life on Earth had evolved from invisible microscopic bacteria to creatures as heavy as half a dozen elephants standing three giraffes tall. Which goes to show you just how big things can get if you have the time. For the dinosaurs, however, time was about to run out. That's because a meteor the size of Baltimore was hurtling toward the Earth at a million miles an hour. The dinosaurs never knew what hit them.

The meteor struck Mexico's Yucatán Peninsula about sixty-three million years ago, creating massive dislocations in the world's climate and landscapes, huge forest fires, and torrential tidal waves. With the food chain reconfigured overnight, many smaller animals perished, never to be seen or heard from again, while big animals lost their food supply. Three-quarters of the life forms on the planet were wiped out.

The descendants of the creatures of the Triassic, Jurassic, and Cretaceous Periods, those lovable hulks in the movies, suddenly disappeared. Only lizards, turtles, and alligators survived from their line, faint shadows of the giants that made the Earth tremble. Birds, also part of the dinosaur lineage, survived as some earlier took wing, escaping the upheaval on the ground. As always, however, there is opportunity in chaos. Back on the ground, some cuddly, bug-eyed poachers were about to take center stage in the long evolutionary saga.

Tailored to Perfection

The first mammals to appear were small, rodent-like creatures that sniffed their way around thick vegetation looking for something to eat. They lived under rocks and in burrows and fed mostly on increasingly abundant insects. When the big meteorite devastated fauna and nearly depopulated the globe, the mammals managed to survive. In a barren, ash-covered planet, this new class of animal would eventually rise to the top of the food chain. We are their direct descendents.

Independent little varmints, mammals branched off the reptilian line some 225 million years ago, at about 11:30 P.M. on the clock. Thanks once again to the workings of mutation and natural selection, mammals had developed two distinct advantages over their predecessors. They were warm-blooded animals, which let them rummage around on the cooler night shift while their predators slept. And they gave birth to infants instead of eggshells.

Live birth allows parents to escape the chores and perils of nesting eggs. Their offspring arrive at a more mature stage, ready to accept nourishment from a clever female innovation called mammary glands, also known as breasts. And while we are on the subject of evolving sexual apparatuses, something called a penis was sprouting on males. Growing by leaps and bounds—all the better to implant the seed—it would eventually boast no end of exotic bells and whistles.

The mammals prospered, adapting to a wide variety of surroundings. Jungles, deserts, arctic tundra, oceans, and forests make vastly different demands on the plants and animals that appear within them. But in the evolutionary equivalent of a long summer, the mammalian eruption triggered a wide number of species we recognize as distinctly modern: bats and whales, rabbits and elephants, dolphins and lions—and some exotic creatures called primates. Each became an expert tailored to its domain.

A bold new enterprise, the primates emerged from the mammalian pack about fifty-five to ninety million years ago, around a quarter to midnight. They were crude tool users with enlarged brains. Twenty million years after they first appeared, the primates diverged into three main lines: apes, prosimians, and monkeys. One of the monkey lines, in turn, split into baboons, orangutans, gorillas, and chimpanzees.

Humans are one of about 350 species in the primate group. Some measure of just how slowly evolution moves can be glimpsed by the fact that more than 98 percent of chimpanzee and human genes are identical. This means we have evolved less than 2 percent away from our common ancestor in five to eight million years. The variation may be more substantial in other DNA material, but this does point out what a big deal 2 percent can be.

The primates were essentially tree-living creatures, initially confined to the tropical zones of Africa. Distinguished from other mammals by more elaborate, limb-gripping hands and feet, they enjoyed superior vision, refined hand-eye coordination, and plant-eating teeth. Nearing the end of our journey at six minutes before midnight, or about thirty-eight million years ago, the primates were thriving across much of the continent and had developed crude kin- and clan-based social units similar to networks observed among modern primates. Most importantly, their brains were getting bigger.

The value of the brain in helping an animal adapt and prosper should be fairly obvious to an evolved brain. Like naturalists who map the history of ancient redwoods by inspecting their inner rings, the layers of the human brain document eons of neural interplay with increasingly complex and demanding circumstances. Not surprisingly, the primitive part that first evolved is located at our brain's base, deep within the limbic system. Some scientists call it the reptilian brain because it is the part we inherited along with them. This is the seat of instinct, the place that regulates the automatic reflexes so critical to survival as well as our visceral sexual drives. Our innate response to a hot stove or the impulse to seek orgasm runs on the same systems that kept our predecessors alive and reproducing when they had little time or ability to think. We continue to depend on this primal equipment every moment of our modern lives.

At last, the hominids, our most immediate primate predecessors, diverged from the distant ancestor we share with the chimpanzee. Like most of the species that have appeared on the planet at one time or another, our common ancestor is now extinct, as it failed to adapt rapidly enough to a changing environment. But the hominids would prove to be among the most resourceful animals in the kingdom—and the smartest. This would fuel their ascent and save them from extinction. At least it has so far.

The Goal Is to Get Better

In the near endless trek leading up to humanity's current predicament, until just yesterday in cosmic time, survival and reproduction were the only games in town. It was a jungle out there, a winner-takes-all kind of world, and staying alive long enough to mate was not only the big thing, it was the *only* thing. Natural selection acted as a brute force, inflicting a simple message: any genetic attribute of body or mind that enhances longevity and creates more opportunity to have offspring is favored. Those who went out of business early failed to become our predecessors.

Nature, of course, can be as giving as it is forbidding. Angry despot or benevolent monarch, nature may be imperial, but it is also bountiful. During the epic journey to the present-day, the natural workings of evolution have left us with a dizzying kaleidoscope of diversity—at last count, more than 1.5 million kinds of animals had been identified; it's estimated that several million more species share our planet including no less than five million types of insects. For all of them, the business of reproduction is at the absolute center of their lives.

Assured of our own personal well-being, the universal gene-driven compulsion to survive takes shape in us as an urge toward sex. The fulfillment of our earthbound destiny, sexual reproduction is survival pushed into the future. If our genes do not find a new carrier, they die out. That is why we cherish life, crave intimacy, and love sex. This biological stimulus is the reason why every culture in the world puts reproduction at its core. It is why we adore our children and get passionate about abortion. Even on a crowded and increasingly dangerous planet, for most of us, launching the next generation is at the heart of our existence, the very essence of our lives.

The job of every animal is to survive, but unless we are content merely to exist, our goal as humans must be to get better. Survival is the first instinct; getting better is the second. In a crucial sense, self-improvement is a form of survival insurance. Becoming healthier, stronger, and smarter means we are better equipped to face the world's challenges. These qualities help us to survive and become successful ancestors.

Four to six million years ago something happened that suddenly changed things even if it didn't necessarily make them better. Nobody is sure why it happened. We can't even be certain about precisely where it took place. It was probably awkward, even feeble-looking, a triumph of hope over fear. Then again, maybe it was just idle curiosity. Whatever the reason, an animal looking a lot like a large chimpanzee clambered down from a tree, moved around on all fours, and tentatively glanced around. Rising and balancing itself against the trunk, it stood only on its two hind legs. And then, for some curious reason, it walked upright and headlong into the future.

BEEP

"Some mornings, boy, it's all I can do to drag myself out of bed and make it to Starbucks for my fix.

"And it was there, as I dawdled over my double-decaf-no foam-

one pump-reverse soy-triple double latte, that I saw her. She was up there, like, in her forties or something? A knockout.

"Anyway, one of her high-heeled shoes is dangling on her toes? A beautiful foot, my friend. Hall of Famer. High arch, sharply defined Achilles tendon, gorgeous trim ankles, long, painted toes playfully bobbing the shoe up and down.

"Which is when it falls off. She's fishing around, trying to get it back on. Curls her toes and tucks them in to grab the shoe? Y'know, like those little toe spasms when you come?

"I was in recovery for half-an-hour.

"Which reminds me, it's been weeks since the breakup of my last relationship—a brutal descent into a living hell of self-degradation and endless, uh, minutes, of questioning and doubt.

"Seriously, the ache is back. Big time.

"I want that connection. I want to be in love—yes, in love!—build a future, hand-in-hand as we stroll on sandy white beaches, the glistening ocean sparkling against a radiant, setting sun.

"That's right. Your big time investment advisor is on the prowl again."

2

POSITIONING SEX

Male and Female Cut a Deal on the Savanna

IMAGINE WE ARE SPECTATORS VIEWING THE EARTH FROM SOMEWHERE deep in space. Soon enough we would discover things are moving around down there, that this perky green and blue dot supports life. We zoom in on what appears to be a vibrant civilization going about its daily routine. Being systematic observers, we set out to analyze their social order and forms of authority. We learn the populace is split into various work and social groups. Tasks are divided, mostly by sex. Even from our distant perch we detect the use of language and various forms of nonverbal communication. We note the efficient exchange of goods and services across the economy.

Over time we learn that the inhabitants place a big emphasis on educating their young. At sexual maturity, fevered courtship rituals and generous gift-giving unfold, not to mention some hot sex. Males mostly cooperate, bonding readily, especially on the job, and females enjoy a powerful sisterhood. Basically law-abiding, residents are courteous and hospitable. Most everyone watches their diet, practices good personal hygiene, and helps keep the neighborhood spotless. Medical care, even surgery, is freely available, and seniors get to work the soft jobs. All in all, it is a happy and productive society. Probably has its dark side but, hey, they all do. It's not a perfect universe.

Perhaps you are wondering where on Earth this might be. A progressive town in Vermont? An Israeli kibbutz? An Indian ashram? Hard to tell because most of what we have observed has a lot to do with the things that count for all kinds of animals—for the birds and bees, for humans—and for the ant colony we have just been observing. No wonder: from the standpoint of evolution, we share a heritage with just about every animal alive. It is one big river of life and every species is a tributary. As we celebrate our splendid human achievements, we might be wise to also honor the animal flesh we inhabit because, when you get right down to basics, we are a lot like ants, not to mention chimpanzees.

Standing Arrangements

From the lowest insect to the highest primate, if things are going swell in your domain, there is no big need for change. There is nothing to adapt to. For a carefree young primate cavorting in trees in luscious jungles and forests several million years ago, predators seem but a faint threat in the distance. Mother and watchful relatives hang out nearby. Fruit and berries are there for the picking. It's like you're living in a 7-Eleven. You don't have a care in the world.

Every now and then you wander down to the forest floor, absently chewing on something, to do whatever small primates do on forest floors. Sometimes you lean against a tree trunk just for the hell of it, but mostly you wander around on all fours just like human infants. Standing up and stumbling around on your hind legs isn't necessary or helpful. To the contrary, it could be a clumsy, even dangerous way to get to the few places you need to go.

Should things change and your situation become a lot less cozy, however, you might have a problem. The kind of problem our distant forbearers faced about seven to ten million years ago. That's about the time the Earth warmed and began to dry out after the last big ice age, causing the dense forests of Africa to fragment and recede. As the ground was transformed to open patches of arid savanna, some not-so-minor inconveniences confronted our tree-loving ancestors. A shrinking jungle means food fights start breaking out. With less foliage and diminishing resources, it gets crowded and competitive. The strange new world at the forest's edge may be no Garden of Eden, but things in the old neighborhood look grim. So, like Superguppy, you take a deep breath and make a break for it. Poised between two worlds, with a longing glance back at the old homestead, you step gingerly onto the foreign grasslands creeping up to your door.

At first it's like you're a fish out of water. Let's face it, moving around in these wide open spaces is scary. Your old routine doesn't work anymore. Hopping around on all fours is no longer safe, let alone efficient, but walking upright is. It's faster, and you can run. It keeps the hot African sun off your back, and you can see things in the distance, things like food or large, hungry predators checking you out as they make dinner plans. More importantly, standing up also frees your hands so you can use tools and weapons—just as soon as you figure out what those are.

All things considered, out on the savanna, two legs and two arms worked much better than four legs. Bipedalism, walking erect on two feet, conveyed advantages. Natural selection favored those mutations that helped early primates adapt to walking upright because standing up conferred benefits in this particular habitat. Of course, we did not bounce from tree-squatting to running the decathlon overnight. Like the slow, step-by-step development of complex organs such as an eye, the evolutionary leap to bipedalism looked more like an awkward stumble. The first hominids to walk upright no doubt dropped down to their knuckles once in a while for balance, if not just for old time's sake.

Over a long time, the process of natural selection favored a straighter, weight-supportive skeleton. Our predecessors' foot, leg, and pelvis bones and their related muscles evolved toward a streamlined, vertical position. As we know, evolution takes its time. It is at least four million years since we stood up to walk, and this reengineering is still going on. Supporting our big upper body is why so many of us have lower back problems; ankle, knee, and foot complaints; and varicose veins in our legs.

As intimidating as the broken field savanna may have been to the first two-legged hominids, the new terrain and the challenges they faced ignited the latent promise of evolution. There's opportunity as well as danger when the ground rules change, and if adversity doesn't kill you, it teaches you. It forces you to get stronger and smarter. Plucking jungle food is one thing, but catching it on the savanna takes skill.

Standing up and walking out of the forest proved to be the beginning of a perilous experiment. The demands of this new turf would oblige our ancestors to start working for their food. They would need to hunt. This would trigger some new arrangements. Much like the first multicellular organisms, ancestral males and females would be obliged to specialize. In fact, things would never be quite the same.

Ordering Peckers

Not long ago, some paleontologists unexpectedly discovered the remains of a petite, two-legged hominid in Ethiopia. They named her Lucy, after the Beatles' "Lucy in the Sky with Diamonds," which was playing in the background as they contemplated their historic find. Other recent fossil finds, stretching back more than six million years, have scientists scratching their heads over just who is and isn't our direct ancestor. Nevertheless, Lucy offers a remarkable glimpse into our hominid past. An archetype of the early female, she was a member in good standing of an ancient clan and a harbinger of our momentous leap onto two feet.

Lucy was also a runt, an uninspiring sight at less than four feet tall and a mere sixty pounds; her male counterpart, a foot taller, weighed in at about a hundred pounds. Her brain, a bit larger than a chimpanzee's, was a third the size of ours, but it was easily the fastest microprocessor of her time. Which was a good thing because she needed all the smarts she could command. Hominid life was harsh, dangerous, and often short. Clan members might make it into their middle years if they were lucky. Lucky and smart.

From our distant contemporary perspective, we may be inclined to view Lucy as a work-in-progress, but evolution doesn't work like that. Lucy's descendants could have branched off in any number of directions—or no direction at all. And the transition to the savanna probably took numerous attempts over many generations. Like any animal confronted by changing surroundings, our early forbearers stayed close to their forest origins, retreating to find shelter and traditional food sources. No doubt they surveyed the new terrain with the same combination of hope and fear that propelled Superguppy toward land and that today drives humans to explore outer space.

In fact, our earliest bipedal ancestors barely knew about hunting since food had always been easy picking in the jungle. Out on the savanna, at first they became vegetarian scavengers, grubbing for roots and other easily available calories. They pursued small game the way chimpanzees still do, and they pilfered the kills of other animals. But as the forests continued to recede and prey became scarcer, these protohumans were forced to develop new ways of securing adequate calories. They had to adapt to their new environment—or die.

The early primates from which Lucy evolved, the ones forced out onto the savanna, lived in casual bands of up to fifty members. Like us, they were social creatures. Many were blood-related, favoring each other with protection and resources, but distinct family groupings as we know them did not exist. So deep do these gregarious, clan-wide roots go that psychologists consider modern social isolation, already implicated in heart disease, cancer, and immune system depletion, to be as hazardous to our health as smoking. As our ancestors adapted to the challenges of the savanna, the casual organization that worked so well in lush treetops began to take on more formal shape.

The early clan was no democracy. Alpha male pack leaders were anything but sweethearts. Blessed or cursed with energy and persistence, they had to fight and negotiate their way to the top and keep on struggling to hold their post. Those with the strength, ability, and wit to protect and lead won favor. As the senior males fended off ambitious competitors and testosterone-addled rookies, they continued to advance their urgent, unconscious survival agenda: get all the Lucys they could pregnant. Then, as now, sexual prowess had a lot to do with access to resources, as the strongest and ablest males gained extra mating opportunities. Over time, the gene pool was fortified with some "tough guy" attributes.

With all its infighting, evolving male hierarchies fostered a sort of harmony. As it is with other primates, including humans, relatively stable pecking orders cut down on destructive male competition. The pickings may be slender down below, but less prominent males are freed from excessive competition and the constant need to defend their ground. Within the middle ranks, they may enjoy a relatively secure position in the troop, the tribe, the company, or the team. And, with some fluidity in the rankings, there is always the chance to move up.

Male status hierarchies—a form of social contract—are protection purchased through service. So long as you play by the rules, you've got security and the comfort of a regular payday in the ranks. It was this way millions of years ago, and it more or less remains this way today. Alpha and beta males are not just the big political or military figures, senior corporate executives, or the leaders of major organizations. The alpha male is atop all the cultural, social, and religious elites. He is the captain of the team, the head of the union local, the guy who owns the store where everyone hangs out, the young tough that all the punks in the gang look up to.

Social cohesion around male hierarchies in the clan was important because, with danger lurking out on the savanna, the early bipedal troop needed all the advantages it could muster. For the most part, everyone pulled together, but there were disagreements and quarrels aplenty. Slackers and schemers were shunned.

Sometimes, when there wasn't enough food to go around, things got really rough. Lower-ranking males who had the misfortune to threaten a leader's supremacy in the wrong way or at the wrong time could also face immediate death or banishment. Compared to the laid-back tropical smorgasbords, the savanna's limited resources meant there would be new winners and new losers.

Over the generations, this male jousting for position began to distinguish the sexes. Drawing on the work of contemporary primatologists such as Frans de Waal, we learn that males angle toward vertical power hierarchies built with replaceable coalition partners while females, from the alpha on down, tend toward a more permanent, horizontal sisterhood of supportive social networks. Since a semblance of order is in everybody's interest, senior females often play peacemaker among agitated males. Gender specialties like these enhance the clan's ability to sustain itself. The sexes complement each other, sharing the same powerful ambition—survival.

Gene Pools

Lucy, her kin, and her troop knew that several pairs of eyes and ears were better able to keep a lookout on the savanna's more threatening predators. A cluster of hairy, two-legged apes puffing up and thumping their chests around a hungry lion can be an imposing sight. Maybe enough to kill its appetite. On the other hand, an isolated ape is a meal. Animals of a species often do better hanging together than working alone. "You scratch my back and I'll scratch yours" is about more than just grooming. Despite showboating by the guys (some things never change), Lucy's ancestors turned the necessity for cooperation into virtue. They needed to be good at working together. Getting along conferred an advantage.

As the savannas expanded and the forests continued to retreat, more prolonged food shortages propelled the tracking of game over ever greater distances. Plucking food had given way to chasing it, and male energies were directed outward. For the first time, they had to leave home and go to the office. Group efforts had to be coordinated, calling for organization, teamwork, and the assignment of roles.

These physically demanding and far-flung hunting chores opened the door to an adaptive division of labor between the sexes. The hunt favored strength, stealth, endurance, spatial calculation, and physical dexterity. Stronger and more aggressive, males seemed nature's obvious choice for the job. Leaving the hearth, tracking animals, enduring physical risk and strain, bonding with allies—all the short-term, competitive elements of masculinity found ample expression on the hunt. There, ferocious bouts of mayhem punctuated lengthy waits in the bush; this left time to diddle around and daydream, things a lot of men are still good at. Yet, over the eons, males were honed for action.

Women, on the other hand, already had their hands full. Most were pregnant much of the time and forever caring for dependent infants. Walking on two legs may have been a great idea, but it favored narrower hips and a smaller pelvic opening. That meant giving birth to younger, less mature infants requiring years of parental nurturing. A human embryo takes only 280 days to mature, but it requires a few thousand more in steady attention and training to turn an infant into a self-sufficient young adult. Savanna females drew naturally to their obvious specialty, the challenges of motherhood, and developed latent talents for network-building among similarly burdened women. Even with drooling, help-less infants in hand, Lucy, her sisters, cousins, and girlfriends were able to form powerful social units. Gathering roots, berries, and nuts, fe-males also accounted for a big part of the clan's menu, providing crucial insurance against the uncertain prospects of the hunt.

Daylight had dawned on the protohuman. Hunters and gatherers were loose on a perky little planet orbiting a mellow sun. And that's the way we hung out for what seems like forever. Until just ten thousand years ago, or seconds before midnight on our evolutionary clock, we were all hunter-gatherers. Some of us still are. Yet backwoods primitive or cyberspace sophisticate, the genetic instruction manual in today's bod-ies all got here the same old-fashioned way.

The Mother of Necessity

Sex isn't fair. Males deliver a microscopic bit of semen, while women contribute an egg that's about a quarter of a million times larger and a nine-month lease on their womb. When a couple climbs down from the haystack, or wherever, a long-term obligation may be swelling inside her. The end of this brief sexual encounter for a man is the beginning for a woman. Pregnancy, hormonal rushes, huge mood swings, the trauma of birthing, lactation, and breast-feeding—all this lies ahead of a pro-spective mother.

How unlike the male. Nothing lies ahead of him. He recoils from the sexual encounter with little more than a limp "tail" between his legs. While the female takes on the evolving seed, he stands there—if he's around at all—with no other sexual function. His fully exposed genitalia dangle out there in front of him like a compass pointing forward, sort of. There is not much for him to do but do it again. Ever the drone, his sexual identity rests on a single, repetitive act. It is no wonder he's so ready to perform it.

Females fulfill their bigger reproductive role with a vastly more elabo-rate body. All of a woman's critical genitalia, particularly her ovaries, are protected within a complex, interior, and refined torso. Grounded by the womb, she is bound to nature by powerful lunar rhythms, cyclical reminders of her regenerative capacities. Carrying a baby to term, nursing it at her breast, the mother-infant bond melds into a tandem unit as familiar and comforting as apple pie and ice cream. Born of a woman, in the wake of a long and natural gender progression, she, in turn, gives birth.

A woman's connection to her fetus is unquestioned, her femininity given meaning and purpose by pregnancy. In a sense, a woman's body, if not her psyche, reaches full maturity as it plays out this reproductive symphony. All manner of hormones and neural transmitters surge into consciousness during pregnancy, activating her protective instincts, helping to build an intimate connection to her baby.

Her infant, like all mammals, will be exquisitely dependent with a deeply imprinted need for immediate and sustained physical attachment. Within seventy-two hours after birth, a newborn shows a preference for its mother's voice. On the savanna, early separation meant death, and it remains a young child's most desperate moment. Human babies don't cling to hair; they need to be held. They sniff out their mother's distinctive scent and, like homing pigeons, search out the postnatal nipple, darkened to provide a clear landing pad.

The bond between a mother and her infant is a connection deeply ingrained in the genetic and hormonal tides of both. Theories about the importance of fathers may come and go but, whatever the fashion of the day, the deeply embedded instinct toward motherhood cuts across every culture, every primate, and every mammalian species. By knocking out specific genes, scientists have transformed normal, mothering mammals into parental derelicts, indicating that the maternal instinct is hard-wired. By contrast, barely 1 percent of male mammals or primates demonstrate even the slightest inclination to assist with parenting.

Not surprisingly, there is no society in the world, past or present, that has redirected the responsibility of infant care away from women. Hardly any have cared to try. Jane Goodall, the eminent primatologist, "looking through the windows" of her lifelong experience with chimpanzees notes that "not until I had an infant of my own did I begin to understand the basic, powerful instinct of mother-love." She commented on what she learned from a senior female chimp: "[S]he taught me to honor the role of mother in society, and to appreciate not only the immeasurable importance to a child of good mothering but also the utter joy and contentment which that relationship can bring to the mother." The mother of necessity is no invention.

For all but the last few decades in the history of our planet, and in all but the wealthiest communities, maternal obligations have kept mothers close to home. If a women has several children at modest intervals, she will be tied to mothering for many years. Lucy's predecessors, surrounded by abundant, lush forest and enjoying a sisterhood of babysitters, didn't need much help handling the burdens of maternity. Out on the savanna, it was a different story.

The Meet Market

The harsh realities of the savanna imposed a heavy price on maternity. Expectant females, vulnerable and taxed by the demands of pregnancy, required protection. Breast-feeding mothers needed as much as one thousand extra calories per day and had to see to it that their dependent infants were fed. Females made the bigger parental investment, and they had a lot to lose from a thoughtless encounter—as in an embryo feeding on their body for nine months and a long-term obligation clouding their future.

Out on the savanna, sex for females turned from a casual jungle frolic into something a lot more serious. The Lucys of the world needed males who could and would help out. With food supplies irregular and infants relying on them, fertile females instigated a sexual selection process. Holding the scarcer sexual resource, they began to play hard to get. Not because they were females, but because they were the ones that bore the cost of sex and made the more serious parental investment. It is for this reason that males initiate the path to seduction. And it is for this same straightforward reason that, amongst just about every mammalian species, it is the female who discriminates, granting sexual access to a jostling pack of competing males—males who need her in the reproductive sweepstakes a great deal more than she needs them.

There is a type of male seahorse that, for some peculiar reason, carries the fertilized eggs in its womb-like pouch. In this rare instance of pregnancy role-reversal, aggressive females compete feverishly for the attention of some very choosy males. Nature, it turns out, grants the upper hand to the sex that incubates the next generation, the gender that delivers the goods and makes the big commitment. For 99 percent of mammals, that means the female.

As the gatekeepers of sexual opportunity, female primates at risk out on the savanna began to reserve sexual favors for supportive males. No meat, no sex. No burger, no, uh, buns. Like males of many species, one type of beetle—scientists have identified more than sixty thousand kinds—has evolved to offer the object of his intentions a delectable treat. Having provided this basic food resource, the female allows him to mount her. Since this little creature needs a relatively heroic twenty minutes to get the job done, the males have learned to bring along just the right-sized meal. Too little and the female takes off, too much and the two of them start fighting over the remains. Less-evolved beetle predecessors, the ones who brought too small a treat, did not get to finish the job and failed to reproduce. The males who got the size down were selected by nature and prospered. It is their descendants who are still around . . . looking for just that right-size burger.

Beetle or *Homo sapiens*, when the cost of intimacy falls more heavily on one gender, opposing sexual agendas emerge. Intimate calculation arises, and sexual strategy enters the equation. For humans, sex became something more than a mindless encounter. A mating dance between competing gene packages, sex became the focus of a delicate form of mutual exploitation. Out on the savanna, a conflict of intimate interests emerged between short-term male seduction and long-term female responsibilities.

Then things got even more complicated. Most nonhuman female primates get interested in sex only when they are ovulating, which is when they get very interested. So interested, in fact, that their genital area swells up and turns fire engine red. This would be a lot like women cruising a singles bar with their foreheads plastered: "In Heat! Looking for Sex!" It is not difficult to imagine men jumping at this opportunity. Or, more likely, jumping over each other to get at the opportunity. An attractive chimpanzee female in conspicuous estrus is the object of constant, scrupulous attention by lots of males keen to fend off the competition and hook up.

As time went by, however, our male ancestors stopped getting worked up over swollen female genitals because there weren't any. Swollen, that is. In their infinite wisdom, or more likely by sheer necessity, females evolved the ability to camouflage the more obvious signs of reproductive readiness. Well, almost. Nature has not quite finished the job. An ovulating woman still reflects a subtle skin glow, a reddening of the cheeks, and slightly filled-out hips. Today's man would have to be watching closely to get such subtle ovulatory messages, which may be the whole idea.

In recent surveys, women report that their partners keep a closer watch and check in on them more frequently during these times. (Even sniffing ovulatory secretions can boost a male's testosterone.) And an ovulating woman might give a man more to see. Cross-cultural surveys reported in the *Archives of Sexual Behavior* confirm that women are still most interested in sexual intimacy when they are ovulating. They show more skin, put on more makeup, and wear more jewelry when they are most fertile.

Back on the savanna, concealed ovulation served to cool the jets of males who are constantly fertile and only too eager to take care of business. It kept them guessing about a female's receptivity, amplifying women's power of sexual choice. Monopolizing a fertile female was no longer a piece of cake. It's one thing to control access for the few days she's in heat; it's quite another to corner her market every day.

With this crucial evolutionary adaptation in place, a female's reproductive agenda was no longer sabotaged by huge ads plastered all over her body. A vehicle of discretion—and indiscretion—was placed in female hands, and sexual selectivity merged with a woman's larger interests. The lack of ovulatory signals made it easier for Lucy to pick and choose. A woman could hold out for a mate who would help provide the things she needed most. In a world where females began to grant sexual access to competing males with resources, an evolutionary arms race of complementary male courtship and mating styles was set in motion. The faint rumblings of relationship could be heard in the distance.

The sexual locomotion that drives us toward conception, and the relationships that nourish the result, raises intense issues for both sexes. It was becoming clear that sexual intimacy had different implications for the two sexes who stood up on the savanna. Although we have mostly compatible goals and much in common, as nature would have it, the biological, genetic, and psychological agendas men and women bring to the intimate party are as different as night and day.

Backwards from Coitus

Animals don't have sex because they have decided it's time to have kids. They don't think about long-term genetic strategies or even realize that sex sows the seeds of pregnancy. They simply obey a powerful instinct. Urges erupt in response to instinctive, hormonal stimuli, and the outcome they seek is an unthinking, seemingly pleasurable release. Meanwhile, nature's business gets done.

Humans, of course, understand the consequences of sex but, mostly, we go after the pleasurable release. According to the World Health Organization, sexual intercourse between humans occurs about one hundred million times a day. Less than a million result in conception, although some studies suggest it's a bit higher.

The joy of sex is nature's way of getting us to reproduce. It is the bribe our genes serve up so we will give them a shot at survival. We're here because our ancestors liked sex, maybe even loved sex, especially at the right time and in the right way. They desired and pursued it most when the female was ovulating, when they were in a safe place and in the most advantageous and effective sexual position. Over time, just about anything and everything that increased the likelihood of fertilization evolved to become a sexual turn-on.

In essence, natural selection has woven the force of the survival instinct and the urge toward reproduction into the exotic delights of sexual intimacy—the energy that powers so much of our contemporary world and preoccupies such a large part of our lives. Adult males, under almost every appealing circumstance, wish to inseminate. Mature females, under the right circumstances and with an acceptable partner, want to be inseminated. Nature starts with the goal of pregnancy and works backward. Just about anything that hints of the finish line can be sexy.

A trim athletic foot, for example, appeals to us for good evolutionary reasons. Long toes and a high arch suggest the ability to hold the ground, extend reach, and pivot quickly. Attached to long, muscular, and well-proportioned legs, a sleek foot promises speed, agility, and the ability to outmaneuver predators even while running with an infant. The modern high-heel shoe shows off these attributes. Accentuating the musculature of a women's legs, they display thoroughbred ankles, hint at a receptive posture, and bring a woman's breasts front and center into adult male sightlines. By hobbling herself, ever so delicately, a woman wearing heels out on a date is whispering submission, drawing out the protective male instinct. Heels may be someway back from coitus, but they are definitely a step in the right direction.

Sexual fantasies of dominance and submission, to take another example, are common to both sexes in inverse proportion. Looking at it from a reproductive perspective, researchers speculate that sexual immobilization of the female near climax is favored because it advances the sperm's mission to impregnate. It is more likely to hit the target if the female is stationary, especially in the few seconds before ejaculation. It's no coincidence that so many men are aroused by the thought of restraining a woman and why many women fantasize about being ravished, restrained, or "taken" by their partner, briefly pinioned under his final panting exertions. This is what brave poets and classical biologists describe as "feminine sexual surrender."

Like virtually every other animal and primate, hunter-gatherer couples did not face each other during intercourse. The male mounted from behind. Since animals are rarely more vulnerable than when they are copulating, it was also the safest position, allowing both partners to keep an eye on potentially dangerous surroundings. Perhaps most important, rear-mounting positions favor the rapid and deep penetration that best assures impregnation. Among all primates, only the bonobos have sexual intercourse face-to-face, and then only some of the time. Men and women facing each other for sexual union is a modern invention.

The missionary position is nurture; mounting from behind is nature. Ever imperial, nature comes first, and what nature wants is not just coitus, but successful coitus. In other words, conception. No doubt this explains why fertility experts often recommend this position and why informal surveys, such as those in *Sex & Health* newsletter in June 1998, report it as an arousing position for both sexes. What's more, some Japanese researchers recently discovered that the hotter the sex, the better the sperm count and ejaculatory potency.

However we get to the next generation, we transcend mortality through sexual intercourse as we pass our genetic legacy to our children. The powerful, instinctive urge to survive and perpetuate a part of ourselves has become sugarcoated with pleasure. Working backward from conception, nature propels our renewal through the joys of intimacy.

BEEP

"It's a jungle out there. It's a dark and lonely world, my friend. Cold. Brutal. Is that what you're writing about?

"Everybody's in such a big hurry. They're even in a hurry to relax. 'Sorry, can't talk now, gotta get to yoga.'

"I would like, y'know, to settle down. I am so tired of this dating business. Already. I'm bone weary. How tired am I? I'm soul-destroying tired, that's how tired I am. It's soul-destroying out there. I know, I say that a lot.

"And furthermore, I'm lonely.

"I want someone I can really care about and who really, really cares about me. We're like connected; we're a unit. A team. We face this ugly world together.

"And we have great sex. Lots of sex. Strange and wonderful sex. Lots of it.

"I know what you're thinking. You're thinking 'shallow'. Your pal's shallow. He's lame. But you know as well as I do, we all have two lives: our sex life—and the other one.

"I want roots. I want a family. Little mop-haired kids running around. One of each. The pitter-patter of little feet. Watch them grow up. Then, when I get old, they'll help me find my walker.

"It's insanity, of course. Complete lunacy. Children cost a fortune. My social life revolves around the sitter, my sex life goes directly in the toilet.

"So this woman I'm going to marry? This amazing woman should I ever find her. She has to be perfect, right? And agree to stay that way. Forever.

"Is that too much to ask? And to put up with me because, as we both know, I'm no day at the beach.

"Did I say lots of sex?

"Which brings me to the point of my call. There is a point, so help me.

"I'm eating at the beach yesterday and, as fate would have it, there are some friends at the next table, not to mention a very attractive woman. Precisely—I do mean <u>exactly</u>—my type.

"I know, there are several 'exactly my types'.

"Anyway, her number now rests in the palm of my hand. My clammy hand. Perspiration rings my neck; my heart's palpitating; my throat's constricted. Goosing myself up here. Ready . . . to make . . . THE CALL.

"Am I the nerdy clod who finds out she's engaged to a three-hundred-pound lineman with a personal vendetta against investment advisors? Or am I the bold heartthrob immobilizing her with my dashing confidence?

"Uh . . . Stay tuned."

Over the eons, a female who succumbed to the sweet lure of sex but was unable to hold a partner, more often failed to raise her infants successfully. Choosing to pair up with a fickle or irresponsible male, or just plain guessing wrong, meant she ended up rearing her children alone. On the other hand, those who secured a degree of male investment prospered. Through this process of sexual selection, nature came to favor female hominids who made intelligent choices about prospective partners.

Like Lucy, today's alert and responsible woman is on the lookout for a healthy male partner, a promising package with a strong genetic pro-file. Survey after cross-culture survey—the most often cited studies may be found in *The Evolution of Desire* by Professor David Buss at the Uni-versity of Texas—reports that she also hopes for a smart, dependable, and conscientious mate inclined to stick around and invest in parent-hood. That generally means a reliable partner with resources, or the likelihood of providing them. A male candidate needn't be wealthy; he needs to be solid, with prospects.

Resources mean assistance and sharing the burden of offspring. To Lucy, this meant food, shelter, and protection. To her distant modern sister carrying around ancient genes, it means something more like a secure environment and future, especially for the mothering task. Per-haps that's why, to the reproductively sensitive woman, there still may be nothing sexier about a man than his ability to hold down a job and cut a check. In contemporary personal ads, online or in the papers, women reveal an interest in their partner's financial capacities more than ten times as often as men.

This should come as no surprise. Women make a bet on the future. They can get just as worked up as men over a good-looking face and body, but the responsibilities of maternity force them to think further ahead. Projecting into an indefinite future of child-rearing burdens means women have to make more deliberate mate choices. This means placing greater emphasis on enduring qualities in a prospective mate such as character and dependability and less on shallow come-ons. Realists at heart, practical considerations drive female desire.

Males, meanwhile, are everywhere on the make in nature. Goosed forward by hormonal rushes, they are agitated initiators with commitment phobias who try to sweet-talk their way into the nest. They do this by displaying the things they think females want to see and hear. For many male animals, this means wowing the ladies with seductive ornaments like large antlers or spectacular feathers.

Implying his capacity to deliver resources, the human male animal mentions where he went to college, boasts about the deal he's about to pull off, or picks his date up in hot wheels. He does these things rather than dragging an animal carcass into the living room or flashing his tax return. He demonstrates how healthy he is by inviting her to watch him play tennis rather than e-mailing her his latest checkup. In the meantime, while he's trying to bowl her over with the sizzle, she's searching for the steak.

On the subject of sizzle, mindful of women's sexual depth, an ancient Islamic proverb holds that, when it comes to the joys of intimacy, one part is given to man and nine parts are given to woman. By way of example, the human female enjoys twice the erogenous zones of her male counterpart. But despite their more elaborate equipment, or perhaps because of it, women have evolved to manage their sexual impulses within more calculated, long-term considerations. Some argue that the availability of effective birth control methods have liberated women from the implications of pregnancy, freeing them to pursue their vast sexual potential. But the few decades since the discovery of modern contraception has to contend with millions of formative years of natural and sexual selection.

For nearly all of our species' long existence, the sexes have been molded by these ancient considerations. Inserting a diaphragm or swallowing a pill will not unhook the womb from a woman's psyche. It can take nearly forever for animals to adapt to new conditions, meaning women will restrain their immense sexual potential for a long time to come. They will continue to hold nature's high ground by linking the burdens of parenting to the pivotal act of intercourse.

Stalking Heads

Meanwhile, back on the savanna, our early ancestors continued to struggle with their new environment. The thing about tree-hugging, berry-picking primates is that they don't need to be all that smart: they only need to know how to hug trees and pick berries. But shuffling around on the broken ground of the savanna demanded a different kind of smarts.

As eons passed and our early hominid ancestors' ape-like bodies aligned themselves with walking upright, nature also selected for other upgrades. Improved vision helped hunters see and track prey and helped gatherers find things to eat. Flexible hands did a better job manipulating tools. But for the purposes of our story and the emerging arrangements between the sexes, it was the three-pound organ we call the brain that delivered an evolutionary turbocharge.

During the extended epoch on the savanna, the mental capacities of males and females had been growing under selective pressures to perform more varied and complex tasks. There were other creatures at large in the animal kingdom which were more adept at particular kinds of physical tasks, but no other species had developed the mental flexibility of our hominid ancestors. Mind you, we were still a long way from inventing money or even building a tent, let alone writing love poems or taking moonwalks. What mattered most back then was figuring out what you could eat and what was poison, which animals could eat you and which ones you could take down. And, of course, how to negotiate the sex part. These were the challenges our predecessors' brains first began to master. They didn't know what came next. It didn't matter what the big picture was. What mattered was getting through the day.

By two million years or so after we stood up to walk, or a mere 2.5 million years ago, the Stone Age hominid arrived. With an upgraded central processing unit evolved to half the size of a modern brain, these creatures looked a lot more like us in face and body. Tool use was the big new item, crudely designed instead of merely stumbled upon. This was likely the contribution not of male hunters but of female gatherers who had begun to use sticks to dig roots and rub them together.

This was about the time fire was first understood and controlled, a capacity to generate heat that would open new geographic and social vistas. Over this vast expanse of time, a sense of nature's patterns emerged, a recognition of the ways of animals and plants, an awareness of the seasons and the rhythms of the sun and moon. Nature's mysterious veil began to lift. We were starting to figure out the world around us.

True to the glacial pace of evolution, mental transformation came gradually at first. By the time another million years whizzed by, the protohuman brain had expanded 50 percent, to one thousand cubic centimeters although, as we will discover, size isn't everything. The first fashion show was still a couple of million years away, but we had begun to wear clothing. Lean-tos were built for shelter. Wood implements and hand axes augmented our already useful and flexible hands. Using stone arrowheads and more polished weaponry, hunters could band together to bring down bigger prey, tracking them over greater distances.

Still, progress out on the savanna was achingly slow. It wasn't until several thousand years ago that our forbearers were finally able to save a few things for a rainy day. Pitiful larders of half-preserved foodstuff, a few animal cloths, crude cooking utensils—this was the extent of their holdings, their shield against miscalculation or famine.

Scientists believe that it was during these long epochs of uncertain food supplies that the hunter-gatherer in us developed the habit of gorging ourselves, storing up fat by devouring high-caloric sweets whenever we could. We didn't know if there would be food tomorrow, and we needed quick energy. We still have these cravings, despite our steady food supply. Since few of us in developed nations are deprived these days, and we burn fewer calories sitting in a car or at a desk, we keep adding on the pounds. By now, obesity has become one of our major health problems.

Half a Mind to Speak

Like our eyes, our brains evolved in stages. In a kind of harmonic cause-and-effect tango, mental capacities—like our physical attributes—adapted to the demands of our changing environment and evolving sexual relations. The less-developed, lower components of our brain were adequate for handling the things animals confront every day, those near-instinctive operating programs for eating, walking, even breathing. But forced to forage, hunt, and negotiate more complex relationships, over the ages we have been honed for brainpower.

As we contended with more complex challenges, our evolving brains developed the capacity for synthesis, reasoning, and abstract thinking. Males and females gained the ability to better contemplate their circumstances, anticipate the future, and develop strategies by drawing on stored memories and impressions. In concert with flexible, evolving bodies, the growing capacities of our brain drove us to the front of nature's pack. But there was one thing missing, one giant step that would kick off an explosion of innovation and diversity. We had to learn how to speak. As we shall see, this would create no shortage of opportunities for confusion between the sexes.

All primates cry out in pain, raise their eyebrows when surprised, quiver when afraid, and flush when they get angry. We glower and bare our teeth to signal anger, yawn when we're tired, grin if we're tickled, and look away when we are offended. Chimpanzees can also communicate more complex emotions such as affection and courtship interests, signaling each other in times of danger and pointing out the location of food. From the dolphin's gentle screeches to the howling of wolves, mammals have been communicating for a long time.

Communication is adaptive. It vastly improves our ability to survive—or line up a date. And language of a more advanced kind can convey deeper meaning and more fully developed intentions. But to build and operate a spoken language, we needed both an advanced brain to organize the exercise and the physical capacity to form a range of sounds. This development was probably preceded by a rich language of hand and body gestures and a range of grunts, groans and clicks. Over a couple of million years, the hominid mouth, vocal tract, and evolving mental capacity finally gave rise to language. It emerged between 150,000 and 400,000 years ago and has by now flowered into six thousand different tongues.

The ability to communicate complex things consumed and challenged a lot of our growing brainpower, but it also freed us from some big limitations. A technique that helps you catch fish, concoct an herbal remedy, win friends, or gain a mate does not die out if it can be passed along. Language is the midwife of education and culture. Storytelling from one generation to another became the first method for transmitting knowledge. The oldest form of entertainment—narratives and fables—are the bedrock of just about every culture on Earth.

Converted to written form, language allowed us to record our history, archive information, and heighten communication between the sexes. This most powerful tool helped us define our clan, its beliefs, its rituals, and its artistry. Knowledge could be transported into the libraries and databases of civilization. In this way, language allowed us to benefit from our wise elders.

With language, the store of human information grew and distinct cultures took shape. We began to climb on the shoulders of those who came before us. If we could accumulate nothing else, we could store knowledge. With this singular achievement, we began to lift ourselves above the daily grind, and the pace of human development quickened. It broke from a slow crawl to a purposeful jog.

Business Before Pleasure

Like most everything else that survives the selection process, language evolved because it helped us stay in business. Once our survival is reasonably assured, however, other less pressing needs begin to demand attention. The psychologist, Abraham Maslow, presented this progression as a five-level pyramid. The broad base of this need hierarchy centers our primal concerns on physiological needs, the bare business of survival, food, and shelter. When survival's at stake, nothing else much matters.

Once our hunger is satisfied, our thirst quenched, and we are reasonably certain our basic needs are looked after, our attention climbs toward the middle levels of the pyramid—to our needs and desires around sex, mating, family, and kinship. This is where nature's selection process becomes sexual and more complex social forms emerge. As these more intimate needs are addressed, our interests then expand toward broader social matters—to friendships, our circumstances at work, and our place in the larger community. These middle levels of the pyramid of needs are where most of us live and love each day. Those lucky enough to cover most of these bases then approach the top of the hierarchy. There they may indulge the luxury of realizing their hopes and aspirations, the full spectrum of human potential.

This ladder of motivating needs becomes more refined and less visible in wealthy and sophisticated societies where basic survival is of less concern to most people. Still, it remains with us in more subtle forms. The need hierarchy also comes into sharp focus when misfortune strikes and we experience it in reverse. Out of a job? Doctor says there's a problem with your test results? Terrorists attacking the nation or threatening us with nuclear horrors? These are not the times when we worry about our status in the community or whether the hot new associate at the office has noticed us.

Instead, with immediate danger upon us, deep-seated stress and fear responses kick in: rapid increases in heart rate pump extra blood to tensing muscles, nonessential functions shut down, and perception sharpens as ancient biological forces prepare us for defense or escape—the well-known fight-or-flight response. In times of peril, as individuals and whole societies, we abandon sophisticated distractions, descend the pyramid of needs, and hunker down around the basics. That's when we are reminded that survival is nature's primary piece of business. In the aftermath of the September 11 attacks, "sex" dropped off the list of top ten Internet search engine terms for the very first time. With danger at hand, we get real in a hurry.

The first few million years of hominid evolution represent a near-eternal trek across the lowest rungs of the need hierarchy. Lucy was mostly thinking about staying alive, mating, and providing a safe environment for her children, not whether pleats are in this year. Even today, life remains a struggle for billions of people. Only recently has a modest portion of the world's population surmounted everyday drudgery. Just a razor-thin layer of our most elite societies has gained the option to pursue a higher call. For everybody else, there is the hope of staying alive long enough to steal a few small pleasures, launch the next generation, and gain a toehold on the future. But no matter our wealth and status, starting a family means we have to navigate the tempestuous avenues of the sexual union.

Mama's Baby, Papa's Maybe

Throughout the millions of years that hominids have walked upright and across the hundreds of thousands of adapting generations that reach all the way to our time, males have been hunters. Things were tough. Life could be short. With their piddling sexual investment and the ever-present risk of death or banishment, ancestral males were in even more of a sexual hurry than the human ones are now. A long-term relationship meant the morning after.

Sex had no consequences for males. Hostage to hormones, they made rapid sexual decisions based on availability and some basic calculations. Is she fertile and healthy? Well-proportioned, with clean, attractive lines? Are her hips full enough to carry a baby, breasts ample enough to nourish it? Is she agile, able to move swiftly with the infant to escape danger? These were the skin-deep mating criteria of men on the run. In fact, they probably were not even conscious of these raw computations.

Most young men are only dimly aware of the primitive evaluations that rumble beneath their desires. They usually just respond to the one urgent sexual barometer they know best: an erect penis. Given the male's superficial sexual ignition system, his lack of accountability for the pregnant outcome, and high historical rates of infant mortality, nature has selected for a male strategy of sowing wild oats—often and widely. Plant a thousand seeds so that a few might bloom.

This crude calculus has governed male sexuality for millions of years. Consider the immense frequency of male masturbation, their extensive sexual histories, cross-cultural obsessions with shallow forms of female display, and pornography. Ponder the general lack of male sexual discrimination, how they screw around, flee from commitment, and objectify women. Nor do they grow out of it. A recent survey for the American Association for Retired Persons reports that the mature, over forty-five sexes sustain most of the sexual patterns that first show up prior to adolescence. Mature males think about sex much more often and masturbate eight times more frequently than women seniors. They are also much more likely to think of sex as a crucial part of their relationships.

Yet, hard as men try to propel their genes into the future, fatherhood is never a sure thing, at least until DNA fingerprinting began unraveling this intimate mystery as well. Of course, we have always been able to see the baby in the swelling stomach of its mother. This crucial, longstanding ambiguity, the gnawing lack of assured paternity, eats away at male security. In several primate species, newly ascendant alpha males go so far as to kill off the young offspring of their predecessors in order to make certain the female devotes her energies to the new alpha male's progeny. Anticipating this infanticide, some pregnant mammals are even known to spontaneously abort a fetus that wasn't fathered by a new dominant male. Given this phenomenon, should we be entirely surprised to learn that a young human child is many times more likely to be murdered by a stepfather, or mother's new boyfriend, than by its natural father?

The male compulsion to ensure the certainty of his bloodline is the force that has driven men's extensive, often bizarre, and sometimes abominable attempts to control the women around them. From veils to chastity belts, cloistered seclusion to vaginal mutilation, even the lenient treatment sometimes accorded men who kill because of their wife's infidelity, paternal insecurity is revealed across every known culture. No matter how much we might lament the consequences of this male inadequacy, regardless of whether it is "fair," nothing is likely to change deep-seated male insecurity. Managing rather than denying this imperial force is how successful cultures have handled its volatile implications.

Inflaming this male obsession for reproductive control is the harsh reality that, at least for breeding purposes, we do not ever come close to needing all the men in the world. A thimbleful of male semen holds the planet's entire annual requirements. Save for a few alpha studs, the rest of mankind could be cannon fodder—worker ants, economically useful for assisting women and children, but otherwise dispensable. This daunting equation of male competition, when added to their vivid biological insecurities, is the source of much male aggression and competitiveness; their fixation on resources, dominance, and territory; even the origins of war. When the world is awash in other men's sperm, genetic survival is at stake.

At the dawn of the twenty-first century, an unidentified couple offered $50,000 for an egg, providing the donor was tall and scored high on her SATs. That makes many young women potential millionaires. Meanwhile, hard as they might try, most men can't give their sperm away. As we will see, this anxious sexual equation works its way into every nook and cranny of our lives. For better and for worse.

Opposite Attractions

We can choose to look at the differences between men and women as something that's unfair. We can bemoan them. Or, like Lucy, we can see in them an opportunity. When the less bountiful savanna pushed dependence into the calculations of female hominids, males won, too. They achieved significance beyond sperm contribution. They were needed by women for resources and protection. An intimate bargain appeared on the sexual horizon.

But if men were to help women and their offspring by sharing the fruits of their labor, they needed something in return. They needed to know that the child they were supporting was their own. Promoting another man's genetic bequest is a dagger pointed at the heart of almost every male instinct. Since males were no longer able to monopolize a woman's camouflaged sexual receptivity and were often away on the hunt, female sexual fidelity became a crucial binding ingredient in the mating bond recipe.

No one knows for sure what our early female ancestors understood about sex and its consequences. But if women were not the first to discover the connection, they were quick to fall all over the idea of attaching men to their infants. Women have gone to great lengths to assure their mate that he is the father. Traditionally taking on his surname, they understood, if only intuitively, the value in holding a man's attention and securing his help. Even today, new mothers and their side of the family draw comparisons between the looks of their child and its father, rather than themselves, up to four times more often.

With the intimate bargain set in place, male sexual interest was massaged past the quickie. An echo of something called fatherhood could be heard as males were connected to their offspring. The pair bond was born.

The pair bond is a compact between a woman and a man built upon mutual need and complementary skills, forged for the strategic advantage of both partners. It was a deal no gender could refuse. As with any good bargain, the pair bond called for compromises but, in the end, it worked for everyone. In return for help protecting and providing for mother and child, the male gained exclusive sexual access and the certainty of paternity. (Well, not quite. Modern testing suggests it's more like 95 percent.) It also worked for the clan as coupling off cut down on male competition and jealousy that could be both disruptive and inefficient. In the embrace of the pair bond, men and women were no longer merely sex objects. The door to an intimate future had finally opened.

There were no social philosophers around to inform Lucy and her clan about how things ought to be. Our ancestors reached out for one another to fulfill needs they did not question and contribute talents that came naturally to them. Males and females were compelled by the raw dictates of nature surging within them. What's more, the pair bond was neither entirely monogamous nor permanent. But even if it fell short of a total embrace, when the sexes united, putting their unique qualities on the table, they compensated for each other's deficiencies and gained the benefit of their partner's special gifts.

Needing each other to complete our desires and dreams, the specialized division of labor between the sexes forces us to coordinate with one another; to share, plan, and use our expanding intellectual capacities to work things through together. With unity of purpose won, the dance of human courtship, from fragrant flowers to racy Ferraris, could take its first unsteady steps.

Though we have long evolved from lives of pure instinct and soared to the mighty heights of reason, powerful ancient drives still prowl deep within us. If we deny this part of ourselves, if we confine these primal instincts to the shadows of our minds and our world, we imperil our ability to be fully integrated human beings. If we fail to attend to the lower rungs that continue to power our base needs, we will not be able to ascend the ladder of our higher ambitions.

We do not rise up by denying our origins. They just come back as unfinished business. Acknowledging what we're made of, and where we've come from, allows us to seek acceptable and enriching ways to satisfy our human passions. In the sweet promise of nature's pair bond, males and females at last gained the chance to turn the excitement of sex and seduction into the precious mysteries of love.

The Rise of Humanity

3

THE TRICKSTER
CALLED LOVE

*Women and Men Are Seduced
into Extended Partnership*

To: HotShotWriter@writersbloc.net
Subject: Sex, Drugs and Rock & Roll

Well, sex and drugs anyway. ;–) May I introduce the investment opportunity of the century for your consideration? Let's begin with ED shall we? That's right, erectile dysfunction. A brand new ailment uncovered in the waning years of the twentieth century by those tireless epidemiologists in the marketing department of the uber drug companies. Used to be, you grow up, you get older, sometimes your organ, the one between your legs develops a mind of its own. Maybe you're tensed up from work? Performance anxiety with a new hottie? Whatever. Mr. Happy just won't stand up when you need him the most.

Yesterday's news? You pop a pill, wait for an hour and hope you don't go blind.

Tomorrow's news? Whip out the lubricating gel, dab it on the nearest available hand and apply to the "surface" in question. Presto! As the

---

lotion is lovingly massaged on your member, you turn into a man of steel.

Now that's what I call a growth stock. Demanding Boomers are in their fifties and they will not take "flaccid" for an answer.

Second round trials underway. Great little O-T-C company. FYI we're loading up your 401(k).

On a personal note, I'm just thrilled to report that my first date with the lovely new candidate was a resounding success. She's hot. Very smart. Funny. Got stuff going on. Little bit of hug-face there at the end of the evening. Definite potential.

Later.

YBTIA

P.S. Thought you'd get a kick out of this cartoon.

"*Trust me—you're more than ready.*"

One of the countless wonders promised by the recent unraveling of the human genome is the ability to trace our ancestry back in time. Following men's Y chromosomes and women's mitochondrial DNA, scientists are working out the details of our natural history as they decipher the tiny twists and turns imbedded in the genes of contemporary humans. Combined with classic forms of archaeology and anthropology, a unified picture of human migration and our own origins has come into focus.

Our direct ancestors, to whom all humans alive today are related, first appeared in Africa around two hundred thousand years ago. Restless nomads in search of better prospects and the next horizon, large human troops and clan clusters headed east, across land bridges into the Middle East sixty thousand to eighty-five thousand years ago. From there, the human family's migration extended into central Asia and north into Europe about thirty-five thousand years ago. Roughly four out of five European men share a common, solitary male ancestor from this epoch—a spectacularly successful ancestor if there ever was one.

After millions of years of prehuman inertia, the pace was picking up. Better tools aided the hunt, lean-tos provided shelter, and rough slings carried a few provisions. Life would dribble on in this fashion until nomadic *Homo sapiens* finally settled down a mere ten thousand years ago with the onset of agriculture.

Whatever was going on between men and women in these loose legions, forging an extended commitment to the opposite sex heralded a big advance in the hierarchy of human needs. What was true then is true now, as there is not much time for romance or building a bond when short-term survival is at stake. But with food and shelter in ample supply, humans want more. We want to mate, to connect with a partner. The sexual bond is the next step up the ladder, the place we turn to after our individual survival needs have been satisfied.

Leaving our ancestors to fumble for countless generations with the trials and tribulations of intimacy gives us the opportunity to take a stimulating side-trip to ponder the evolutionary and biological forces that influence men and women, and their mating choices and strategies, then and now. We begin our escapade by figuring out why we find certain people attractive, what love has to do with it, and why this pathway so often leads to a baby carriage. We then trace the human odyssey from conception and infancy to childhood and the sexually ripe, seemingly invincible modern-day adolescent. By chapter's end, we'll pick up the trail of our recent ancestors.

The Look of Love

The pair bond. It was probably signalled by no grand moment in our history, just some couples choosing to bed down beside each other. No doubt they slept around. The one-night stand, after all, is still with us. In fact, the sexual bond was a fragile thing, all the more precarious when the couple's child was old enough to be lodged with the other kids, which wasn't very old. Still, there was no denying that the basic building block of every subsequent human culture to come—the devoted sexual pairing—had at last emerged.

No one knows for sure when the pair bond first showed up, but anthropologists do know that extended relationships were in place by the time *Homo sapiens* put in an appearance. With the male drawn into the semblance of a connection and a whiff of paternal responsibility in the air, couples could begin contemplating their future. A new organizational energy was set loose. A stable society was the pair bond's promise, the modern family its gift.

It should come as no surprise that we spend a lot of energy trying to fulfill the promise of regeneration. Mating is still the business of survival. It is survival "going long." Begetting progeny means we have achieved an indefinite reach, a potentially unending future. Some of our genes survive, hitching a ride with the next generation. The survival instinct handed nature an anvil, shaping our bodies and the lower ranges of our intellect. But the new business of lining up and holding onto a mate drove the higher powers of our minds.

Negotiating the minefield of sexual pairing would take all the cleverness, guile, and discernment our little central processing units could summon. It would push the limits of our intelligence into the more subtle realms of intimate calculation and compromise. Courageous acts, desperate deeds, and majestic sacrifice would be committed in the pair bond's name.

Because we desire the best for our offspring, we have a powerful incentive to make promising mating choices. After all, the other half of our child's inheritance, and much of its prospects, will be our partner's gift. This sexual selection process is engaged every time we size up a member of the opposite sex, check out the competition, assess our daughter's boyfriend, notice a "mismatched" couple at a party—or, better yet, gain a glimpse of the future in a new lover's eyes. We are all genetic engineers.

We make breeding judgments on the street, at the coffee shop, and in the boardroom. This seems especially true of men who, prompted especially by visuals, are busy assessing women the instant they arrive at the party. Women at least seem to wait until they sit down. In making up our minds about something as important as finding a mate, we activate every intuitive capacity seeded during our evolutionary odyssey and all the mental calculation we can command. People may only be packaging for genes, but when we're trying to swap them with the opposite sex, some packages look better than others.

Humans take in most of their initial impressions through vision, and a well-balanced face and body suggest some crucial things to both casual and not-so-casual observers. An evenly proportioned face and figure go together, and, according to biologists, we find this symmetry appealing because it suggests a healthy genetic inheritance, a kind of uniform and untroubled downloading of parental archives. Physical regularity and balance imply health and the absence of developmental stresses in the womb. Symmetrical features advertise genetic fitness; they are nature's hint that having offspring with this person will more likely result in a healthy child. In other words, symmetry has bedroom eyes.

Asymmetry, the absence of structural balance, suggests the opposite: an irregular genetic inheritance, a lack of nourishment as a fetus, an early childhood disease, or perhaps an impaired immune system. Less symmetrical males score lower on IQ tests; they are less proficient at sports, report greater health problems, and display more frequent outbursts of anger and jealousy. What's more, this instinctive preference for symmetry crosses all cultural and racial boundaries.

We start early on this, well before society's values can instruct us. Infants, for instance, smile longer and more often at balanced faces. And it's not just us. Many species use symmetry as criteria during mating. Birds favor symmetry in selecting their partners, and bees go for the most symmetrical flowers. Beauty may be in the eye of the beholder—except most of the beholders are looking for the same thing.

Studies at the University of New Mexico report that, on average, symmetrically framed men gain more sexual partners and produce more sperm; they have their first sexual encounters up to four years before their less well-proportioned peers. Evenly proportional men have more orgasms, more of which are achieved simultaneously, which leads to improved sperm retention and an increased likelihood of achieving pregnancy. (Measuring these things must be a fascinating line of work.)

We desire physical beauty, as well as agility and strength in a mate, because they are the qualities we want to pass to our children. These are the features that helped us survive and prosper on the savanna, and when passed to our offspring, they increase our chances of having grandchildren. Slender fingers, high arches, and agile joints appeal to us for their dexterity, grace, and economy of movement. Still other features, such as a long neck, may be admired because they most distinguish us from the nearest, related species. A woman's long mane of hair suggests youth and health while full, red lips suggest . . . well, red lips.

When we get in closer, we use our sense of smell to nose out the best candidates. Like most mammals and primates, we're trying to determine genetic compatibility. Though we seek familiar smells, we don't want them too similar because different scents imply beneficially diverse genes. From an evolutionary perspective, closely related genes compromise our offspring, while fresh blood rejuvenates the chromosomal mix.

Mating Games

Consciously or not, we are looking for good genetic bets. This means a lot more than looks. In every culture, people long for a pleasing personality, dependability, intelligence, and generosity of spirit in a mate. But once we get past these basic qualities and the physical markers of a healthy and pleasing partner, the mating interests of men and women begin to part company. The dilemma—as well as the challenge and much of the excitement—is that when it comes to sex and partnership, men and women are not playing for the same stakes.

We all want to mate "up," to advance and improve our genetic stake. The male seems to take what he can get over some crude minimum threshold and, like the Energizer bunny, just keeps on going.

For him, upward mating is infinite, plagued as he often is by the sense that there is something more, something better out there—like the perfect woman. Spared the investment of incubating an embryo, males of almost every species can get worked up in a hurry. Sexually speaking, males are skin-deep. Reading female bodies like road maps, men seem to run potential candidates through a rapid "go/no go" breeding turnstile. For many males, the minimum level of attraction is low, which begets a wide range of sexual possibilities. And whatever else may grab men's immediate attention, hardly anything counts as much as fertility and its youthful signs.

Whether a man wants to be a father or not, even if he's quite sure he doesn't want to be one, the ability of his prospective partner to conceive a healthy infant is sexual priority number one. The physical markings of youth are what captivate male attention: wide, glowing eyes set over rosy cheeks on a symmetrical face; tight, unblemished skin; full lips revealing white teeth; lustrous hair; erect posture; a lively gait and a slender waist in pleasing proportion to womb-bearing hips. Miss America has gotten almost a third skinnier over the last few decades but her waist-to-hip ratio hasn't budged. Mature men may be aroused by mature beauty. Youth is always in style.

Packaging counts for women, too. In cross-cultural studies of young couples, 85 percent of observers place lovers within two points of each other on a one-to-ten beauty scale. In fact, big imbalances in the looks department often mean big trouble down the road as, according to this research, couples who widely differ in beauty are more likely to break up. In addition to symmetry and other universal signs of health and good form, women are usually attracted to men who are taller than they are as height is a kind of proxy for a man's ability to protect, provide, and avoid domination by other men. Reporting in the journal *Nature*, an international team of scientists found that, on average, bachelors are an inch shorter than married men and childless men are an inch shorter than fathers. Even in a world where brain clearly trumps brawn, studies confirm that, on average, taller men make more money and command higher status. The taller man rarely loses the popular vote in American presidential elections.

As usual when it comes to sex, dessert for men is just the appetizer for women. Given the weighty physical and parental investment of pregnancy, a woman is motivated to look past the glossy envelope to see what's inside. Pretty boys can be feckless, their heads turning at each passing fancy. As a result, good looks may get a man in the door, but not necessarily into bed.

According to recent studies, a woman's idea of a good-looking man can even shift depending on where she is in her menstrual cycle. Women experience a rise in testosterone during ovulation, which may account for a feistier sexual appetite and a preference for more rugged, masculine features. The rest of the month, a woman is more likely to prefer men with softer, smoother faces. These subtle variations will often play across a woman's menstrual cycle if she's not taking oral contraceptives, yet another example of the female sexual symphony versus the Johnny-One-Note male.

Sitting on the scarce commodity, the object of persistent male attention, and less urgently compelled to act on her impulses, the attractive, fertile woman disposes of male proposition. Not held hostage to immediate gratification, women are on the lookout for signs of sincerity, reliability, and endurance, and are more inclined to project their intimate lives into a responsible, maternal future. As she contemplates motherhood, a woman may prefer to delve into a potential mate's prospects for parental investment and resources. In other words, as men get worked up over looks, women start checking references.

Pleased as a woman may be to find herself the object of lustful attention, women around the world view intimate possibilities from the heights of relationship. Looking past the come-on through to character, they set the deliberate pace of the sexual tango. Through their evaluation of male candidates, women have, over time, helped shape masculinity. This is also true throughout the animal world where female emphasis on genetic fitness and resource provision sculpts the opposite sex and the mating strategies males employ. Giving form to her incubative instincts and responsibilities, extended female time horizons turn male sexual urgency into something more enduring than a one-night stand.

Nature drives us toward the jackpot of pregnancy. How we manage to get there, however, depends on who's calling the shots. Without the responsibilities of the womb, men are sexual anarchists. Driven by urgent hormonal rushes and boundless wells of sperm, men the world over ini-tiate and propel sexual activity. Posing, posturing, and strutting, men coax, wheedle, flatter, and sweet talk. They tell heroic tales and make promises they don't keep. Their pursuit of intimacy is often one part reason, nine parts seduction.

Until, that is, they are struck by lightning. Seduction sizzles into romance. Casual turns to serious. Giddy with passion and the promise of a future joined together, men as well as women get high on infatua-tion. It is an electrical, full-body experience. We daydream, fantasize and project like crazy into forever. We ache for one another. We may even forget to eat.

We are in love.

Enter the Magician

Being "in love" is a wonderful thing, but we mustn't be fooled: love is here to do nature's bidding. For women, capable of bearing the child of only one man at a time and inclined to look into the future, love has become focused and exclusive. As a woman fixates on her partner, her interest in other candidates ebbs. She draws her prospective mate to-ward a relationship. Love becomes the bedrock of her partnership, a long-term commitment requiring patience, fortitude, and vulnerability. She prepares to stick it out through thick and thin, to stand by her man. For a woman, love is of the heart. It is a form of feminine completion.

A man's love is a signal of devotion, a willingness to expend energy and resources. Having wandered the lonely alleyways of masculinity, the modern man revels in finding Miss Right and commits himself to a single beloved. This time he makes promises he would like to keep. He exhibits the innate urge to protect, to provide for his lover and their offspring, making sacrifice upon sacrifice. In this way, love tames a man, channeling chaotic male energies toward relationship. Anchored by love, he dreams of a bright future, a world of achievement and respect. Love is an inclusive circle for women, but Cupid's arrow gives men direction and propels them forward. They set out to work for something. Sexual anarchy is stilled, masculine rivalry is cut short, and harmony between men is fostered.

Well, mostly. The fiery heat of passionate love unleashes other tempests as jealousy travels in league with desire. Ready to pounce at any sign of disloyalty, male jealousy erupts from the uncertainty of fatherhood. Back on the savanna, even a hint of female infidelity raised the stakes. If a male was going to hang around and invest in parenting, it had better be his kid, since he certainly wasn't interested in supporting someone else's. According to researchers at the University of Texas, this uncertainty makes men keenly sensitive to any inkling of their partner's sexual involvement with other men.

On the other hand, though they may be distressed by isolated acts of infidelity, women in a committed relationship seem far more threatened by their partner's wandering into an emotional, and perhaps financial, relationship with another woman. When we become jealous over infidelity and outside attachments in our "sophisticated" third millennium relationships, we confirm the contemporary power of the ancient emotions and calculations that still rumble beneath our civilized exterior.

All this fire and brimstone around Eros erupts because, in the hard light of day, love is a con artist. A seductive hypnotist. Love is both the pair bond package wrapper and its glue. The survival instinct embodied as hope, love is a whisper of eternity. Cloaking the object of our affection in an amorous mist, love seduces us into glossing over our partner's less appealing qualities, blinding us to blemishes and helping us find excuses for inadequacy. Our partner's assets are magnified, his or her liabilities diminished. Overwhelmed by hormonal rushes, the scents, essences, and pheromones of the alchemist, love carries the reproductive game into the end zone.

Flights of Fancy

Where there's love, there's sex. Which is the point, so to speak. But as has always been the case, men and women bring their own particular agendas into the bedroom. This divergent sexual energy is prominently displayed when we consider sexual fantasies—flights of intimate fancy that act like x-ray vision, revealing our unfiltered urges and the ancient biological calculations that propel modern romance. Zooming in below the mantle of civility, intimate fantasies can be a safe outlet through which we can express the erotic, even strange reveries most of us harbor.

Evolutionary psychologists Bruce Ellis and Donald Symons at the University of California, Santa Barbara, have summarized a wide variety of international studies. For starters, men everywhere have about twice as many sexual fantasies, whether they are awake or asleep, perhaps because their flights of fancy don't go very far. Male sexual fantasy plot lines range from nonexistent to simple. There is no flirtation or courtship, hardly any foreplay. Interested as always in rapid connection to a wide variety of prospects, three-fourths of men's fantasies revolve around women with whom they are not involved.

True to the arithmetic of savanna reckonings, men's fantasies are big on quantity and variation and short on nuance. They frequently change partners within any given episode and fantasize about group sex twice as often as women, even if they hone in on one lover at the moment of orgasm. Male sexual reflections are visual, centered on easy, dominant access to attractive, exposed, and wanton women. We're talking sheer graphic lust, wide open positions, and body parts—a fast track to copulation. There are no commitments or encumbrances.

Less than a fifth of men report having any feelings at all during their sexual fantasies. This is worth repeating: More than four out of five men experience *zero*, nada, *zilch* in the way of emotions—nothing even close to love—during their sexual fantasies. Unless, that is, you think pure lust qualifies as an emotion.

When it comes to women, almost all these proclivities are reversed. They have fewer fantasies but, then again, they can nurse one all day. Their fantasy partners are most often familiar, as almost 60 percent relate to someone a woman is already involved with—twice the rate of men. There is usually a buildup and much thicker plot lines. Romantic closeness counts big time. For women, sexual intimacy is about emotional connection, romantic settings, and the quality of the experience. In other words, it's about relationship.

Women rarely change partners during a single fantasy episode. Nearly half never do, and they don't come close to men in thinking about the opposite sex through explicit visual cues. At the center of their fantasy resides the sweetness of heart and soul. They yearn for strength, protectiveness, and bonding, often to be swept away by a dashing, masterful partner. Journeying to an intimate inner world, women open the floodgates when they feel trust. Vitally interested in how their partner responds to them, they fantasize about being the exclusive focus of a favored man's nearly uncontrollable desire.

All of this should help explain why pornography grabs male attention and why women purchase so many romance novels. With two thousand new titles each year, romances account for 40 percent of fiction sales, or nearly one in five adult books. Pornography is the male romance novel.

Navigating the ancient business of love and sex in real life, as opposed to fantasy, leaves many of us understandably bewildered at least some of the time. Depending upon culture and circumstances, the dance of sexual pairing can be a casual fling that is scarcely removed from coitus, or it can be fashioned into an intricate minuet that barely looks like sex. Surely one measure of a culture's sophistication is how far back from intercourse the intimate dance of romance begins.

But whether the buildup to sexual union is a jitterbug or an elaborate waltz, a one-night stand or a pair bond that lasts a lifetime, the melody meant to linger is a baby's lullaby. The blessing a newborn child bestows on its parents transforms their parental sacrifices into acts of devotion. In this way, the magician called love becomes a servant to the next generation.

The Point of Conception

Orgasm may be the end for men, but it's just the beginning for women. With an egg fertilized, a woman embarks on a lengthy reproductive odyssey. Life stirs in her womb.

The instinctive drive among women to realize motherhood, rooted deep in their genes and charged by hormones, is one of the deepest of all animal urges. Only a tiny fraction of women report a complete absence of maternal desire. Despite the many other ways a woman may find fulfillment in our modern world, for many, if not most, connecting to a suitable mate, getting pregnant, giving birth, and nursing an infant go a long way toward achieving the essence of feminine potential. Typical of nature's ways, answering this call delivers a wide variety of health and psychological benefits.

Pregnancy grounds a woman. It sharpens her maternal focus and rounds out her body. It may permanently and favorably alter brain function, often heightening awareness. Depression and suicide are lowest among pregnant women; in fact, they are less likely to be admitted to psychiatric facilities than at any other time in their life. Medical research has pumped out ample and growing evidence that pregnancy and lactation afford crucial breathers for ovaries and hormones. Contemporary female gatherers in Africa and Australia, for example, average six pregnancies and breast-feed each child for more than two-and-a-half years. As a result, they have about 160 menstrual periods over their lifetime, while the average Western woman endures the strain of about four hundred.

Pregnancy reduces nearly every type of reproductive cancer. Ovarian cancer is cut in half among women with three pregnancies. Breast cancer is highest in nuns, lower in mothers who nurse three or more months, lowest of all among females who get pregnant in their teens. Pregnancy also correlates with a lower incidence of colon cancer while birthless females are two-and-a-half times more likely to develop brain cancer. Mothers who breast-feed gain some protection against type 2 diabetes later in life. Early pregnancy, multiple pregnancies, and breast-feeding are simply healthy. Childbirth carries risk, of course, but so does crossing the street or taking an aspirin. *Not* giving birth seems riskier still.

Lucy was pregnant at eleven and may have been dead by the time a lot of Western women even begin thinking about motherhood. As women age, the complications of pregnancy increase significantly. By age forty, a woman is much more likely to carry an impaired fetus and miscarriage rates soar to more than one in three. Her chances of experiencing a difficult birth rise substantially, and she is three times more likely to have a Cesarean section. The chance of high blood pressure problems for the baby, and mother, is heightened among older mothers, and the risk of giving birth to a child with Down's Syndrome increases ten times between the ages of thirty and forty. Most women who have carried their first child in their twenties, then a second child a decade or so later, describe their early pregnancy as a piece of cake, the last one as a serious endurance test.

The intimate bond between a mother and her child is forged through the lengthy human gestation period. While hormonal rushes sweep through a pregnant woman's body, mother and unborn infant share blood and every breath. Their link is further welded in the tumult of giving birth, the intimacy of breast-feeding, and the mother's fondling and care of her utterly dependent infant. Actually, not quite utterly dependent. A baby's cries announce a clever evolutionary adaptation, one that makes their mothers seek *them* out. Babies, as well as puppies and kittens, have evolved to be adorable because of the loving attention it gets them. Being cute at birth, if not later, confers an advantage. A 2005 study at the University of Alberta suggests that parents take better care of attractive children, perhaps sensing a more promising genetic legacy.

A key player in this orchestration of mother-and-child affection is a body chemical called oxytocin. It has a knack for showing up at all the right moments. Working with estrogen, oxytocin can trigger an instinctive, sometimes intense female urge to be "filled-up." Seeping into receptor sites in the brain and throughout the reproductive system, oxytocin—which spikes at orgasm in both men and women—also triggers uterine contractions at labor, heightening mothering impulses and a woman's readiness for breast-feeding.

Oxytocin, the "cuddly hormone," unleashes an affectionate openness that intensifies every new mother's maternal devotions. Our evolutionary heritage extends even to the time of day women give birth as oxytocin usually initiates labor after dark, when our ancient predators were asleep. Fathers also experience hormonal shifts, even if they are less pronounced; testosterone levels back off when his mate gives birth and estrogen levels rise to encourage nurturing instincts in new fathers.

The true depth of this maternal instinct in nature is most vividly on display when a mother is called upon to defend her young, the only time female primates can be prodded into acute levels of aggression. It seems there is nothing a mother will not do to protect her child, even if it means acting like an aggressive male. The potent and enduring bond between a mother and her infant is honored and reinforced in every known human culture. Whatever else the female contributes to the pair bond, her role as nurturer and nest-protector is beyond question.

Mothers are not the only ones who benefit from honoring nature's call. So do their children. Medical evidence increasingly suggests that infants benefit most from mother's milk, which contains nutrients and fatty acids not easily reproduced in formula. Mother's milk is nature's cheap, healthy food source. It is all an infant needs to survive during its first six months. Although formula improvements are in the pipeline, breast-feeding is also associated with lower infant mortality, fewer infections, easier introduction to solid food, and better childhood performance in several other ways. Breast-fed children are less likely to become obese, are generally healthier, and test up to five IQ points higher than formula-fed babies.

Although two-thirds of new American mothers choose to breast-feed, most give it up in a few months. While some breast milk is preferable to none, the longer the better for the child. Which is important, because the infant emerging from its mother's womb is something primal and urgent, earthy and mysterious—a brand-new entry in nature's evolutionary sweepstakes. It will need all the help it can get.

Chance and Circumstance

Like all complex animals, human embryos pass through stages that resemble some of the creatures from which we have evolved. On the way to developing hands and lungs, the human fetus first develops things that look like fins and wings, which are eventually transformed into arms and legs. The embryo floats in the amniotic sac, a body of fluids chemically resembling the sea water from which we came. Even today, an occasional newborn human arrives with some tiny vestigial tail structure before it's surgically removed.

Within weeks of conception, the embryo's blood cells can be separated from its mother, revealing the fetus' own genetic profile. Inside the nucleus of this blood cell, or any other cell in our body, can be found our own version of the human genome, the how-to manual for creating and sustaining human beings like us. Mapping the genome, it turns out, was more a beginning than an ending. When it was finally sequenced in

2001, humans were revealed to have barely more genes than some very "simple" animals. Although estimates of the gene count have been rising ever since, this humbling news serves to point out our similarity with other living things; it also brings to light the complexity of genetic research.

As it happens, gene sequencing is only part of the story. Gene size, positioning, and composition, as well as huge stretches of seemingly repetitive "junk DNA," may also play a role. More important, genes are recipes for making multiple proteins that, in turn, manufacture the hormones and enzymes that activate our cells, and trigger growth, illness, healing, and aging. There may be as many as three hundred thousand proteins in our body, and their structure is complex, unlike relatively simple genetic "strings" of nucleic acids. This makes epigenetics and proteomics, the hot new study of proteins, an extremely complicated, lengthy, and challenging undertaking that will occupy biologists and their computers for decades to come.

Even with all our genes finally identified, scientists are left merely with a list of recipe ingredients, only some of which are understood. That is not unlike a catalogue of the thousands of parts that, for example, go into a jetliner. The simple list doesn't tell you what role each part plays in assembling the craft, how they fit together, why the plane works, or where it's headed. Exciting as the current revelations are, there is a lot of work ahead for geneticists as they move from churning out raw data to pinning down what each gene does, let alone deciphering the many three-dimensional proteins that genes command.

As scientists uncover the meaning of these scrambled genetic codes and the mechanisms they command, the origins of many of our biological and behavioral traits will be revealed. That's why we've been treated to a stream of scientific reports in the last decade linking aspects of our physical and mental makeup to our genetic heritage. Skepticism is in order since a lot of these announcements cite suspiciously exact percentages of heritability and many studies are later disputed. Most importantly, in the arcane world of molecular biology and behavioral genetics, complex personality traits are usually not traceable to a single gene.

Nevertheless, by manipulating simple genes that mice share with humans, researchers have so far turned lab rats from timid to daring, from loners into party animals, and bumped up their IQs. They have fended off some forms of cancer with gene manipulation, vastly extended animal life spans, knocked out the mothering instinct, and shored up male fidelity. Which suggests some intriguing, if not disturbing, possibilities about our biological underpinnings.

The genetic influence on what and who we are seems to run wide and deep. In addition to some of the obvious physical traits long known to be largely inherited, such as height or eye color, the influence of our genes appears to be extensive. Mental and psychological tendencies as diverse as excitability, creativity, obesity, and even criminality have been heavily attributed to genes. So have some forms of addiction, a bent for novelty-seeking, and religiosity. Shyness, conformity, a worrying nature, aggressiveness, the extent of our extroversion, or a happy disposition are all reported to be genetically influenced to a significant degree.

Psychological ailments also have been traced to genetic, chemical, or biological roots, as well as the uterine environment of the fetus and parental handling in infancy. These include phobias, depression, mania, obsessive-compulsive disorders, and some forms of neurosis.

In all, geneticists propose that overall "personality" is anywhere from 30 to 70 percent genetically derived, "intelligence" at least 70 percent. In fact, a study at UCLA reported in 2002 suggests that the size of certain regions of the brain closely related to intelligence are tightly defined by genetic factors. Researchers are also uncovering unique gene clusters correlated with longevity. It seems the gene combination we were bequeathed by our parents at one very particular point of conception has a lot to say about our hardware and software configurations— and the way we experience the world around us.

The Borders of Freedom

Studies of identical twins who share the exact same DNA, or gene recipes, reveal remarkable and consistent similarities between the twins, even when they are separated at birth. Despite vastly different upbringings with different adoptive parents, many of these identical twins share not only specific aptitudes as adults, but even particular social and cultural values. And in spite of intensive parenting, adopted children, whether twins or not, often bear no resemblance to the people who raised them; in fact, studies suggest they are much more likely to possess the behavioral patterns of the biological parents who gave them up for adoption at birth.

Most parents have no trouble quickly identifying their own children's core temperament and unique personalities. They readily determine that their children are, say, cranky, fearful, or outgoing in just months, if not weeks after birth. They can tell in a hurry that one of their children is brighter or more easygoing than another. Despite even concerted attempts at redirection, girls seek out dolls and boys find a weapon or a projectile in most every toy. These are ancient patterns at work.

Most of us know, if only by intuition, that we have inherited many of our features—good, bad, and indifferent—from our parents and earlier generations. We see it all around us at family gatherings or when we meet the parents or kids of our friends. It appears that some key aspects of our personality can no more be altered than our blood type. And, if so many of our aptitudes and so much of our makeup is programmed by nature and planted in our genetic makeup, a lot of the things we like to think of as "free will" are open to question. The judgments we make and the things we do are obviously affected by our intelligence, our personality, and our psychological state of mind. If these guiding elements of our thinking process are largely predetermined, volition or our own free will looks to be deeply influenced by our evolutionary and genetic heritage.

It is increasingly believed, for example, that most forms of homosexuality have a biological or genetic origin affecting brain metabolism, or may be influenced by conditions in the womb. Although preliminary attempts to locate specific "gay genes" have so far failed, the identical twins of homosexual males are more than 50 percent likely to be gay, compared to 20 percent of nonidentical twins. Since twins, whether they are identical or not, usually share the same family and environmental influences growing up, genetic factors, neurochemistry, or uterus hormone levels are assumed to account for the difference. Other studies point to minor anatomical distinctions, especially among lesbians, and suggest that certain neural responses of homosexual males, including their reaction to odors, appear more similar to females.

The steady stream of discoveries about the biogenetic source of our behavior is accelerating, which makes it all the more imperative to keep in mind what these revelations do not mean. Genes may initiate behavioral tendencies and inclinations in us, but these are leanings and penchants. Rarely do genes dictate specific forms of behavior. For instance, genes do not "make us" nervous or anxious. Most people become anxious under appropriately worrisome circumstances. Some of us may be inclined to get anxious more rapidly than others, or in situations where it is not fully warranted. Or perhaps we are unable to calm down after the danger has passed. This is what behavioral geneticists mean when they attribute a tendency, such as anxiety, to inheritance. This is also why they constantly point out the crucial interplay between our genetic predispositions and the environment we inhabit.

Even our height, which is more than 90 percent inherited, is not intractable; undernourished, it will fall a bit short of projections, while good nutrition and exercise may push it up an inch or two. As it happens, genes, or their mutation, may inflict particular burdens on some of us and bless others with exceptional possibilities. They may frame the outer limits of our potential, and the hormones they ultimately instruct may nudge us in distinct ways as they propel our most basic desires. But genes are direction, not destination; affinity not fate.

Genes are the factory-installed hardware that drives our central processing unit. They may determine our memory capacity and define our processing speed but, powerful as they are, our particular genetic bequest is expressed in the unique ways we use our capacities and relate to the world at large. Yet whatever the influence of our evolutionary legacy, of all the ways that nature impacts us, none is more profound than which sex we turn out to be. For this, more than anything, colors every aspect of our existence.

The Tyranny of Testosterone

We all start out as females. Well, sort of. Should father contribute a Y chromosome, at about eight weeks into pregnancy, a series of biochemical events trigger the first rush of testosterone that will transform potential ovaries into testicles. The fragile male embryo is set off on the act of becoming something different as it is exposed to two more hormonal washes: the first dousing helps shape the embryonic male body, the second, occurring in mid-pregnancy, tweaks the masculine brain.

Testosterone is the masculine chemical rumbling at the restless core of maleness. It contours the male body, propels the masculine temperament, and instigates a wide, defining range of male behaviors. Present in much lower levels in females—roughly a tenth—testosterone impacts everything from our muscle-to-fat ratios, to people's strength and energy thresholds. Testosterone is a survival fuel that compels the sex drive. Agitating for release, it especially sends males into fits of arousal. Libido, it seems, is a hormone.

Propelling the hunter-warrior to competitiveness and acts of dominance, testosterone was and is the source of the "take charge" male attitude, the penchant for aggression, the origin of prickly male anger and incautious acts. Testosterone is a tyrant, an itch that will not go away. It drives men to take on projects, to achieve and to succeed, kicking its heels even higher with triumph. Extensive surveys of men taking large doses of injected testosterone point to short-term but near-universal reports of an invigorated sense of confidence and assertiveness; a livelier, focused intellect; increased mental clarity; tenaciousness and positive thinking. The hormone generates boldness, a risk-taking bent that can tilt toward fearlessness, even acts of valor—and fearsome excess.

Direct research connecting a specific hit of testosterone to particular acts of aggression remains skimpy. And hormone replacement therapy, by gentle patch or gel, is unlikely to install a brazen new personality. But the circumstantial evidence of the hormone's role in buttressing male assertiveness is overwhelming. Castration, which turns off the testosterone manufacturing process, transforms most males, of most species, into pussycats. Boost their testosterone and feeble male lab animals morph into tigers.

The adolescent male is another testimonial to the hormone's power. Formative young males absorb testosterone rushes two to three times that of a vigorous male adult and up to twenty times their female counterparts. Trial lawyers, those windup aggression dolls who battle at court, register higher testosterone levels than their nonlitigator associates. Studies report that blue collar workers have more than white collar workers. Blacks have more than Caucasians. Violent prisoners, male or female, have more than the soft cases. Military professionals register higher than new recruits.

Working women have more testosterone than housewives. What's more, their *daughters* have more than the daughters of stay-at-home moms. The "butch" end of the lesbian spectrum has much higher levels than the average woman. So do the daughters of some women treated with progesterone, a kind of testosterone clone, in the 1950s. Women who, for one reason or another, have experienced high-dose testosterone injections report experiencing acutely masculine responses, from intensely heightened sexual arousal to a feisty overall aggressiveness.

The ebb and flow of this pungent hormone also plays a role in social cohesion. Winning sports teams and their fans experience a spike in testosterone levels, while the losers suffer a reduction. This has the effect of easing postgame tensions since the brazenness among the defeated is cut back. While the winners dance a jig in the end zone, the losers nurse their loss. And get ready for the rematch.

Married men, reined in by wife and responsibility, score lower on testosterone than bachelors, especially in the weeks after their wives give birth. This is nature's way of promoting fatherly nurturance, cutting down the wandering male eye, and boosting marital fidelity. Hormones also may play a part in holding couples together as they age. Men escape the tyranny of this demanding hormone as they move deep into their thirties. As testosterone fades in maturing men, their estrogen levels gain added emphasis. The edge comes off. This turns older men toward mentoring and nurturing, and makes grandfathers a softer touch than dads. Conversely, as estrogen levels fall in mature women, their testosterone reserves take on greater importance. They pick up a boldness that harmonizes with their husbands' offsetting hormonal drop. Men get softer as they get older, women get harder.

Yet women never get close to male levels of testosterone. Nor is it apparent that this is a bad thing. But this difference certainly helps explain why so many of the social, economic, and cultural imbalances between the sexes seem so resistant to change. It's not just about adopting new attitudes and beliefs. Males and females approach life with different biological, evolutionary, and hormonal legacies. Out on the savanna, female requirements for boldness and risk-taking were limited mostly to protecting the nest. The same can't be said for hunters and warriors.

Men needed to be confident, even bold, prepared at times to throw caution to the wind. They needed to focus sharply and be tenacious in pursuit of resources, a mate, and status. Testosterone, for all its can't-sit-still restlessness, continues to confer advantages upon men in charged, competitive environments such as athletics, the military, and the risk-oriented, firing-line slots of modern organizations.

Not surprisingly, homosexual men are far more promiscuous than their lesbian counterparts. In their case, the urgency of testosterone is not tempered by female restraint. In fact, a world that was dominated by a male sexual agenda would look a lot like gay sex, at least before AIDS put a partial brake on its more frenzied forms of masculinity. Male sex is testosterone freed of the estrogen leash—short-term and without emotional depth. Conversely, lesbians gravitate toward female patterns of long-term relationship.

Testosterone initiates the male journey and makes the world go round. The chemical of initiative, it can also drive male energy toward chaos. In that sense, it may be the most dangerous drug in the world. As modern mobility shrinks the planet, drawing the neighborhoods of our Global City ever closer, and technological advances extend the destructive scope of individuals, we need to watch out that unbridled testosterone doesn't send the world spinning out of control.

X, Y, and Me

Melding X and Y chromosomes, it turns out, is a tricky piece of business, an exercise the female fetus is spared. Blending different things together is more difficult than matching a pair. There is more opportunity for mistakes—and not much backup. These complicated male chromosomal mechanics, together with acute masculine testosterone rushes, means that the male fetus is exposed to many things that can go wrong—things that don't take, or invert, or deviate, or fail to happen in the right sequence. Mutations are usually no big deal but, then again, sometimes a mutation can be a big deal indeed. Whatever its impact, human males have mutation rates several times that of females.

The sexes also develop distinctive brain patterns early in the womb, a process that modern technology permits scientists to observe in action. Much of the activity is similar but, when averaged out, the brains of males and females show significant differences in some of the ways they function and are organized. Based on everything modern science knows about evolution, these differences are there for a reason. The female brain develops more rapidly in embryo, especially the frontal lobes, which negotiate many of our cognitive and interpersonal tasks. The female cerebral cortex also divides into two hemispheres earlier and forms thicker connections, while the embryonic male's connective fibers instead turn back to reinforce the right side of the brain that men so favor.

As a result, the female brain is structurally more refined and better balanced between hemispheres. This may account for both the superior capacities of females to integrate mental functions and their greater ability to maintain a soft and wide focus. Not only do women pick up more proximal data with their superior peripheral vision, they have an eye for detail and draw more information from taste, sound, smell, and touch. All these mental capacities echo a woman's ancestral specialty: the alert, take-it-all-in awareness of the female gatherer and her ancient, multitask job description of preparing food, keeping an eye on children, and fending off intruders.

Women generally activate more parts of their brain more of the time, even when it's idling. At rest, a woman's brain maintains about 90 percent of the alert state's electrical activity. In other words, women are constantly processing their environment. They also have longer attention spans, are more patient, and are better equipped to read emotions. This is natural selection and sexual selection at work. These are female adaptations for coping with several things at once, including dependent infants and potentially dangerous males out on the savanna.

The male brain at rest (clearly one of its favorite states) is more or less completely shut down. With less than a third of its fully active juice levels pulsing around up there, the resting male is on autopilot. Wakened to full throttle, however, males can get alert to danger in a hurry. They can show flashes of awesome, single-minded concentration; rapid deduction; even imaginative abstract thinking.

In studies where subjects listen to simultaneous conversations, men filter out one of the voices while women hear bits of both. Females have evolved the capacity to juggle multiple tasks while listening for a baby's cry. Switched "on" for solving a particular problem, male attention operates with tunnel vision, filtering out the background. Just like their ancestors out on the hunt.

Vive La Difference

Celebrate our sexual differences or loath them, they will not disappear anytime soon. Well before they poke their heads into the world, the sexes are already staking out separate ground. For example, female fetuses display more varied and longer mouth movements, while male embryos exhibit more frequent and forceful limb movements. It's as if the first inklings of female relationship skills and the male penchant for action are already on display in the womb.

By the time they're born, female infants are already more mature; on average, they are six weeks ahead of males developmentally. As a result, female "preemies" have a better chance of surviving and are generally more resilient than their male counterparts. Infant females register fewer incidents of brain damage and are much less likely to suffer developmental disorders such as cerebral palsy and autism.

Baby girls can distinguish their mother's voice at one week and hold her in longer gazes, showing greater interest in people from the outset. Girls are quicker at reading faces for cues and emotions as well as sensing the needs of others. They boast early skills in dealing with emotional issues and exhibit better affectionate and temperamental control. Girls also display early nurturing tendencies. They take a keen interest in infants and younger children, often mimicking maternal behavior at a very young age. Their games reflect these attitudes as they grow up, involving dolls, playing house, and dressing up, as well as the expressiveness and exhibition of dance. Girls draw flowers and huts.

As girls age, the balanced, integrated female brain is expressed through better verbal and linguistic skills across all cultures. Girls talk sooner. They are more adept with words; use longer, more sophisticated phrasing; and build larger vocabularies more quickly. In areas of the brain impacting verbal fluency and listening skills, researchers have discovered that females have denser neuron concentrations. Young females are more observant of their immediate surroundings, more practical and grounded, and more capable of synthesizing several thoughts simultaneously. They are emotionally sturdier.

From the outset, girls are more conscious of building networks and relationships. They send twice as many e-mails as boys, for example. Girls seek inclusion and equality, crave popularity more than dominance, and take less pleasure in abstract measures of achievement. As young females mature, they tend to define their problems along personal, family, or relationship lines. Given to shyness, a bit more fearful, and prone to depression, girls are generally more obedient and respectful of authority, and more generous in their dealings with others. These are the ways of the nurturing gatherer.

Boys, as not everyone seems to appreciate, are a different story. In just about every culture, they exhibit slower mental development, often apparent in the first months of their lives. Boys gaze at people for shorter spans, preferring objects and activity. Movement and irregular shapes hold their attention; their favored toys are spatially oriented action figures. Innate aggressive tendencies are displayed early by boys around the globe. As kids, boys suffer three to four times the developmental disorders, take more chances, get injured, and die more often.

With age, boys become much more competitive. They develop more hostile fantasies, fight, and seek to dominate more often. Boys enjoy rough-and-tumble play in large spaces with bigger groups. They like games with rules, authority lines, and winners and losers. Boys are mostly indifferent to younger infants. They prefer acting out to expressing their feelings. (Actually, they prefer just about anything other than expressing their feelings.) Well before adolescence, boys begin to pull away from their mothers and enter an emotional cave. As they mature, young males trade in their tears for action, problem solving, and silence. These are the training wheels of the once and future hunter and warrior. Dreamers and risk-takers, boys are less socialized, less obedient, and more determined to go their own way.

These sketches are of average boys and girls, typical descriptions and generalizations. Any adult in regular contact with an array of children can point to vivid exceptions. Nevertheless, these gender qualities turn up consistently in cross-cultural studies. They also show up early in childhood, before parents, much less the culture, can impose their will. Often these sexual distinctions persist in spite of zealous and unrelenting attempts to deny or reorient them.

When a big toy company set up a strictly "unisex" playhouse for observation, the girls played house, dressed dolls, and "made nice." Meanwhile, the boys were on the roof launching toys. "The No. 1 reason girls don't like computer games is not that they are too violent or competitive, it's that girls find them incredibly boring," said the female CEO of Purple Moon, a game producer. "They aren't really interested in games where the point is just to get a high score. They think dying and starting over is pointless, and they don't really care about speed and action. What girls want are characters they can relate to, story lines that are relevant to their lives."

These unyielding gender patterns may be why, in 2001, the National Academy of Sciences recommended studying "sex differences from womb to tomb," concluding that they are "an important basic human variable that should be considered . . . in all areas and at all levels of biomedical and health-related research." It can't be an accident that these childhood attributes are expressed, more or less, universally. It defies logic to believe that every culture on the planet just happened to shape its boys and girls in the same specialized ways.

It is far more likely that culture takes its cue from biological and evolutionary forces and that these universal social attitudes toward males and females emerge in sympathy with their innate differences. In any event, should these unique gender aptitudes and interests not be suffi-ciently apparent during childhood, we could hardly fail to notice them at the onset of puberty.

Coming of Age

Like all female primates at puberty, girls experience rapid and uncom-fortable physical changes and some unsettling hormonal rushes. Grow-ing up is rarely a day at the beach. Yet, from the awkward and uneasy stage of adolescence, a girl will blossom into a fertile young woman like the mother who bore her. Visibly rounded curves, developing breasts, the onset of menstruation—these clearly evident and rhythmic aspects of femininity fortify her sense of womanliness and amplify her future worth as a mate and mother of her own. The increasing sexual attention of boys and young men further propels her growing sense of sexual iden-tity and maturity. Girls make it to women well before boys make it to men.

Jane Goodall describes how the young male chimpanzee, unlike the budding female, is forced to undergo a tortuous separation from his mother, his younger siblings, and the nurturing females of the troop who have watched over him. The account is touching in its description of the young male's innocence and fear. It is a rupture that contrasts sharply with the young female who learns almost everything she needs to know safely at her mother's side, in the supportive company of other mothering females. There she can touch and learn, "aping" the more mature females of her troop, even peeping in on their sexual encounters.

In cold contrast, the young male chimp is nudged or pushed out into the brusque company of older males. There he must figure out how to hunt, search for food, and join in defense of the group, things he cannot learn with, or from, his mother. Older males may mentor a youngster, but he must work his own way into their elaborate status hierarchy. Cast out of the comforts of the hearth, he will encounter mostly indifference if he's lucky, chilling brutality if he isn't.

While things may not be quite that tough among human primates, the adolescent male rides a rough, less-protected road to adulthood. Under siege from testosterone rushes many times the level endured by females, a male youth may experience half a dozen acute hormonal surges a day. Forced in his youth to differentiate his sexual identity from his life-giving mother, and without the supportive network enjoyed by girls, he may be surrounded by emotionally absent men with whom he, too, will someday be competing.

The adolescent male is mood, chaos, and aggression. He is almost certainly erecting a massive fantasy sex life, masturbating frequently if not incessantly. While his teenage sister uses the Internet for homework and chatting, he's playing games and clicking around the sex filters. With his equally unsteady young male friends, he may show signs of acute homophobia as he attempts to master his budding masculinity. He can be counted on to bump into things with his gangly new body, practice acts of near random aggression, lose his temper with little provocation, attempt to monopolize the space around him, and seek quick and easy gratification in the way he eats and behaves. Powered by enormous bursts of energy, the teenage male also can be earnestly antisocial and disrespectful of authority. One way or another, he's heading to his own male place.

The Odd Couple

The precariousness of masculinity tells us something important about men. Males are nature's wild card, its unfinished business. Men are energy perpetually seeking completion, battling hormonal chaos as far back as the womb. Yet, if the composed female is the handmaiden of our survival, it is mutation that drives human change. Mutations mostly happen in males—for better or worse. Males are at the edges; they are on top and on the bottom. A "bell curve" charting any society's intelligence levels will be a bit wider and shallower for males, meaning more geniuses and more dunces. Though there will be some females at these extremes, too, they will be more heavily represented in the hefty middle ranges.

We can choose to regard the innate male compulsion to be assertive as the fountainhead of the hero's journey, or the unhappy roots of male belligerence. We may choose to see the relatively supine female fetus as the origins of feminine passivity, or view it as the source of women's rich confidence in nature. However we elect to assess these qualities, and acknowledging the great variations *within* each sex, the natural distinctions generally observed between the sexes seem deep-rooted. More than the object of celebration, these natural features are vital attributes that can be deployed for our gain.

Whether a bonded couple is living in an archaic human clan or a complex modern society, every human grouping benefits by taking advantage of the specialized skills of each sex. Specialization makes for efficiency, and efficiency gains nature's reward. The most skilled person at a task does the job easier and better, improving his or her specialty with each new experience. We don't need a partner who does the things we do well. Real and mutual benefit is achieved when our partner is strong where we are not.

Millions of years on the savanna forced a primitive kind of specialization upon hominids. Across thousands of generations, nature has selectively carved out the ever more refined skills and interests of the sexes. Sexual selection has further amplified these specialties, differences that serve to draw males and females into closer partnership since handling separate tasks requires planning and teamwork.

Among our predecessors, and throughout the animal kingdom, a division of labor between mating pairs is both obvious and universal. Different, of course, doesn't mean better or worse. It means different. But differing gender capacities suggest unique skills and motivations. The specialized sexual legacies honed during an eternity on the savanna permeate every culture the world has known. In a classic study of basic functions among more than two hundred human societies published in 1965 by the anthropologist G.P. Murdock, for example, hunting remained exclusively a male task in more than 90 percent.

Most of us no longer live in forests or on the savanna, nor do we hunt for food. Men can gather up veggies at the market, and women can bring home the bacon. But watching paint dry is like taking in a three-ring circus compared to the glacial pace of evolution.

The genetic recipes contained within our human instruction manual were encoded during the 99.9 percent of the interminable evolutionary history our forbearers spent in archaic domains. We are assembled for and shaped by ancient circumstances. Having leaped from primitive foragers to urban sophisticates in a flash, our individual happiness, as well as the success of society, may well depend upon how we reconcile this ancient primal heritage with the imposing demands of modern life.

4

UNIVERSAL DISTINCTIONS

A World of Cultures Celebrates
Marriage and Family

B EFORE SOPHISTICATED CIVILIZATIONS ERUPTED ONTO THE WORLD'S
stage, watching primitive human bands traipse around the Earth
would have been a pretty dull job. That's because almost all of them
looked and behaved in the same ant-like way: find food, make shelter,
fend off predators, manage the clan hierarchy, hook up and have sex,
and keep an eye on the children.

Wherever our wandering forbearers wound up and made camp, the
world's people were still tied to the bottom of the survival pyramid. After millions of years of sluggish, hunter-gatherer subsistence, and a painfully slow build-up of computing power, this was about to change.
Humanity chinned its way over the threshold of subsistence and drudgery. Our ancestors found a few minutes to doodle and dance, paint on
walls, carve an ornament, and tell a story.

Just thirty thousand years ago, the Neanderthals, not directly in our
line of evolution and victims of some real bad press, heralded this monumental leap forward before they died out on the European continent
after briefly overlapping our own species. Living close to the bone meant
that our ancestors' first crude stabs at creativity were about meaningful

matters such as diagrams of how to kill a deer, carvings of voluptuous mothers, or ceremonies for burying the dead. Sometimes, at places like the Caves of Lascaux on a French hillside, this early imagery was astounding in quality and impact, hinting at the promise of grand human artistry to come.

As coarse as most of this primitive artwork may have been, humans had finally won the luxury of experimentation. Imagination took wing. Inventiveness was the invention. Creativity was the gain, and cultural diversity the eventual result. The fruits of this evolutionary leap would take thousands of years to ripen, and there was no telling where it might lead.

In what amounted to a kind of technological big bang, humanity would be catapulted from a primitive hunter-gather eternity to the edgy frontiers of cyberspace. With the pair bond foundation solidified and foraging clans freed from the struggle to survive, it's as if humanity was emerging from a maddeningly long adolescence and beginning its sprint to maturity.

Universal Expressions

As humans scattered around the globe, building different societies and novel cultures, they carried one vital legacy with them: the seeds of their evolutionary past. Human cultures everywhere base their values on natural impulses and innate drives. Customs and traditions may have become unique to each culture, as anthropologists have pointed out, but they have been woven from the same basic fabric of human nature. In nearly all known societies, the intimate pair bond has formed the basic social building block.

In every society we might visit across time to the present, we would also learn that people favored their own kind, especially those with whom they share a lot of genes. In every culture, we would witness a celebration of puberty rites and the presence of the incest taboo. "Eating up one's blood" is how one aboriginal chief describes incest. Men, it turns out, are more sexually aggressive in all societies. Rape is always a crime. Prostitutes can be found in almost every culture, but, whatever their age or gender, their clients are nearly always men.

As we traveled from one human society to another, facial expressions would be easy to recognize, especially primitive emotions like anger, disgust, and joy. Around the globe everyone uses a calendar, tries to predict the weather, and plans for the future. Promises are made and broken in every culture. People in every society use their bodies as billboards: from painted faces and wedding bands to tattoos and nose rings. These adornments will be found even on humans who are not teenage mall rats.

Everywhere in the world we would hear the sounds of music, feel the rhythms of dance, listen to poetic speech, and pay witness to athletic competition. Dream interpretation is practiced and folklore recorded in all cultures. As we move around the planet, most of the people we meet will be right-handed and just about every one of them will love sweets. In every culture people use mood-altering plants. Religiosity and spiritual yearning may be in our genes, too, even a belief in the supernatural and faith healing.

Across every culture we would notice that men construct elaborate pecking orders. They dominate almost every society's political system, especially at the top and when negotiating with other tribes and societies. Males are everywhere the instigators and the principal victims of aggression, violence, and warfare. Women outlive them—partly for these reasons—in every region of the world; they almost always stay closer to home and help promote peace. A study of forty-four nations, released in 2005 by the Pew Research Center, confirmed women's continuing and universal caretaker role noting, perhaps not coincidentally, that they are happier than men with their lives in every country.

Over time, as humanity picked up the pace and human groupings grew larger, social issues became more complex. Mutual courtesy, a pragmatic, "do unto others" kind of morality began to lubricate human interactions. Across the globe, people give gifts, share food—and expect something in return. Every society has cheater-detection systems and ways to redress wrongs. Binding rulings of disputes are another human universal phenomenon. Almost all communities endorse some concept of individual property and develop rules of succession and inheritance. Rights, obligations, and responsibility for personal actions are attached to individuals in every part of the world, as is the person's intention and degree of control over their behavior when punishment is handed out.

So powerful is the continuing pull of the savanna that, even today, given the choice of various landscapes, people from every corner of the globe show a consistent preference for open grass, scattered trees, foliage, and water. They love places where they can see without being seen, have a panoramic view for safety and lots of ways to escape. Our desire for these landscapes is so fundamental that researchers at Texas A&M University report hospitalized patients recover faster and require fewer painkillers when they are able to view trees from their windows. Even fake trees . . . in fake windows.

Seeds of Originality

Natural historians date the beginning of modern times to about ten thousand years ago. Considering we took those first tentative upright steps more than four million years earlier, the birth of the modern era seems like just yesterday. By this time, the tropical and temperate zones had expanded much further away from the equator and every continent except Australia and Antarctica was inhabited. About four to seven million people were trekking around the planet.

The earth's human inhabitants were still confined mostly to small bands that encountered each other rarely and then only with suspicion. Clans had stabilized at around 100 to 150 men, women, and children drawn together mostly by loose kinship arrangements. This was the optimum size for defending the hunter-gatherer troop and sharing its primary tasks. It is also about the size of many modern social networks and work circles, a comfortable head count for weddings, funerals, and informal organizations. Beyond this rough limit, groups become more rigid and bureaucratic, segments split off, and new troops form. Just like on the savanna.

Humanity's geographic dispersal had also brought about the first visible racial differences even though modern humans emerged from common hominid ancestors. Our modest racial and ethnic shadings are minor forms of evolutionary adaptation, tiny adjustments unfolding in response to different environments and climatic stresses. As the cooler regions of the planet such as present day Europe became populated, darker pigmentation, nature's sunscreen, was no longer needed for protection from a searing equatorial sun. Paler skin also admits more vitamin D in sun-scarce temperate zones. A feature like the sharpness or flatness of the nose relates to a climate's relative dryness and the need to moisturize the oxygen we inhale. Most of the other racial variations—anatomical, metabolic, and disease susceptibility—can also be traced to geographical adaptations.

The thing that really kicked us over to modern ways about 8000 B.C. was agriculture, a discovery of the food gatherers. It appeared at more or less the same time all around the world. Scientists theorize that, as women foraged and gathered on familiar grounds, the reblooming of discarded seeds spawned the idea of planting them for a future harvest.

Some animals had also started to get friendly. The first of the many modern breed of dogs had been domesticated from wolves toward the end of the nomadic era. They earned their keep with an acute sense of smell that paid off on the hunt, and their barks helped warn the clan of intruders. Soon afterwards, the disposal of small amounts of about-to-spoil food drew more of the curious from among the tamer creatures nosing around newly fixed agricultural encampments. Sheep, goats, and pigs were reared, beasts of burden were yoked for plant cultivation, horses and camels mounted for transport.

Stationary agricultural compounds fostered greater variation in the kinds of tasks that people performed, and they required some elementary organization. Over time, a more elaborate human social structure emerged. Refinements in language and a broadened vocabulary enlarged our thinking capacities and encouraged social complexity. We began to pass on a bit of knowledge, a few rules and traditions to help establish and regulate social order and prepare succeeding generations.

Social cohesion in the clan was fortified by something that just about all of us still like to do: gossip. Like most other human universals, gossip promotes survival and plays a big role in sexual selection. Gossip is how we find out about important things like status and infidelity, conniving males and loose females, what she's really like and what he actually does for a living. Gossip was the evening news for primitive clans, and the provider of it gained influence. You were in the "in group" simply by being chosen to receive it, and ancestors who were out of the loop took a hit. Knowledge, after all, is power, even if it is embroidered sometimes.

BEEP

"I know I say this all the time, but this could be the real deal. I'm gonna pause here until the laughter subsides . . .

"I mean it. She's outstanding. Whip smart. Hot looking. Laughs at my jokes. Has a career together. Wants kids. Comes from a happy kind of family, which is amazing in itself, and which happily lives far, far away. Cool friends, it sounds like. Very hot looking. Did I say that? This is starting to look like the whole package.

"And, the excitement builds because, dear valued client and friend, the proverbial fourth date is at hand. Yes, the fabulous fourth date. We all know what that means, don't we? Why it's the disciplined man's payday.

"Last time out was some serious kiss-face. Some dreamy phone calls since then. Do I have to paint a picture? Dinner at her place tonight. She's cooking. Told me to bring some wine . . . and some attitude. Well, she didn't exactly say that last part.

"Verily I say unto thee, ah but how I love the fabulous fourth.

"On a more pedestrian note, I'm happy to inform you that your investment portfolio is doing brilliantly, swelling, even engorging under the professional tutelage of your big-time investment advisor.

"We are positively loading up on the erecto-gel stock. Trust me on this. Nobody ever lost money delivering a board-certified hard-on to the American public.

"And, on that uplifting note, I'm outta here.

"No, I'm not. I remember. I have a very juicy piece of news about a mutual acquaintance. You won't believe it. Too outrageous to record. Besides, this one will cost you.

"Sending you another cartoon.
"Later."

The early agricultural encampments were flimsy and often failed but, eventually, with the jagged edges of survival blunted, a growing sense of security took hold. People settled into fixed communities. Cycles of planting and reaping and the presence of animals focused attention on reproductive rhythms, the harmony of nature, and the patterns of the seasons. The birth of a child developed into a sacred event, a symbol of regeneration offering the prospect of another productive clan member. Obstructing birth became the closest thing to blasphemy, perhaps helping us understand the universal fervor that has fueled anti-abortion sentiments across all of human history.

Built around her life-giving capacities, a golden age of woman emerged from roughly 7000 to 3000 B.C. Magical powers were ascribed to women. Sex was fused with fertility and pagan ritual. Some women became healers, shamans, and priestesses in addition to fulfilling their maternal roles. Women were seen as touchstones of life, and their powers of propagation inspired the earliest forms of creation myth and religious observance. Mother Earth and the great goddess spirits invoked awe. Female deities begat life even if, in their fury, they sometimes snatched it away.

By contrast, male images of virility from this period are scarce. Only a handful of crude phallic symbols have been discovered in a sea of voluptuous feminine images. Yet women did not rule these budding communities. The consensus view among classical anthropologists is that there has never been a pure matriarchal society of any size. Which does not mean women were without power. The archeological evidence infers that during this time women were fully honored partners. In the world's new pastoral encampments, a guarded mutual respect had emerged to govern the relations between the sexes.

Still, life remained harsh for everyone. As with mammals and primates, a sickly human infant was put to death, a weak child abandoned if it imperiled the clan's survival. Big investments in child-rearing could not be squandered on poor survival bets. Ancestral divisions of labor were also reinforced in these agricultural settings. Women concentrated on tasks that could be carried out near infants: gathering and preparing food, harvesting, laundering, pottery making, stretching and sewing clothes, and collecting fuel. Meanwhile, men were busy with the heavier physical demands of agriculture, shepherding, fowling, animal butchery, and stonework, as well as smelting ores, clearing land, and constructing housing.

After the unchanging eons as hunter-gatherers, this brief, inventive horticultural epoch advanced most of humanity. Village encampments grew larger. Kinship ties tightened into stable, multigenerational families. Growing social complexity, settled pastures, and the control of shepherded animals ushered in the first concept of personal property. Which meant ownership. Which in turn meant regulations, inheritance and law. Which could mean only one thing: men and the assertion of masculinity.

Rights of Passage

The force that propels men beyond the safe, sure, everyday business of survival may be the engine that pushes the envelope of our species, but no matter where you look in the world, masculinity can leave a lot of pain and destruction in its wake. For better or worse, men remain burdened with the legacies of the hunter and a hit-and-miss attitude toward sexuality. Dragging around ancient genes and edgy hormones, men are still mostly wired for action and variety, the chase and the kill—and a lot of idle daydreaming in between. Together with their penchant for risk-taking and aggression, testosterone-driven compulsions can render even well-balanced and successful men hostage to dangerous behavior.

Despite the vast diversity of the earth's unfolding civilizations, every one of them has found it a good idea, if not an outright necessity, to dull the jagged edges of aggressive masculinity, to direct young males and harness grown men. As Margaret Mead pointed out, pregnancy and motherhood can alone convey a sense of adult achievement for a woman, even if some seek more out of life.

There is no such tranformative passage in the life of men. Providing sperm is their only sexual task. The challenge, as Mead observed, is to channel exuberant male energies into socially productive avenues. As we shall see when we examine the world today in later chapters, it is an even more important question in contemporary societies where muscle-bound tasks are no longer required or valued.

Unmanaged masculine tension and anxiety is a challenge to civility. How have most previous and contemporary societies dealt with it? Since boys are slower to mature and settle into their sexual identity, the vast majority of cultures segregate them from girls until they gain a confident gender footing. Youthful, male-only events are created to provide outlets for boys' competitive instincts and give older males the opportunity to be mentors.

"You know, in some cultures the male does things."

Healthy societies set targets for young men and erect hurdles for them to overcome. Achievements are rewarded and male youth encouraged to gain the next rung toward manhood. As any parent knows, boys purr when they get a well-deserved pat on the back.

Male tournaments and initiation rites are a universal phenomenon. From the vision quests of South America and the Jewish bar mitzvah to modern fraternity hazing, these rites of passage are emblems of entry into manhood. They are a kind of compensation for the gender confirmation women derive from pregnancy, a place to cross over. And the benefits for the entire community are palpable.

Male initiation provides socially acceptable means for male youth to gain status and position, something they seek the world over. These rites act as social pacifiers. By channeling and cutting down on excessive male competition, and fostering a disciplined response to exterior challenges, these celebrated passages help stabilize society, drawing young men, who are every community's most aggressive and precarious element, into the fold. Contemporary studies of male prisoners suggest that those with the greatest sex role anxieties commit the more predatory and violent types of felony.

Encouraging responsible masculinity through rites and initiation, testing men and maneuvering them into adult accountability, is a worthy goal for every culture, because responsible masculinity does more than promote civility. Cultures that compensate for masculine vulnerabilities and draw males into circles of civility gain greater participation by men in the community and in the rearing of children.

It is when young men turn their fervent attentions to winning a mate that the community gains its best chance to contain the excesses of masculinity. Societies that challenge men to earn a woman's hand reinforce the importance of the intimate bond and the value men place on it.

The Rules of Engagement

Sex, it turns out, is too important to be left to its participants. Survival and reproduction are matters so crucial that society at large, let alone family and kin, impose heavily on this most intimate of behaviors. Communities have an interest in order and growth, in encouraging stable family units, in fostering regeneration and in discouraging what is perceived as wasteful or disruptive activity. Though rarely enforced, even the most sophisticated societies still have laws on the books that make some forms of nonreproductive sexual behavior a felony, even between married partners.

For example, homosexuality has occasionally been cultivated and sometimes tolerated but throughout much of world history it has most often been condemned. Homosexuality exists in many species, if only as a stage in male maturation. It also shows up in most human cultures. Yet according to the National Opinion Research Center at the University of Chicago, less than 3 percent of males and females report exclusively gay activity in the year preceding its surveys.

The evidence mounts that homosexuality is largely a biological predisposition. This allows us to say, in one sense, that homosexuality is natural, that it exists in nature. But however generously we may wish to view it, no animal or human society organizes its social axis around a biological orientation that fails to foster survival. No species *designs* for extinction. Still, we live on a packed planet, and we don't all have to be breeders. Every one of us has a contribution to make as well as a right to go about our lives undisturbed, enjoying as many rights as possible short of imposing upon the central foundation of human regeneration.

Whether it is a repressive culture of antisexual fanaticism or the most permissive of contemporary societies, the collective sexual attitudes of the community play a big part in setting the tone and the limits of its members' activities. Due to its importance, sexual education starts early in most cultures and everyone knows the rules by the time they reach puberty. Most often these standards define courtship rituals that lead to marriage, which opens the door to sex and children. The further back from sexual union this courtship promenade begins, the more room there is for cultural invention and human creativity.

Throughout every known culture, however, the weighty imbalance in the reproductive contribution between the sexes invites casual, seductive, and aggressive mating strategies by men. Among mammals, primates, and humans, males compete, in some way or other, for the chance to breed. With nothing consequential at stake, goosed forward by acute testosterone rushes, it is no wonder men make the opening moves in courtship. From one end of the animal kingdom to the other, klutzy or classy, males knock first—and at almost every opportunity.

Because women are the more prized sexual resource, most cultures winnow out male suitors, challenging them to earn a bride's hand. Through initiation challenges and productive competitions, men are called upon to display character and resourcefulness— demands rarely, if ever, required of a bride. These tests are a sort of proxy for hopeful suitors that often seem to come down to that age-old question: "Just how do you intend to support our daughter?" Recent studies at Chicago University report that merely viewing photos of attractive women heightens men's estimate of their career prospects and generosity or, in other words, their capacity to be resource providers.

Females, of course, are not passive in the dance of seduction. They just sway to different rhythms. Selectively, and sometimes not so selectively, women flirt, show off, and advertise their capacities. Exhibitionism, almost always a female specialty, is featured throughout the animal and human world. Not surprisingly, it is among the most frequent sexual fantasies reported by women—in perfect harmony with men's visual hot buttons. In sophisticated parts of the world, women choose how much of themselves to show the lunch crowd, the client, or a hot fourth date. Heels and hemlines, shoulders and cleavage, hair up and hot lips, women get the ball rolling in countless subtle and not so subtle ways.

Women also readily take sexual initiative in a committed relationship. But given their heavier investment of pregnancy, discriminating women in search of an appealing partner remain more cautious and reserved in nearly every culture. Capable of restraint, the prospective bride, or her agent, holds the high ground and gains the leverage to select from ever-prepared male candidates. In nature, female selection determines which males get to advance their genes. Males propose . . . females dispose.

From as far back as our hominid days, when Lucy refused sexual favor if meat was scarce, to today's sophisticated displays of male financial power, fertile women show a consistent, cross-cultural preference for a mate who can deliver resources and make parental contributions. If he is deemed acceptable, the courting man gains the award of a woman's exclusive devotion and the promise of progeny. By committing to his wife and children, he escapes the solitary outposts of his gender, relinquishing sexual chaos to gain a stake in tomorrow.

No matter the local matrimonial custom, the contemporary bride is still "given away" at the altar. She is dressed in virginal white and symbolically cloistered behind a veil until the moment of betrothal. And whether the groom's teeth are sanded down in Bali, or someone throws him a bachelor party in New York, the husband-to-be is harnessed by wedlock. The "honeymoon," too, bears testimony to our evolutionary past, offering the sugar-laced groom exclusive access to his bride for a full menstrual cycle. Nine months later, he may be as sure as any man can be that he is the father.

Negotiating Nuptials

Whether the path of courtship is short or long, a delicate seduction or a stark proposition, despite all the exotic variations on managing repro-duction, almost every culture in the world has ended up with the insti-tution of marriage. Matrimony is the pair bond's end game, the universally sanctioned foundation of the family. A public undertaking recognized by the entire community, wedlock is enforced by law and is everywhere surrounded by social supports.

Negotiating between sex and love, merging short-term masculine and long-term feminine interests, matrimony fuses the competing sexual agendas and provides a hopeful platform for regeneration. Marriage consecrates love. As an economic partnership, it builds a supportive and dependable environment, extending our solitary lives into the larger realm of family, kinship, and community. Most of all, matrimony pro-vides the container for rearing the next generation.

Somewhere along the way marriage came to offer the evolving male an inviting alternative to sexual profligacy. He could help provide a few well-trained and prepared children with the protection and the tools they needed to succeed rather than indiscriminately attempting to spread his seed. Marriage meant that, for men, the quality of their offspring's preparation began to trump the quantity of hormonal chaos.

Making our way to marriage by falling in love appeals to our modern values of egalitarianism and freedom-of-choice but Euro-pean-based courtly love is the new kid on the block. That's because there is a problem with magic: you can't trust it. We may be momen-tarily beguiled by love's sleight-of-hand, but many cultures decline to hand their reproductive agenda to a trickster.

The majority of the world's marriages are still arranged. Those with a direct stake, aside from the bride and groom, are their par-ents, whose genetic future rests on the fruitfulness and endurance of their children's union. Preferring their own instincts—or the sea-soned calculations of a matchmaker—rather than the huckster called love, in many cultures parents impose lifelong intimate partnership on their children.

Barely half the men in the world and a little over a third of the women get to choose their spouse. This gender disparity arises because, in stark evolutionary terms, the family of the bride is generally understood to have the precious asset, thus the more valuable bargaining chip. Just who calls the shot, how it is negotiated, at what age and on which terms, is open to a wide range of possibilities. Father, mother, tribal chief, or clan elder may make the decision. In some cases, the bride and groom will not set eyes on each other before they are united in eternal union. As in, forever.

In the rest of the courting world, the blossoming of romantic ingenuity along the universal road to wedlock knows no bounds. Luscious treats, romantic melodies, rhythmic dance, and lubricating aphrodisiacs are among the universal ingredients people use to cook up a sizzling brew. In fact, humans are the most sex-conscious animals on earth. We are unique in the total amount of energy we devote to intimate relations, and we are unmatched in nature for the variety of our sexual interests.

Aside from being immensely enjoyable, if not at times exquisite, the romantic path to intimacy is a quality-assurance obstacle course. Courtship gives us the time and opportunity to calculate the worthiness of a prospective mate. Yet caution is in order. The Trickster, after all, is a master of illusion. And in many of the ways that really count, choosing a mate is the most important decision of our lives.

BEEP

"Well, I'm just absolutely head over heels in love! Ga-ga. Out of my tree! Unable to form a complete sentence.

"While you sit there in your Fruit of the Loom underwear, hovering over the keyboard, probing the dark recesses of your brain for some killer phrase, I've been out in the real world losing my entire mind.

"The other night, she serves this great dinner, right? Candlelight. Hot dress. The works. She's wearing high-heeled mules that are, like, they go 'clop-clop' when she walks? The

sound gets me so worked up, it's, I dunno, the promise of dirty sex, or something. Y'know, skin pounding leather?

"Anyway, over the bananas flambé, she goes, 'I think men should take charge in the bedroom and leave us alone everywhere else, instead of doing the opposite.'

"Now you have to love a woman for a remark like that. I'm, like, ready to run downstairs and set up neon lights across the street: 'YOUR SEARCH IS OVER. I'M THE GUY!' Where do I sign?

"And then, all of a sudden, I get this really warm feeling? In the general area of the groin? Like dinner is great but, as we both know, the way to a man's heart is <u>beneath</u> his stomach. Right?

"That's when we smell something burning! This is because my pants are on fire! Something dripping from the flambé.

"Well, dousing the flames? Suffice it to say, a good time was had by all.

"She's everything I've ever wanted. She's a dream. I'm starting to think about her all the time. I walk down the street and I'm just, y'know, happy. For no reason. People look at me—I'm smiling like some idiot retard. Some jerk gives me a hard time at the office? Hey, it's okay. No problemo.

"Why? Because I'm connected to someone, that's why. I have a partner and we're . . . in love.

"To tell you the truth, I feel kind of invincible really.

"It's awesome, dude. Can't wait to see her again."

The worthy institution of marriage, encouraged and supported by all vital societies, is hardly perfect. No matter how hard we work at it, the effort to extend committed, matrimonial partnership keeps bumping up against some stubborn remnants of our ancestral past—male biology in particular. Testosterone is a despot that will not sit still, even for a splendid institution like wedlock. It persists in oozing out from under all our neat assumptions about how things ought to be.

Ninety-seven percent of mammals are polygamous, open to mating with numerous partners. Until recently, before modern Judeo-Christian practices took hold, more than 80 percent of the planet's cultures practiced some form of it. A tiny fraction of these cultures permitted women to have extra husbands, nearly all the rest allowed extra wives to men so long as they could provide for them. Yet polygamy has never been widespread. It has generally involved only a razor-thin edge of prosperous males, and it usually means a couple of wives, not a harem.

Despite its cost and complications, however, polygamy remains the goal of nearly every man in those societies that still condone it. Men in positions of authority, not unlike contemporary heads of state, often egged on by the hormonal spikes that accompany power, take particular sexual advantage of polygamy's opportunities. Ismail, a seventeenth century Moroccan king, may have pushed the envelope, fathering 1,056 offspring with more wives than we would care to imagine.

For many women in polygamous societies, being the second wife of a resource-rich male can be a more appealing possibility than being the first and only wife chained to miserable prospects. In places where it is no longer legal, this deep-seated male urge persists. Across many contemporary societies, men leave a trail of divorced spouses and children behind them in what amounts to serial polygamy. Other married men may support a mistress. Still others rent one for a night.

Disappearing Acts

There is, of course, a double standard around male and female sexuality. The problem with comparing the sexual behavior of men and women is that it's like comparing apples to oranges. We use different standards to judge different things. We regard women and men in distinct sexual ways because their physiology and their psychological needs are different, and because the implications of their sexual activities are not the same.

Consider adultery. If women are at home, going about their activities in an extended network of children, family, friends, and community, they are much less likely to be enticed by their superficial encounters with men. At work, they are seldom flooded with provocative images of the opposite sex, and when occasionally they are, it rarely seems to faze them. One-at-a-time pregnancy and a woman's evolutionary instincts toward relationship insulate her from the kinds of skin deep arousal that so easily agitates the male libido.

On the other hand, temptation for the shallow, variety-driven male sex drive is everywhere in modern cultures. Assaulted by ubiquitous sexual imagery, men may sense the limitations of fidelity *every day* of their lives. Surveys in the U.S. and Europe suggest that about half of all married men are open to an extramarital affair—eight to ten times the number of similarly inclined married women. The flashy openness of Western societies and the nubile single women working around them means that the deep-seated male inclination for variety and the opportunity to act upon it often comes together.

The same insecurity that drives male philandering lies behind their paradoxical attempts to control females. Everywhere on the planet men attempt to guard their mates and restrict their display and availability. Hypersexual jealousy in men, despite its reprehensible extremes, is a naturally selected strategy designed to help assure paternity. When a woman "plays around," even once, it potentially compromises paternity.

This biological divide between fatherhood insecurity and the pregnant certainty of motherhood shows up in every world culture. It is on display in crude forms of female cloistering and repression and hides behind more sophisticated nuances in the West. It is often revealed in laws that tend to forgive, or only lightly punish, men who attack adulterous wives and their lovers. Sensing this male insecurity, women everywhere display acts of fidelity toward their mate at several times their husband's rate.

Female jealousy tends to erupt out of fears of abandonment. Cross-culturally, while women report being disheartened by single acts of unfaithfulness, they are much more disturbed by signs of an emotional attachment to another woman which threatens to redirect their mate's resources and attentions. By contrast, men report less concern over their mate's outside emotional attachments, yet they are acutely disturbed by even a hint of sexual dalliance.

These uneven attitudes around sexual fidelity may be one of those things that seem terribly unfair, but marriage is a long-term contract that calls for compromise by both parties. There are things about wedlock that do not seem fair to men either. Men may understand the modern notion that concentrating on a couple of well-prepared children makes the most reproductive sense. They may even agree that sticking to one partner offers the best prospects for long-term emotional fulfillment. But our modern epoch—these last few thousand piddling years of cultural refinement—goes up against millions of years of hard-wiring. In crude testimony to evolution's staying power, men still act out sexually a whole lot more in every culture.

Given these persistent differences in how men and women approach long-term partnership it is hard to avoid the conclusion that females simply tower above males in this area. More responsible about sex and relationship, more practical, rooted in commitment, and focused on raising the next generation, women are the stewards of regeneration, the guardians of survival.

On the other hand, males often look like procreative pygmies. Sexually chaotic, men appear to be one-note drones, forever scratching compulsive itches. Sometimes comical if not downright dangerous in their urge to copulate, men are carnal accidents waiting to happen. Loaded with potent if not necessarily focused vitality, males require the guidance of culture. They need to be pacified and socialized, their rash energies directed along productive paths. Otherwise there's no telling where they will end up.

The Dizzying Heights

Whether marriage is achieved through stark calculation, hard negotiation, or stumbled into by freelance lovers, wedlock is an alliance, a deal to be each other's reproductive partner, companion, helpmate, and survival unit. If this union results in children, the partners' genetic archives are melded together. Two lineages become one.

Yet no conjurer, however gifted, can hold men and women in thrall forever. We are dazzled by love for only so long. At the outer limits of the illusion, our attention begins to wander. No longer mesmerized, new and wily sorcerers and enchantresses pop up on the screen. Divorce is yet another human universal. Infidelity and money remain the foremost reasons to exercise it.

It is then that the Magician of Eros pulls off its last big trick and brings down the curtain. Before our very eyes, love disappears. The chemistry is gone. We are left scratching our heads, or is it the so-called "seven-year itch"? According to recent research of married couples, love fades gradually over the first four years—or more abruptly after the first child is born—before it stabilizes, then drops off around year seven for many couples. This is the time it took to get a newborn child or two into circulation. It is roughly the span of the ancient pair bond.

Whether love lasts an hour or a lifetime, by demanding a price for their lopsided sexual contribution, women have become the agents of social stability, converting the urgent male libido into romance, love, and commitment. In this way, women soften the hard edges of masculinity, connecting men to their offspring, molding husbands and fathers out of vagabonds. And anchored to home, family, and community, settled and bonded to their partner and children, men were free to pursue the hunt in worldly domains.

For better or worse, innovation propels us forward. Mutation is the change agent, and males are its breeding ground. They are where most of the genetic "mistakes" happen. For all their primitive sexuality, or maybe because of it, men have been bequeathed the reins of invention. From everyday technological wonders and modern conveniences to the heights of breathtaking scientific discovery, men have driven humanity out of the warm hearth to explore and construct our modern world.

From the beginning of the Bronze Age six thousand years ago, the scientific deciphering of the universe and our position in it began steadily picking up steam. Liberated from the soup kitchen of daily survival, human energy and creativity took off in a thousand different directions. Like huge mountain tops thrusting through the hazy fog of primitive agricultural villages, the grand civilizations of recorded history arrived on cascading waves of innovation.

In an evolutionary sprint, an archipelago of tiny, drab settlements scattered around the planet was eclipsed by magnificent metropolises. Bristling with activity, fueled by written language and other technological triumphs, these capitals would climb to the dizzying heights of empire and become the focus of unprecedented masculine power. The impact on men, women, and their relationships would be profound.

During this transformation, the primitive world's loose economic and social structures would turn from casual and horizontal to vertical and formal. Rural would give way to urban. Our direct ties to nature would be severed. Charged by a growing intellect, we broke free of instinct's chains. Anchored in the evolving pair bond of wedlock and family, propelled by a surge of creativity, humanity launched a bold adventure of reason and diversity. Our modern history is a spectacular epic of wondrous achievement and dismal failure.

It's the greatest story ever told.

5

THE SHADOWS OF TECHNOLOGY

The Rush to Modernity Rocks the Intimate Bargain

ANY WAY YOU LOOK AT IT, FOURTEEN BILLION YEARS SINCE THE BIG BANG is a long time. Even if things move at a crawl, it is enough time for some monumental developments to take place: the Earth logs a permanent address, the first multicellular organisms morph into life, plants colonize land, and Superguppy makes it to the shore. Then, at last, a mere four million years ago, one of our distant relatives climbs down from a tree, wobbles on its hind legs, and stumbles onto the savanna. The rest, as they say, is history.

Or, at least, *our* history.

In its purest interpretation, evolution dictates no particular outcome. With the chemical preconditions of life in place, a planet's natural environments propel organisms toward increasing levels of complexity. Yet adaptation and selection, the contouring forces of nature, do not bring about predetermined results. Evolution is energy and locomotion, not destination; natural selection is a process, not a conclusion.

Like every living thing, our primitive impulse toward survival first spurred us forward. The mental capacities of men and women have been extended to include both sexual and social selection. The brains we've built along the way have blossomed further into a kind of cultural selection process as well. We use our intelligence to filter useful innovations, develop customs, and build ever more sophisticated cultures. In these last brief shining moments of our story, barely six thousand years ago, our species escaped millions of years of a subsistence heritage and ignited a dazzling pageant of human ingenuity—a male-driven mad dash from the agricultural epochs that succeeded the hunter-gatherer eons all the way to the present-day.

Men and women have had to adjust to the promise and peril of modern civilization in the blink of an evolutionary eye. Though we may be removed from the timeless natural settings familiar to countless generations of our predecessors, ancient instincts and proclivities remain within us. Through it all, the intimate pair bond bargain, torn and tattered, has struggled to survive.

The Reason for Reason

When Bronze Age tools finally propelled *Homo sapiens* through its pastoral transition around 4000 B.C., just a few million humans populated the planet. This compares to six *billion* today. In any event, humanity was on the move. Wheel transport had been invented, and men were cast upon the seas in exploration.

By the time Iron Age smelters superceded bronzework a couple of thousand years B.C., the world's peoples had generated written languages and boasted their first libraries, the early data banks of civilization. For the first time, information was catalogued and archived, and succeeding generations could build on a platform of knowledge. In a quantum leap, grand civilizations erupted onto the world stage.

The informal clan systems that had solidified during hunter-gatherer and agricultural times proved inadequate to the task of organizing and managing this complex activity. Regulations, laws, and central governance were needed. Who better to fill these slots than a rising class of male officials, the merchants, traders, and new landholders?

In an evolutionary minute, property replaced meat as the avenue to resources and power. Wealth, in turn, would foster rapid technological and cultural progress. In a breathless sprint of just a few thousand years, humanity managed an astounding transformation from foraging, hunting, and simple agricultural settlements to the sophistication of Babylon and a bustling Roman metropolis.

This surge of innovation is magnificent testimony to human brainpower. Almost any single human capacity is surpassed by one animal or another. Some fly, others breathe under water, run faster, or see better than we do. Others have a superior sense of smell, climb more skillfully, or pull more weight. Humans, however, are blessed with a remarkably efficient and flexible body—a body directed by a world-class brain.

Intelligence is the big weapon in our survival arsenal. Its ongoing task, of course, is to act in our service. Our brain is there to help us satisfy our needs and desires by assessing our circumstances, determining our options, and crafting effective strategies for a favorable outcome. Other animals live only in the moment, bound to instinct and a few simple calculations. We have gained the freedom to think ahead and contemplate our motives, which are often anything but simple.

History speaks volumes about human ambition and attempts to control territory, gain resources, and secure heirs. At the center of these related activities, we find the male. Human history is replete with men who sought to hold and enlarge their ground and, in one way or another, to lever power, prestige, and sexual prowess. But land is finite and often hard to command in crowded cities.

Over the eons, and especially in the latest chapters of human development, the male penchant for territorial influence was redirected from more casual horizontal spheres into vertical status hierarchies. The modern man's home may or may not be his castle, but worldly power and prerogatives are still often determined by his financial and social ranking.

Among the countless possibilities and obstacles on the way to creating these bold, new civilizations, masculinity found its opportunity. The drive for adventure, conquest, dominance, and status afforded by the emergence of empires opened boundless avenues for masculine expression. Every early, grand civilization was led by men. Many of these leaders exercised awesome and arbitrary powers used without fail to enlarge their wealth, gain access to concubines, and advance the interests of their kin.

On the savanna, everyone had to work for their lunch, and the clans' arrangements were simple. But as modern civilizations developed, growing prosperity began to foster more complex social structures. Humanity's organizational template shifted from horizontal to vertical, from loose to regimented. The rough and ready subsistence-level grind on the savanna turned into an arduous climb for power and position. Broad social divisions appeared and widened ominously. In just a few millennia, the small uncomplicated clan had morphed into an elaborate class system draped over huge geographic realms.

Interior Women, Exterior Men

The appearance of modern civilizations and vast empires meant that the circumstances affecting men, women, and the pair bond would, for the first time, have to account for the big differences in social standing and the varying economic conditions under which people lived. While it was high-ranking men who were asserting themselves in the world at large, the quality of life for either sex had a lot more to do with wealth and position than the particular burdens of gender. In empires East and West, the lives of upper- or middle-class women were hugely preferable to the harsh drudgery of male laborers, not to mention the hordes of the poor and enslaved.

By 1000 B.C., wedlock had become a publicly announced legal bond formalized by contract. Among the select few in the upper levels of society, marriages were arranged. Matrimony had become a way to foster the birth of a male heir in whom the hopes of both the bride and groom's family rested. Much conniving went on but, generally, the teenage bride's father had the final say. Polygamy, in the form of concubines or multiple marriages, was still an established practice, though not widely exercised.

Life was venerated, and abortion widely condemned as the birth of a child meant future hands to advance the family's interests. Through the early classical and middle ages, infant mortality remained high, even in elite circles. Weaning a child was a tricky, potentially lethal passage, and a quarter of newborns would die within a year. Unsanitary cities incubated death and disease at every social station.

The high-born woman of these classical times was educated at home, but to a level approaching that of her male siblings. As her husband, the undisputed head of the family maneuvered to advance its fortunes, his wife administered a household of servants and slaves and oversaw the upbringing of their children. Not confined wholly to domestic management, she also may have supervised the family's extensive agricultural holdings, even its commercial activities. Recognized as both a social and legal entity, the upper-class woman could enter into contracts, spend time in public and at court. But her real sphere of influence was the household.

At the lower socioeconomic levels where the vast majority toiled, there was good news and bad news for women. The good news was that things were a bit more equal. The bad news was that most everybody suffered. Among the downtrodden the sexes were not segregated and they worked at similar jobs. They lived brutish, often short lives, often at the mercy of the privileged classes.

At the cradle and hearth, where a woman's role remained paramount during these times, things were hardly changing. It was a different story on the outside. For men clever or lucky enough to escape common labor, there were worlds to explore, continents to conquer, contraptions to invent, and flights of inventive fancy to be realized.

In His Image

Until a few thousand years ago, there were few recorded efforts to explain our existence on earth. Early hunter-gatherers had neither the capacity nor the inclination to address these questions. When our forbearers finally settled into fixed encampments and gained some control over their immediate lives, their first stabs at uncovering the meaning of existence came down to a simple, primitive veneration of life. This devotion was gradually enlarged to embrace the grander rhythms of nature. Some of these pagan and animist celebrations were then absorbed into Western religions and endure to this day.

With the arrival of language and settled community, traditions of folklore began to be handed down by elders, generation to generation, to be embellished and recorded. A grand menagerie of gods and goddesses imbued these early fables. Under a night sky of brilliant stars tracing animals and deities, what stories they must have told! In these primitive cultures, humans were thought to have a personal relationship with the mythical divinities found in nature. If the gods of the lakes and rivers were not generous with their bounty, perhaps the goddess of the harvest could be induced to bless feeble larders. If the goddess of fertility abandoned them, maybe the gods of war would deliver new concubines.

As humanity continued to crawl away from the subsistence edge of nature, there was time for a bit of ceremony and further musings about our origins. Branching off in many directions, fledgling religious dogma, featuring interpretations of our human genesis and proposing moral imperatives for how we ought to live, won the devotion of the world's dispersed peoples. Evidence of belief in a unitary omnipotent god first appeared in India and Egypt, even before it was recorded in the scrolls of the early Hebrew cults. Christianity and Islam, the great religions that followed in Judaism's wake, would carry this monotheistic belief forward upon the teachings and pronouncement of their prophets.

A few thousands years B.C. the world was a much simpler place, and scientific knowledge was limited. Powers of imagination were relatively meager. It would be five thousand years until someone figured out that the earth was round and that it was not the center of the universe. To the early chroniclers of folklore and the authors of religious scrolls, ten thousand years seemed an eternity. They were certain the Earth could not be any older. They gathered the strands of wisdom that came down to them in legend and myth and described a universe constructed in six days. They scratched out sacred writings to explain many of the mysterious, as yet undeciphered workings of nature, and claimed them as miracles. They wrote parables and poetry, much of it common sense and high in virtue, some of it inspirational, even majestic.

Given the primitive state of knowledge, it is no wonder that a bold new god, the creation of man's imagination, was presented in simple, direct human terms. How to imagine and describe a single deity? As there was but one, this god needed a recognizable gender, as opposed to the previous assortment of pagan deities that displayed the many sides of human experience. Man in god's image, god in man's. Sympathetic to the human plight, tough on wrongdoing, merciful but all knowing. This would be one omnipotent god. A male god.

Mother Earth to Father Sky

Judaism, Christianity, and Islam, the religions of Abraham, were born in and around barren deserts and harsh domains. While their original scrolls and bibles are punctuated by sensual passages, the male clergy eventually spurned nature's voluptuous business of reproduction and went on to promote an austere, masculine theology instead. The sensual, animalistic elements of humanity were suppressed.

In a flash, the spiritual world passed from earthy Mother Nature to forbidding Father Sky; from intuition to rational deduction; from lush animal instinct to cold abstraction; from inclusion to hierarchy; from tempest to tyrant; from sexual richness and the unruly tumult of creation to the barren realms of chastity and moral rigidity.

Fearful of losing themselves in the luscious, chaotic embrace of nature and the feminine, the early male clerics sought refuge from the frightening chasm of animal instinct. They fended off the bottomless pit of the womb by wrapping themselves in fierce, rigorous, and frequent rituals of devotion. By a few hundred years after Christ's birth, when two-thirds of the world's people were still hunter-gatherers, the church had determined that the everyday urges of sexuality were disgraceful. We are born sinners, the clergy proclaimed, wretched prisoners of instinct. Shame lay with the body and its functions. The flesh is weak.

In the end, they took what was natural in humans and cast it as sin. The very essence of our survival mechanism, the sexual union between a woman and a man, was shunted to the moral dungeons. The newly ascendant Western religions held women to be inferior for their sensual connection to nature. Rigidly puritanical, the male clergy seemed increasingly repulsed by the animal tides of menstruation, birthing, and breast-feeding. The clerical servants of god would themselves forswear sex. They would rise above fornication as sanctity lay with the chaste.

Jesus, they said, was born by immaculate conception. Only the briefest, get-it-over-with intercourse would be tolerated—and then only with eyes averted. Sex only to procreate, sex as the necessary evil.

In the fourth century A.D., the Christian church emerged from the pack of religious cults that were scuffling for position when the Roman emperor Constantine realized a prophetic battlefield vision and converted. With the fervor of a new believer, he built churches, constructed a new Christian capital, and pounced on pagan ritual and treasures. We are left to wonder at the fate of Christianity and the world had the prophecy failed.

Beneath the light and shadow of these sky-god religions, the Western world stumbled through the Middle Ages. Masculine economic hierarchies hardened into feudalism, an interlocking arrangement of class rights and obligations. Sovereign leaders ceded land to local headmen-turned-nobles in exchange for their loyalty, service, and money. In turn, the newly landed aristocracy granted peasants and serfs the uncertain privilege of tilling its acreage in return for protection and a portion of the harvest. The concept of individual rights, especially among the lower-born, did not exist. Privilege and license rested on family ties and kinship relationships.

The world's population had swelled and spread out, forming dense pockets along lush valleys, bustling riverways, and busy ocean ports. Unlike the isolated clan settlements that preceded them, the packed unsanitary cities were ideal breeding grounds for disease. By the middle of the 1300s, Europe was ravaged by the Black Death, a massive plague that swept over the continent. By the time the epidemic was contained, between a third and a half of its population had been wiped out. Ever imperial, nature had unleashed another challenge in the obstacle course of human progress.

The Rise of the Individual

Marriage had become solemnized by religion during the Middle Ages. For the elevated rungs of society, wedlock remained the center of political and social organization, legitimizing offspring and securing the family's holdings. Matrimony was still arranged, pregnancy remained a special event, and motherhood secured a woman greater privileges. Among the tiny but growing middle classes, married women gained more time with their children.

Wealth is the midwife of culture. It is when we gain the luxury to look up from our daily toil that we can afford to pursue higher vistas. Only then are people able to contemplate their circumstances, indulge in amusements, ponder and portray the big questions of life. This is true both for individuals and for societies. Much like the Internet revolution of today, fifteenth century printing presses triggered a wide democratization of information and knowledge. Literacy, like cyberspace, became a new divide. Brute strength yielded further to intelligence as information and knowledge commanded the pathways to material wealth and reproductive success.

But it was the world outside the home that was energized. Science, commerce, political order and administration, geographic exploration, competition, warfare, and hierarchy—these were the challenging domains of men. Not all men, of course, but male elites of many kinds. Their wives and daughters, educated in scholastic convents or at newly founded universities, continued to lead elegant, even influential lives directing their children's upbringing, overseeing family estates, running salons, and gaining impact in government circles. But the exterior world that lay beyond the hearth kept turning intently and pervasively masculine.

While privileged and aggressive males confronted the outside world, women at most social levels increasingly endured legal, commercial, and political restraints, often suffering under demeaning, widespread stereotypes. For those at the bottom, life was so brutal that equality hardly mattered, while women at the top had it so good that they hardly noticed. It was the women in between, the wives and daughters of middle-class craftsmen, shopkeepers, merchants, and functionaries, who most felt the stings of inequality.

Building upon the foundations laid during the Renaissance, the Enlightenment's celebrated thinkers, notably John Locke and Jean Jacques Rousseau, rejected the notion that human nature springs from primitive animal origins. These philosophers believed that humans are born a blank slate, that we are molded entirely by the culture that surrounds us and by our experience. Humanity's less appealing sides—greed, aggression, jealously—did not arise out of any innate disposition but from our exposure to a corrupt society. Contrasting thinkers of this era, such as Thomas Hobbes and Voltaire, incorporated our primal and ancestral legacies within their philosophies and presented a less romanticized view of human nature. Thus was launched the modern nature-nurture debate.

Whatever their assumptions about the origins of human behavior, most of the era's thinkers argued for elevating the rights of the individual. They saw it as their duty to question prevailing superstitions and unmask widespread prejudice. They challenged the arbitrary abuse of political power, arguing for greater educational opportunities, even-handed justice, and fair taxation, and set their hopes on democracy and individual freedom. The rightful object of government, they argued, was not to serve the elite, the modern clan leaders, but to promote the greatest happiness for the greatest number of citizens. Male citizens that is, because many of these philosophers retained unenlightened beliefs about women's intellectual and ethical capacities.

Meanwhile, over the centuries, the plight of the poor had risen from worse all the way up to merely bad. Both sexes began working as children. They labored under terrible conditions and often died young and penniless. In order to support themselves and their families, increasing numbers of women took in piece work or were forced into flourishing pre-industrial workshops; more than one in seven headed her own household, an often dangerous circumstance. Marriage may not have been blissful among the impoverished classes, but, like today, it served to shelter a lot of less fortunate women from predatory masculinity.

The Enlightenment's steadfast drive to reveal nature's secrets had set off a race to uncover humanity's origins. An English naturalist, Charles Darwin, returned from a five-year voyage to South America, in 1836, with an ark of exotic plants and animals and found himself pondering the curious similarities and distinctions among the creatures he encountered on the Galapagos Islands west of Ecuador. Although scientific thinkers had been closing in on the answer for more than a century, with *On the Origins of Species*, published in 1859, Darwin was the first to propose that species evolve through a self-regulating system called natural selection. An instant smash, the book generated both astonishment and savage attack. Critics within and outside the religious establishment vehemently rejected the notion that humans and other primates share the same ancestry.

It is hard to exaggerate the importance of Darwin's contribution. Newton explained, among other things, why apples fall to the ground. Descartes said we think, therefore we exist. But Darwin, in concert with the monk Gregor Mendel's discovery of the mechanics of heredity, told us how we got here and a lot about what we are made of. A century and a half later, we have barely begun to realize its implications.

The Best of Times, the Worst of Times

Since the savanna clan faded out, men and women of the most advantaged classes had enjoyed abundance. The big news was that the Industrial Revolution, which drew to a close at the dawn of the twentieth century, created a rapid expansion of the middle class, the bourgeoisie. For these small-time male entrepreneurs, artisans, white collar minions, and bureaucrats, family was enshrined at the center of their lives. Home was a place of order, the secure seat of vital kinship networks, the launching pad for children. Success was marked by becoming prosperous enough to free a man's wife from having to work outside the home, just like the upper classes they were so keen to join.

The middle-class wife could then run the household, minister to her children, and otherwise advance family prospects. The newly arrived bourgeoisie, like the aspiring middle classes of every subsequent age, were motivated to work hard and live frugally in order to build a better world for their children. These values and the family model they promoted were reinforced on all sides by the church, the state, and other influential elements in society.

Not everyone shared in the good times. As far back as anyone can tell, *Homo sapiens* have shown anything but kindness to strangers. To the contrary, we have often visited violence, war, and bondage on one another. Seeking land and riches in the service of a thousand masters, humans have regularly subjugated each other, killed, raped, and pillaged. There is no major civilization that can boast of a history free of bondage. Slavery is as old as the human race, appearing in sophisticated and primitive societies alike.

Our nomadic, hunter-gatherer ancestors, traipsing around a modest chunk of territory in a sparsely populated and insular world, did not encounter many outlanders. Meeting up with strangers could herald a dangerous passage, especially if the strangers were men. Over a huge expanse of time, cautious alarm when confronting "others" became encoded as a survival mechanism. Our guardedness, even hostility, toward outsiders is an unhappy legacy born of the brutal realities on the savanna. Racial, ethnic, tribal, and religious animosities are still with us everywhere, from the Balkans to Africa, from Asia to the Middle East. According to the best estimates, there remain today about thirty million slaves on our planet and more than one hundred million children under the age of fifteen who labor full-time.

With today's incredible mobility and ubiquitous media, the world has shrunk dramatically. We mostly live in crowded cosmopolitan neighborhoods of the Global City where all kinds of people, from all sorts of places, live and work close by. Natural wariness of strangers was selected as a life-preserving advantage, and this legacy of caution is still with us, but we are not enslaved by ancient shadows. The grace of human empathy can be summoned through education and reason. After all, genetically speaking, we're more than 99.9 percent the same.

A Woman's Place

In the several thousand years of modern, recorded civilization, the Earth has been convulsed, time and again, by violence, mayhem, and war. By and large, human history has been carved in battle and etched in savagery. There has been no shortage of flashpoints but, in the thick of them all, we find nature's wild card. Throughout the entire animal menagerie, males are the risk-takers, the sex that just won't leave things alone. They are the change agents, the single-minded hunters, tinkerers, and innovators. Host to the most mutations, men are the vast majority of our break-out geniuses, nearly all of our scientific and cultural Goliaths.

Then again, if most of the world's historic and artistic triumphs have been produced by men, so too have the horrors. We find men at the top, and we find them at the bottom. Though some women will earn a place among them, it is men who are the magnificent leaders and the hideous despots, the discoverers of mighty technology and the first to turn invention to slaughter. Men are the saviors and the serial killers, capable of majestic sacrifice and unspeakable horror.

Tracking all the way back to the savanna, the larger issues of clan government have been almost exclusively a male preserve, a facet of nearly all historical and modern cultures. Power is concentrated in most societies, of course, and relatively few men achieve the heights. History suggests that, politically at least, it is not so much men over women as a few men over everybody. Women have found places in the ruling circle, or under the imperial tent. They have flourished on a few smaller stages and have even sparkled there as leaders. No man could have done better in many of these circumstances; few could have done as well. But, among the leading nations and empires, while women have occasionally reigned, just a dazzling few have ruled.

Elizabeth I, the daughter of Henry VIII and Anne Boleyn, succeeded to the throne in 1558 when England was isolated, in turmoil over religious strife, at war with France, and deeply in debt. She was crafty, smart, and a political genius, qualities she needed in full measure to hold on to her crown—and her life. Elizabeth steered Great Britain through the dangers of the Reformation and was instrumental in unifying her nation, shaping it into a global force, and presiding over a vibrant artistic and cultural era that bears her name. Declining to marry, she deflected the pleas of parliament for an heir by playing diplomatic charades with promising and hopeful European princes. Educated in the manner of male royalty, she triumphed regally over the Tudor-era handicap of being a woman. "Her mind," opined her tutor, "has no womanly weakness," and, in a boast no historian would deny, she famously declared herself to have "the heart and stomach of a king."

Catherine the Great, another majestic female ruler, was banished to St. Petersburg, the intended bride of a mentally infirm Grand Duke. Without a drop of Russian blood coursing through her German veins, at thirty-three she orchestrated his assassination and seized power through a coup organized by her lover in 1762. She was a spectacular sovereign who dragged a backward Russia kicking and screaming into European modernity. Becoming more Russian than her people, she left behind a much bigger and better-defended empire.

It is the rare male leader who commanded Elizabeth's authority or was Catherine's equal in boldly reshaping his state, or in the breathtaking promiscuity of his bedchamber. Near the end of Catherine's thirty-four year reign, the sight of her enormous, pasha-like body hoisted to the royal bed on hydraulic cranes must have shaken the ardor of even the hardiest of the Russian officers regularly procured for her sexual enjoyment. Elizabeth, on the other hand, died a virgin at seventy. Easily the most dynamic female leaders in history, they were in some ways among the most masculine. If exceptions prove the rule, Elizabeth and Catherine were two magnificent exceptions.

The Time of Perils

The twentieth century arrived on the vibrant coattails of Victorian England. Building on an ever-expanding information and scientific base, each dazzling new discovery and technological breakthrough sent many more innovations in motion. Boldly climbing on the shoulders of those who came before, the world breached a stunning scientific threshold.

The century that began with ink wells, blotters, and hand copying ended with e-mail flashing to a thousand points around the globe from hand-held computers. The century that opened with the Wright Brothers' twelve-second, 120-foot flight ended with a dune buggy trundling around Mars, seen live via the Internet. By the middle of the twentieth century, male-driven technologies had even split the atom—the smallest known thing—and found within it the greatest power on the earth.

The power to dispose of us all.

The World Today

6

THE CULT OF THE INDIVIDUAL

An Army of Ones

YOU HAVE BEEN CALLED BACK TO THE DOCTOR'S OFFICE. IT'S NOT good news. You know it. That's why you went to the clinic in the first place. You just shouldn't have done it. Sure, you got excited, y'know, a little carried away. It happens. You're only human. But it was too soon. These days you have to get to know the person better. Yup, it must be an STD.

Twenty-two and a half agonizing minutes in the waiting room and it's starting to feel like a near-death experience. You have been staring at the same article on the thrills of needlepoint technique for the last quarter hour. You're so nervous you're ready to settle for something like genital warts, even herpes. Anything, except, y'know—

"The doctor will see you now."

Any last vestige of hope that it's just some dinky thing ("No more bacon cheeseburgers, I swear") evaporates when the doctor greets you with a serious face. As she shuffles through your file, beads of perspiration trickle down your neck. She clears her throat. It sounds like a scream. *"We have a little problem."* ("Oh, god, no! And whadaya mean, 'we'?")

"You've tested positive for . . . syphilis. It could be a false reading but, to be on the safe side, you're going to have to—"

Your head is swimming in adrenaline-addled confusion. You rush out of the office. Syphilis!? Who gets syphilis, for chrissakes? Isn't it, like, just old Mafia guys? A thousand riffs parade across the vortex of your brain. Your sex organs will seize up and die. You will be sent to a leper colony. No one will ever want you. No more sex! Life, as you've come to know it, has ended.

Stumbling into the house, you collapse on the stairs. Be rational! Think for a minute! Think for two minutes. That's it! Fire up the laptop. With trembling hands, you type in "S-y-p-h-i-l-i-s." Anxious milliseconds and . . . twenty-six million hits! Okay, okay, let's get more specific. How about, "Syphilis for a clean-living person who made one dumb mistake and will be good forever." Oh, great . . . only 126,319 options.

You persist. A few refinements and—kazaam!—the entire history of the disease is on the monitor. Most importantly, you discover the miracle of penicillin. Death is not imminent; it's merely a distant possibility. You hyperlink to "Proud Kids of Syphilitic Parents," which thoughtfully provides the toll-free number to four support groups in your area code. Two clicks and you're at the site of an activist organization lobbying for inclusion of syphilis in the Americans with Disabilities Act. The bumper sticker is on the way: "We're here. We're syphilitic. Get used to it."

Every known medical intervention, from the Mayo Clinic to aromatherapy, is now at your fingertips. You can express-order ointments with your credit card from countries you have never heard of and they will be here tomorrow. There's a clinic in Tijuana that will handle everything—very discreet, fix you up and have you back in action in a flash. You can fly in tomorrow. No sex for a week they say, but, hey, you'll make do.

The blood is starting to come back to your face and a joyous serotonin rush begins to bathe every synapse in your cerebral cortex. I . . . will . . . LIVE! You feel a thousand times better. Except of course, you're emotionally drained. No, make that exhausted. You flip on the CD player, glancing at a sidebar on the screen called "Syphilis Over the Centuries." You slap on the earphones, close your eyes, and breath deeply—very deeply.

Soon all is hazy confusion. Nothing is where it's supposed to be. You can't find your laptop or the cell phone. You can't access the Net because there are no computers. You can't send a fax because there are no phones. No flights to Tijuana because there are no planes. You can't drive there either because nobody knows what a car is. Worst of all, a strange man in a white coat keeps telling you there's no such thing as penicillin.

Smoke is billowing from boiling cauldrons. Hideous devices line the walls. Strange little creatures float in jars. The man in the white coat is now explaining that if the mercury drops don't work, he will have to fire up the "fever box" or maybe use what he calls "the leech treatment." As a last resort, he mumbles something about attacking your genitals with a hammer and chisel. If that doesn't work, it's off to the loony bin and a slow, agonizing death.

The phone's RINGING.

You wake with a start! You're soaking wet. You dozed off after all the excitement and dreamt you had syphilis a hundred years ago. The machine answers. "Hi! It's me. That was soooo special, baby. Can't wait till next time."

No Time Like the Present

A hundred years ago, you could have died from a lot of things. Fifteen million people in the United States will contract a disease from a sexual partner this year, a quarter of them teenagers. According to the Centers for Disease Control and Prevention, sixty-five million Americans now carry an STD, and the one in four who will pick one up at least once in their life can usually go in for a shot and avoid the nightmare. Medical progress is just one example of how technological innovation over the past few generations has revolutionized our living conditions and greatly extended life expectancies.

Up until recently, the human odyssey unfolded painfully slowly, deep in the wildness of nature. We were permanently camping out or, more briefly, tilling the land. Most families in the prosperous parts of the world have long since packed their bags and moved into the cities, far from creepy crawlers and things that go bump in the night. The stepped-up pace of urban migration is clearly evident in the United States where, a hundred years ago, more than half the population was engaged in some form of agriculture, compared to less than 2 percent today. In 1900, just 14 percent of the world's people lived in cities. Today, it's more than half.

The flight to the cities has been a push-pull phenomenon—people pushed out of country pastures and pulled toward the city lights. Family farms could be split up and handed down only so many times over the generations, and exceptional advances in productivity means we need fewer hands tending crops. There are benefits to living in rural areas and small towns, of course, but also steep disadvantages. Industrial jobs and eligible mating prospects may be in short supply. Life can be strenuous. And your dirty laundry hangs out for everyone to see.

The big bad city promises so much more: cosmopolitan sophistication, boundless opportunity, discreet anonymity, and urban adventure. Whatever the reason, cities have mushroomed with more than 360 metropolises around the world supporting at least one million people. The largest, greater Tokyo, is home to a staggering thirty-four million, a population greater than 86 percent of all nations.

With the help of twentieth century technological marvels such as telephones and television, satellites and the Internet, the world has dramatically shrunk. Distant continents are as close as a cab to the airport and an in-flight movie. Multimedia transmissions take seconds, and silicon chips drive ever-faster microprocessors, digital monitors, and cellular phones. We can check e-mail from the palm of our hand and hold a live video conference with the other side of the planet.

Twentieth century technology has set the table for a grand leap in sophistication, prosperity, and world health. Innovation, on the other hand, has also set loose some ominous possibilities. Traditional social boundaries are disintegrating. We live more isolated lives in more complex, faster-paced, and crowded cities, where the pair bond and family, the ancient anchors of civility, confront ever more daunting challenges. The social and environmental circumstances of humanity have been rapidly and radically altered. What hasn't changed are the eternal forces of the universe that govern the planet and prod our personal lives.

The evolutionary odyssey we've taken has been a long one—from the Big Bang and the formation of microscopic organisms on Earth to the evolution of complex modern life forms. So far on these pages, we have journeyed through our ancient past while casting only an occasional glance on contemporary life. Now we reverse the focus. In the chapters ahead, we concentrate on dissecting the varied aspects of today's high-tech living, using the perspective of our natural history. But before we undress modern- day sex, romance, and family issues, we begin by assessing the overall social context in which women and men now live.

Acts of Kindness

Our story leads up to the present-day with a look at the political and economic conditions prevailing after World War II. Broadly speaking, we find two ways of organizing human behavior: socialism and free enterprise. Based on differing assumptions about human motivation, two generations later only one has survived. A look at these divergent ideologies from an evolutionary perspective suggests that this has everything to do with the gut issues of personal motivation, how we feel about our families, and why we go to work every day.

Socialism was inspired by the lamentable working conditions of early industrialization, but its philosophical roots lay with the romantic philosophers who emerged during the Enlightenment. Adopting the notion that we are born innocent, a clean slate, socialism assumed a large and wishful degree of human openness and purity. Society becomes the ultimate parent. Just program in some hospitable values and gentle manners and—presto!—you've got the utopian dream. In this starry-eyed universe, human animals will willingly sacrifice and work extra hard so that others may improve their lot. "From each according to his abilities, to each according to his needs."

Altruism is the word biologists use to describe generosity among animals; bees committing suicide to protect the hive; squirrels exposing themselves to danger in order to warn others; gazelles bobbing up and down to alert the herd to danger, drawing lethal attention to themselves. These and many other examples of animal activities appear to be unselfish, even self-sacrificing, forms of behavior. Not long ago, the scientific explanation for this was that animals, under certain circumstances, would put themselves in peril for the benefit of their species. But looks can be deceiving, even to the experts. As the mysteries of DNA were unveiled, biologists began to reposition the engine of survival a lot closer to the bone. Altruism, it turns out, is not so much simple generosity as an evolutionary strategy designed to preserve the donor's own family legacy.

Animals risk their lives but not for just anyone. The closer the relative, those carrying more of their own genes, the greater the animal's willingness to risk life and limb. A screeching female rodent sounding a warning to nearby offspring, sisters, brothers, nieces, and nephews is, in effect, helping many kin who share and can propagate its genetic legacy. A modest increase in the chance of being someone else's lunch might be worth the gamble if it helps relatives to survive and prosper. J.B.S. Haldane, the great biologist, famously explained these priorities by declaring that he would lay down his life for two brothers, four nephews, or eight first cousins. Likewise, mothers throughout the animal kingdom protect their own child first, their siblings' children before a cousin's, and a cousin's child before that of a stranger.

Animals also practice reciprocal forms of cooperation that, out of context, can look a lot like altruism. Animals join forces to attack large prey they could not bring down alone, or defend against formidable predators. Acting cooperatively, each gains a meal—or avoids becoming one. Animals also share food, especially when they have a lot of it, but, then again, they expect something in return. They keep track of who's naughty or nice, use cheater-detection systems, and shun chiselers.

In fact, among our close primate cousins there are only the slightest trappings of civility, just a vague notion of sharing, an elementary, tit-for-tat kind of reciprocity. For some strange reason, male primates share more of their food with females who just happen to be in heat. They also may exchange food for a bit of political alliance-building, tenuous deals between senior males who gain increased breeding access in return for resources or the protection they offer subordinates. Nevertheless, those who keep chimpanzees under observation report that they are only too ready to concoct an excuse to avoid sharing a tasty morsel, or to dart into the bushes to snatch a quickie. Sound familiar?

Then there is that gazelle, hopping conspicuously up and down as a hungry lion approaches. Some people who study these things believe she may not be warning other gazelles: instead, she may be talking to the lion, advertising the fact that she's a tough cookie so he better pick on someone else. As the big cat chews this over, the gazelle melts into the protected center of the herd. Pretty sneaky stuff.

In the strict sense of sacrifice, none of these are acts of unconditional generosity. Every one of them is in some way calculated to benefit the donor. Animals do not sacrifice themselves for their species. They do not die for their gender, or for their fuzzy friends or distant family. Animals act in self-interest. Which means first seeing to it that their genes, and the progeny and family who carry them, survive and prosper.

Home of the Brave

Mercifully, human generosity is not so easily dismissed. Sometimes, of course, jeopardy comes with the job. Firefighters, cops, soldiers, and secret service agents, among others, know that they may pay a deadly price for bravely living up to their oath. Still, most of us are familiar with acts of heroic sacrifice that are not in someone's job description or confined to saving the immediate family. This capacity is one of the unique traits that make us human.

Animals will not die for a cause, but humans will. Relatively rare but persistent human examples of pure sacrificial bravery stand as elegant testimony to the range and fervor of our intellectual and spiritual beliefs, the importance of our emotional attachments, and the bravery propelled by hormonal spikes of valor.

When push comes to shove, almost all of us approach the possibility of serious personal sacrifice with the utmost reluctance and calculation, a self-centered mix of hesitation, guilty conscience, and strategic deception. How much we have to gain and how much we have to lose colors these decisions. And like all primates, even our interest in relatives is, well, relative. One-eighth of our genes may be shared with first cousins. Past them, to more distant relatives, we share no more than one-sixty-fourth, not much greater than we do with a likable stranger. This is why our sense of family dissipates sharply when we get beyond this ring of first cousins, even if we're crazy about the second cousin we met at our niece's wedding.

The reality is that most of us are prepared to lend a helping hand to other deserving people—indeed, we may feel good about helping others—but most of us put ourselves in real jeopardy only for close family. Should we be called upon to put our lives on the line we are forced into a dilemma in genetic reckoning, an exercise most people fervently hope they will never have to confront. When you get down to it, we are more likely to risk death for our child than for a parent or sibling. And, just maybe, for a romantic partner. Because, as Romeo and Juliet proclaimed, sometimes we will die for love.

To propose, as socialism does, that the general populace will see the fruits of their hard labor freely distributed to unrelated others because "they need it" is a genetic non-starter. Looking through an evolutionary lens it is hard to imagine a formula of animal organization more out of touch with a biological understanding of motivation. Most of us do not particularly want to work all that hard to begin with. When we do, we want ourselves and our family to profit from our efforts, not some people we don't know, just because some other people we don't know say they need a break.

Most of us seek to live in a civilized world. We may be blessed with a genuine sense of compassion for those who are in distress, especially through no fault of their own and particularly if they are trying. Cold as the truth may be, we have to climb a long way up the ladder of human philanthropy before we willingly sacrifice a big chunk of our hard work, our safety, or our genetic advantage in order to lift up the anonymous multitudes.

Except for a few individuals insulated from the burdens of everyday life by wealth or extreme spiritual or psychological detachment, we all want to get ahead. We may not wish to succeed to the detriment of others, but we do want to see a direct relationship between our efforts and our rewards. To deny this powerful, self-centered human predisposition is not to adopt some higher morality—it is to contravene a vital natural force. Charity and a whole lot more begin at home.

Socialism and communism, its cynical cousin, crumbled in the last decade of the millennium because people within these systems saw no fair connection between what they put out and what they got back. Attempting to organize society against our natural instincts, these philosophies of economic and social leveling have created countless personal, political, and community distortions. Directed from the powers above, economic activity is dictated by political consideration. Goods and services are not shaped in the proving ground of a free marketplace. Instead, bureaucracy and corruption stifle economic efficiency while informal gray and black markets emerge to meet real, unserved needs. Inevitably, the rigid, swollen cadaver of socialism bowed to the more powerful forces of human nature and imploded.

BEEP

"*It's positively scary, my friend. We've been talking about the 'M' word. M-m-m-m-m-m-m-m-m-marriage. There, I said it. Big whopping changes. A wife, two-point-three kids, a dog, and a mortgage.*

"*I mean, I love her, but wedlock is, like, forever. The 'lock' part, that is. Many, many fiscal quarters. Fiscal quarters for as far as the eye can see. Infinite fiscal quarters.*

"*Talking about fiscal matters, the answer to your question about the markets is that the big thinkers around here figure they're going to churn for awhile. Consolidate, build a base for the next push.*

"*Which gives us time to reflect on the state of the world.*

"*Let's face it, it's not a pretty picture. People are greedy, nobody cares about anybody else. There's no loyalty to anybody or anything. Everyone's a free agent.*

"*Dating sucks. We know that. Everybody lies.*

"*Aren't you glad I called? I'm just getting started, actually.*

"*No matter what I do at work it's never good enough. Competition is insane. Every time I turn around someone's stealing my clients. The backstabbing, the lying and conniving—and that's from the home team here in my office, let alone the jerks across the street.*

"Everything moves at hyper-speed. You notice that? I can't keep up anymore. Who can keep up? Can you keep up?

"You can't even afford to buy a house anymore. It's a joke.

"The ice caps are melting. It's a screwed up world.

"However, bearing in mind the abominable world we're living in, it sure feels good with a partner. At least you're not battling it on your own.

"What do you think?"

By the end of the twentieth century, the world's capitalist economies had triumphed. A free market may not be a perfect place but it represents the closest economic model to the basic operations of adaptation and natural selection and the unstructured conditions that prevailed in our ancestral domains. In the kind of open market where competition freely reigns, new economic organisms survive and prosper if they are appealing or useful. If they serve no valid purpose, sooner or later they fail. By this process of commercial selection, successful innovation is rewarded with enhanced opportunity for growth. Until, that is, the marketplace changes.

Despite all of the well-intentioned attempts to order and manage human activity, deep-seated self-interest drives almost all of our actions. Most of what is useful about our modern world was generated by encouraging and channeling the innate desire to better ourselves rather than attempting to deny or direct it. The Internet, to cite one vibrant example, arose and thrived largely because the American government got out of the way, providing resources to scientists so they could pursue their own interests instead of following a predetermined course.

Although the socialist command system occasionally threw up an achievement of big science, such as the first manned space satellite, the dinosaur of centralized economic and social planning is now just about extinct. The juice of free enterprise lubricates the economic generators that drive the world toward greater prosperity and closer union. Encouraged by a free market system, technology and innovation become catalysts of growth. In the process, multinational corporations, instant world-wide communication, and sophisticated, interlinked financial markets have begun to eclipse geographic boundaries in our digital universe.

At the outset of the twenty-first century, the diverse neighborhoods of the Global City are being put through a blender. Historic, geographic, ethnic, and bloodline attachments are fading as the entire world, not just the local clan, is now at our fingertips. We straddle the planet with a click of the mouse, watch space stations hook-up, chat with strangers from far away places, or buy much needed STD ointments from exotic countries.

Our ancient anchors have broken loose. The pull and power of tribe and kin, bruised and battered in the move to the big city, are disintegrating in the Web of modern communication.

The Savanna in Cyberspace

We are crossing over from analog to digital in a hurry, a transition most dramatically on display in the anonymous terrain of the Internet. The most far-reaching of our recent technological breakthroughs, even the Web seems a stellar example of nature-based principles at work; its early formation is not unlike the savanna topography that greeted our ancestors. Cyberspace has the feel of a natural domain, a more or less level, if chaotic, playing field.

Innovative energy and self-interested calculation abound on the Internet. Digital "organisms" replicate, mutate, adapt, evolve, and grow more complex while others are driven to extinction. New ideas, technology, services, and products emerge to face an immediate harsh filter of utility. Productive innovation is rapidly and abundantly rewarded and weaker entities brusquely eliminated. All manner of destructive forces, from worms to viruses to renegade hacker terrorists, lurk at its edges.

As in the biological world, initial cyberspace chaos evolves toward stability. Rules of interaction and standards of etiquette emerge, informal networks develop, and Netizen gossip circles distinguish the valuable from the wasteful. Rating systems appear. Families of interest arise. Talking shops develop; customs evolve; dysfunctional behavior arises and is punished. Internet archives are maintained and, with them, the body of knowledge expands. Bouts of innovation and anarchy beget excess, calling forth spasms of regulatory response. Web users join faceless tribes driven by shared interests. Inevitably, the new landscape is maneuvered toward commercial advantage.

Whether we are navigating the virtual world or hanging out at the actual mall, twenty-first century consumers enjoy options that would astound their grandparents. Just about everything we could possibly desire is for sale. The immense range of goods and services, the countless shadings of style, price, and quality on offer in the modern marketplace are remarkable. Like the eight-page deli menu, we risk being overwhelmed by choices that bombard the simpler, savanna-oriented consciousness sitting on top of our heads. From an ordinary ATM to the hottest handheld device, a free market system, powered by technological innovation, has granted us exquisite control over our lives, even as the hectic pace of life makes us sometimes feel *less* in control.

Consider the pace of change. The first contraption that might be thought of as an electronic computer took up half a basketball court, weighed in at a dapper thirty tons, and housed eighteen thousand vacuum tubes. That was fifty years ago. A quarter of a century later, PCs ran at 2 MHz and boasted a whopping 256 bytes of RAM. By 2000, top-of-the-line versions were running at twenty-thousand times the rate of that first huge clunker and held three million times the memory of their twenty-five-year-old precursors. From the size of your house to the palm of your hand in a couple of generations!

Exceptional innovation, however, can also give rise to unforeseen circumstances as gift and curse are technological twins. The hand axe can be used to build a log cabin or slaughter innocents. Miniaturized silicon chips put the world's libraries in your lap and ballistic missiles in the hands of today's barbarians. Genetic manipulation can enrich and extend our lives or set hazardous monsters on the loose. Where there is technology, there is light and shadow.

Despite its many blessings, including the prosperity and convenience it has fostered, technological innovation can also distance us from the natural world. Analog to digital numbs the senses. Are you reading this on a monitor or do you have the feel of paper in your hands? With the gateway to modern power resting at neutered keyboards, human interaction can be reduced to "0s" and "1s," digitized bits of on-and-off data.

The Internet itself fosters isolation, reducing the need for face-to-face contact.

Trekking into the cities, cut loose from nature's steadying hand, we run the risk of getting lost in a remote, sexless place, a world of techno-androgyny, a place where we no longer have a grounded connection to our biological core, even though it insists on bubbling to the surface. As we attempt to massage our primitive psyches into the hectic, quickening, and disorienting pace of contemporary life, it would be comforting if we had a sturdy moral compass to guide us.

The Borders of Faith

The digital revolution yields a lot of data but few answers, reams of ideas but few values. As an anonymous Internet posting put it, we have learned to make a living, but not a life; we have added years to our life, but no life to our years; we have conquered outer space, but not inner space. For so many of us in today's high-tech wonderland, the old answers to life's big questions are just no longer adequate.

The Abrahamic religions of monotheism—Judaism, Christianity, and Islam—served a critical purpose when they were founded and first propagated. Civilizing and positive forces in the human odyssey, they provided comforting answers and decent instruction to a world that did not and could not know any better. Most of us would agree that "do unto others as you would have them do unto you" is a worthy and constructive principle for organizing human society—whatever we may believe about the origins of the universe. For many of us today, biblical stories are not taken literally but are more likely regarded as useful parables. Religious ritual continues to offer us sanctuary during the most important and stressful passages of our individual lives and that of our communities.

There are now about eleven thousand recognized religions—nearly a dozen considered major. Although many share a common perspective and historical foundations, their individual teachings are often contradictory, their specific doctrines forming not so much a harmonious chorus as a cacophony of competing voices. Adding to the confusion is a clergy that has often distorted the words of the founding prophets in order to accommodate their own religious establishment. Over the centuries, huge bureaucracies have enveloped many of them.

The Roman Catholic religion, for example, is administered through layer upon layer of hierarchy, almost all the province of males vowing celibacy. Inevitably, corruption and perversion have ensued. Consider the vile Inquisition or the sale of indulgences, a license to sin that Catholics could purchase ahead of time. Having declared that what people wanted to do was bad, the clergy then sold them the right to do it. (We used to call these people priests; now we call them therapists.) In spite of their vows, religious nobles have succumbed regularly to male frailty. The history books have illuminated some very hot clerical orgies. Pedophile scandals continue to plague the church.

Animals are not inclined to be celibate. If everyone was, the species would fade to extinction, which is perhaps why chastity has been described as the greatest perversion. Abstaining from sex takes a female out of the reproductive chain of survival. Meanwhile, zesty male hormones do not go away but lurk shifty-eyed and unresolved in celibacy's shadows.

Many religions fire up their adherents' passions and compete feverishly for new followers; religious conflict, fueled by fanaticism, quickly topped the list of reasons why humans go to war. Staggering legions have died in the name of someone's god, and fundamentalist terrorism once again comprises the greatest threat to contemporary societies.

For a lot of us, the steady scientific unveiling of the planet's natural laws has eaten away at the "once upon a time" teachings of orthodox canons. Science has uncovered enough of the workings of the universe to predate—by millions of years—the religious folktales about our origins with many of these verifiable discoveries having been revealed in just the last few hundred years.

As a result, it's difficult for most educated people to believe that the planet was formed in a week, or that Noah managed to round up and load every kind of dinosaur and millions of species on a solitary ark, two each, perfectly matched, accounting for every type of creature ever to appear on earth. Since we have figured it out, more or less, from the Big Bang to today, clearly if there is an intelligent design to the universe, the designer must have let go of the reins a very long time ago.

Simply put, literal dogma no longer contains our doubts. Many of us see the traditional faiths as the triumph of hope over reason. In fact, commencing with the Renaissance, traditional religious observance has been in gradual overall decline in the West. Despite periodic retrenchment, especially in troubling times, nearly every poll starting from early in the twentieth century confirms the gradual waning of religious faith.

Although there was a significant rise in church attendance in the two decades after World War II, confidence in organized religion had fallen from more than 40 percent of the population in the West as recently as 1966, to less than half that number by the 1990s, a precipitous drop in less than two generations.

With the millenium and George W. Bush's presidency, the religious right has enjoyed a modest revival. Deftly commanding the levers of political and media influence so skillfully mastered by the social engineers on the Left, the fundamentalists on the Right are demonstrating the power of a mobilized minority. While they may be making a lot of noise, so far they are limited to nibbling at the edges of the culture; their impact on the nation's huge educational, economic, and social institutions appears muted. Yet, given the fervor and newly organized political potency driving America's current evangelical resurgence, it may be hard to see the overall trends in religious observance but most broad indicators continue to point downward.

Roughly one hundred million Americans now have no connection to a church or temple according to some pollsters. A 2002 report by Gallup's Princeton Religion Research Center indicates a clear majority of Catholics, Protestants, and Jews agree that despite the zeal of the fundamentalists, religion is gradually losing its influence in America. Nearly two-thirds of young adults also believe religious influence is waning. Tithing reportedly fell by 17 percent in the last three decades of the twentieth century during which weekly attendance by Catholics fell from 50 to barely 25 percent.

Overall religious attendance, just half of what is claimed in telephone polls, is reported to have fallen by a quarter over the last three decades of the twentieth century. It is now mostly the habit of the orthodox, the elderly, evangelicals, the less educated and less prosperous. And women.

Men are far less religious, abandoning even the patriarchal churches in droves.

Europeans are much more skeptical than Americans whose religious fundamentalism is periodically emboldened. Less than one in ten believes in a literal Bible compared to four in ten in the U.S. Although the events and immediate aftermath of September 11 occasioned a modest 5 percent return to churches and temples, attendance rapidly fell back to earlier levels. Reflecting on the perpetrators of the attack led many to see religion, or at least its fanatical devotees, as less the answer than the source of the problem.

Except for their most fundamental and orthodox segments, major religions are grasping to retain their influence in the face of massive and persistent scientific sabotage. Only in 1994 did the Catholic Church release Galileo from purgatory for having made the heretical claim, in 1616, that the Earth rotates around the sun rather than the other way around. In 1996, the Church again bowed before the inevitable when Pope John Paul II declared evolution to be "more than hypothesis." If evolution is more than a theory, then life has existed for a very long time and theological doctrine, taken at face value, must be folklore. Which is perhaps why, within weeks of his passing in 2005, the church dismissed his declaration on evolution as "vague and unimportant."

Even if they do not comprehend its exact workings, many people sense the basic idea of evolution. As a result, while most of us would choose to live in a society respectful of private religious beliefs, in our fast-paced and complicated world the theological bargain is rapidly breaking down. For the majority in many Western nations, literal religious dogma looks increasingly like man-made teachings. We may attend the obligatory holiday service and choose a religious wedding or funeral, but the doctrine just doesn't deliver. During difficult times, many people seek organized religion's comforts, not so much for guidance, it seems, but for solace and, perhaps, because there is nowhere else to go.

Seeking new avenues of fulfillment for the meaty answers we still crave, for many of us spirituality may be up but dogmatic religion is down. As a result, many of us in the West operate in a kind of existential void, groping for answers on our own, finding inspiration in things like popular psychology and self-designed ritual. For some, the quest for meaning has only intensified as scientific explanations debunk previously held beliefs. But the sectarian shrines have become devoid of meaning. There is an empty place where our purpose ought to be.

The Cult of the Individual

Whether religion is failing to provide answers or science is unsettling the doctrine, surveys report about two out of three Americans believe the nation is morally misguided. The traditional canon of ethics—hard work, marriage and family, steady progress to well-defined goals—is eroding. Polls suggest we are increasingly suspicious of others, and, except for those who came of age soon after World War II, each succeeding generation has reported a greater mistrust of human nature. Periodic polls by *U.S. News & World Report* and others find that about eight in ten Americans consider incivility a serious prob-

"I mean, hell, sure, Superman is cute, but Batman looks like he's got money."

lem that is getting worse, confirming a growing sense of cultural coarseness, an increase in cheating and rudeness.

As the baby boomer generation arrived at middle age, a young aide to President Bill Clinton described it as "the most self-centered, self-seeking, self-indulgent, self-aggrandizing generation in history." Surveys report the boomers' kids are arriving at college, record numbers of them the product of divorce and enveloped by apathy, particularly when it comes to political and social issues. Membership in civic organizations has eroded, while the clergy, the courts, most government agencies, and many other institutions are increasingly looked upon with suspicion.

Despite sustained prosperity, Americans say they are overworked and underhappy. According to U.S. Department of Labor data and international reports, Americans were toiling seventy hours more a year than even the hard-working Japanese, seven weeks longer in just the last decade, and a remarkable nine weeks more than the average European. "Stressed out" is now the norm.

At any one time, in what is sometimes referred to as an epidemic, a fifth of Americans report being depressed, lonely, or upset, most often resulting from relationship problems and marital strains. It is estimated that as many as thirty million Americans take an antidepressant in any given year. Although definitions of mental illness can be exceptionally broad, one study conducted by the University of Michigan reported that fully one in four Americans met the criteria for having a mental disorder in 2004. More than a third of Americans will experience some form of sexual dysfunction, and a quarter of the nation's population admits to having approached the edge of mental breakdown at least once. Most doctor visits now involve stress-related complaints, while big segments of the American public endure acute anxiety, experience panic attacks, or suffer from major phobias. More than twenty-six million people live alone.

The overall shift to detached, high-tech urban lifestyles has cut us off from the rhythms of nature, distanced us from the wisdom of instinct and the innate sense of our own bodies. We have relinquished the moral anchor of traditional religion, and in an anonymous cityscape of vertical caves, we have become unhooked from our kin and clan as well. Many Americans feel like strangers in the crowded Global City, floating digits in cyberspace. Accountable to no one, morality becomes whatever you can get away with. We drift like ethical flotsam on a sea of moral relativity. Finally, ego alone triumphs.

The elevation of the individual articulated during the Enlightenment was a welcome and revolutionary achievement. But a scant few hundred years later, it appears we have taken the concept to ridiculous extremes.

A mantra of our time, "be all that you can be," has come to mean, essentially, "I gotta be me." Many of us, especially youngsters, find ourselves navigating through permissive value systems that spurn responsibility in favor of personal fulfillment. We don't think we owe much of anything to anybody; too often we think we're entitled. In a free-agent economy, we change jobs and neighborhoods without a second thought. In a moral funk, unable to draw deeper meaning into our lives and disconnected from family, we have regressed to a culture of selfishness, to the cult of the individual.

Most Americans intuitively sense that social bonds and a feeling of community are disintegrating, suspicions supported by overwhelming evidence. Social capital, the wellspring of supportive neighborhood resources, the rich density of our social networks, has been in steady decline for decades and is wearing thin despite recent signs of modest reversal, especially in Web-based virtual communities. This collapse of American community life is chronicled in *Bowling Alone: The Collapse and Revival of American Community*, an exhaustively researched book by a Harvard University professor of public policy. Membership in community organizations such as the YMCA, the Red Cross, and the PTA has been falling steadily, as has political participation, civic engagement, religious affiliation, overall citizen volunteering, and philanthropy. Surveys measuring social reciprocity and interpersonal trust are at historic lows. By almost any measure, it appears we have forsaken the community for the individual.

Lousy at discipline, we have become a culture of privileged hedonists with much to demand about rights, but little to say about obligations. Vessels of self-centeredness, we outsource our elderly to institutions and our children to daycare; we eat out more and get together as families less. Between 1980 and 2000, the practice of gathering for family dinner fell by a third in America. By a ratio of three to one, young adults say they are less family-oriented than their parents. Big on the individual, we have jettisoned family, clan, and community.

Water Is Thinner than Blood

During the millions of years that our ancestors moved around in small groups devoted to survival and mating tasks, our roots took deep hold in tribe and kinship, the sturdy blood network that is our genetic legacy and the place that feels like home. This simple family base may explain the common yearning for an uncomplicated life and why so many people feel uneasy in huge cities with their screeching sirens, high-rise buildings, and big, impersonal institutions. In the ancestral habitats where so many of our instincts were forged, our focus was much less complex and our support system of kin and clan was secured by enduring relationships that lasted a lifetime. Now they're mostly gone.

In just a few decades, we have abandoned the extended family. The three-generation household is nearing extinction as less than 4 percent boasted a grandparent at 2000, according to the Census Bureau, despite the mushrooming of the elderly population. A third of American adults, or roughly seventy million people, are grandparents. There will soon be more people in America over sixty than under twenty, more grandparents than grandchildren. Few will be living with each other.

Once again, technology and urban pressures account for many of these patterns. Along with the erosion of stable, family-oriented agriculture and the trek to big anonymous cities, human mobility has become a defining characteristic of modern life. Across town or across country, more than one in seven Americans moves every year, nearly one in three of those is in their '20s. We are also marrying five years later than we did just a few decades ago, which is five more years out there surviving on our own after moving out of the house.

As our involvement with the larger family dies out, our allegiance shifts from kinship to less permanent constellations of friends and co-workers. We build urban tribes and artificial families based on issue groups and around things that interest us. From fantasy baseball leagues and local amateur theater to Internet chat rooms and STD support groups, our pleasures, fears, and passing fancies have become the hubs around which we connect. The Global City is built on households of convenience, neighborhoods of interest, and online communities.

But these new allegiances, important as they may seem, are often tenuous, temporary, and conditional. They are not the rock of kinship. They do not pick up the enduring ties of family. Rather than something you can depend on and choose to be loyal to, these circles of interest are impermanent, changing over time—when we move, when our interests change, or when we need a different support group. Many people now seem to prefer the less burdensome obligations and the easy escape routes these transient groups offer. In an undisciplined world, they are much less demanding than family. In this sense, water is thinner than blood.

In fact, for the first time in recorded history, the family has pancaked, flattened out and gotten smaller. Family organization has gone from vertical to horizontal, and, while all sorts of lateral living arrangements are in vogue, few extend beyond two generations. When we discourage the elderly's presence or farm them out, we lose their wisdom, not to mention their help raising kids. Children, in turn, have fewer mentors and are deprived of experiencing the full spectrum of life's critical passages.

By reducing the outer reach of family, cutting off grandparents, aunts, uncles, and cousins, we narrow our support structures and lose the reassuring sense of connection to a larger identity. Many studies report that people who are socially isolated and disconnected from kin are among the least happy and least healthy segments of society. Severed from the fullness of family, we squander a supportive steppingstone to the larger community. Without our kin, we lose the safe half-way house to the crowded, aggressive, and threatening world outside our door.

Say "I Don't"

The big thing disrupting the extended family is the erosion of its core unit—matrimony. Deferred marriage and modern mobility means losing touch with the folks back home. Living together, rather than getting married, means fewer settled connections. Frequent divorce means having to keep score of the in-laws. No point investing too heavily in your extended family when it may soon be reformulated.

Through much of the cosmopolitan world, marriage has ceased to be a commitment to perpetuate life. Recent surveys suggest a majority of Americans no longer view having children as the main reason to get married. Having lost "child-centeredness" from the heart of our community, matrimony has become an easily delayed vessel of personal development.

Wedlock, the formalized and extended version of the pair bond, the solid bedrock of the male-female social contract, has taken a serious hit in just two generations. As a result, humanity is regressing to less permanent, makeshift mating patterns and living arrangements. Nowadays, at least in America, departure to college is followed on graduation by a move out on your own. Many young people work apart from where they grew up, often cohabitating in horizontal groupings with roommates, live-in lovers, or a combination of the two.

In many developed countries today, a majority of twenty-something's have not tied the knot. More than delaying marriage, a lot fewer people are attempting it in the first place. In 2005, the Census Bureau reported that, by the year 2000, households of people living alone, without children, represented the largest segment of the population. Between the end of the 1960s and the middle of the 1990s, the number of unwed adults nearly doubled in America, to 44 percent of the population, according to Census Bureau data. By 2003, almost five million unmarried couples were cohabiting, a tenfold increase in two generations. In Europe, especially in Britain, France, and Germany, an even higher proportion of domestic couples are not married.

One aspect of the flight from matrimony is the dramatic rise in single motherhood. In the last few decades, the practice has gone from generating acute social ostracism to general public acceptance, even celebration in some quarters. There are now more never-married single mothers than divorced single mothers. From 1960 to 2005, out-of-wedlock births in the United States rose precipitously—from 5 percent to more than one-third, or almost 1.5 million babies in 2004, according to the National Center for Health Statistics. It gets worse.

The number of recorded divorces in the United States nearly quadrupled from the end of the 1960s to 1995, by which time almost half of all "I do's" ended in "I don't"—three times the divorce rate in less than half a century. Four out of five women married in the late 1940s celebrated their twentieth anniversaries; barely half married in the early 1970s got that far.

These cold statistics translate into unprecedented human wreckage both painful and costly. When it comes to society's core institutions, observers are used to measuring tiny changes over an eternity. To social scientists, these recent tectonic shifts in the matrimonial landscape look like screaming avalanches. Marriage, the indispensable center of the family, is rotting to the core, and it's doing it in record time.

Together Through Thick

At center stage in the modern culture of selfishness is "no fault" divorce, available at a courthouse near you in all fifty states, though a few are at last retrenching. There are surely legitimate reasons to seek a divorce as some marriages descend to states that are beyond repair, and nobody should live under the threat of tangible violence. It's also true that many adults and their children function superbly in single-parent households, especially after a seriously dysfunctional person has been removed. In fact, women initiate 60 percent of divorce proceedings. The most often cited reasons are financial problems and infidelity, echoing archaic issues around resources and the wandering male libido.

Easily obtainable divorce, however, cripples partners who want to fight for their marriage. And whoever files, the unpleasant truth is that divorce is lousy for just about everyone, including people who are not directly involved. The exceptions seem to be wealthy males who leave behind a tip for the "ex" and pick up a new bauble; "family practice" lawyers who mostly practice laughing on the way to the bank; and the booming self-storage industry, which gets to keep everyone's stuff.

Divorce sets men loose again without the stabilizing connection to a wife and family. Women, especially those with children, almost always face reduced living standards, their social and economic options severely restricted because potential partners are often reluctant to live with and rear another man's children. Then there are the children, forced to endure emotional pain, the absence of a supportive parent, and financial strains that frequently result in the dislocation of their home and peer group.

Although psychologists continue to debate divorce's longer-term influence, the children of divorced parents are much more likely to experience emotional and mental disturbances and do more poorly on almost every social and academic measure. Through a kind of "sleeper effect" children may then carry the heavy baggage of a broken home into their own future marriages. No fault they say?

Divorce also means that what is left of a couples' extended family, their parents, siblings, and in-laws, lose the connection to their genetic future. Instead, they are often forced into wrenching choices of allegiance and a lot of personal complications. When society's primary building block erodes, everyone has to pick up the wreckage of abandoned families. As the social reserves of the community unravel, we all pay the price of a transient culture.

An institution that draws the roots of two families together to seed the future with their children is not something to fool around with lightly. Breaking families apart incurs a big cost in money, time and civility and it inflicts incalculable emotional damage on individual men, women and their children. Some of this cataclysmic social decay in the state of marriage has begun to stabilize, but the attitudes and values that originally promoted these problems still pervade many of our basic institutions. Although a recent Gallup poll of young women reveals a deep-seated desire for a lifelong soul mate, many women and men are now ambivalent about marriage and look favorably on alternative arrangements. Given what they have been taught about marriage and see around them by way of wedlock, this is not all that surprising.

As recently as the 1950s, the American government was doing just about all it could to encourage family formation. The GI Bill offered mustering out pay for soldiers, providing a lot of men with the wherewithal to marry while also funding dependent allowances and subsidized family housing and education support. The post-war golden age of the American family was also fortified by a broad range of government laws, policies, and institutions that fostered marriage and reinforced stable households.

Although healthcare and retirement benefits continue to favor married couples, since the 1960s much of the nation's supportive marriage-centered structure has been dismantled. Accommodating single parenthood and its effects consumes billions in federal and state subsidies. There have been helpful revisions more recently, but tax code provisions still penalize some marriages, and family support payments have been substantially reduced.

Despite some pulling back, the broad cultural attack on marriage and the family is relentless and unprecedented. Social acceptance of casual intimacy discourages matrimonial commitment in the first place, and easy divorce promotes its destruction. Women have been encouraged to make it on their own, and men have been liberated from troublesome responsibilities. Instead of treating motherhood as the central axis of our lives and our community, we have run it down. Rather than trying to attach men to their families and their children, we are driving them away.

Life Without Father

Our natural history reveals that hunter males, like virtually all male primates, barely bothered with offspring. Prehistoric males did notice and protect the clan's children as they matured, even mentoring and socializing favored young males. But most of the time, adult males were busy hunting, defending the troop, or just stargazing. Nurturing may not only have looked unappealing to them, it might have blunted the hard edge that hunting and warfare require. Chasing animals for dinner is not exactly breast-feeding.

Despite all the splendid diversity on display in the primate kingdom, mother-with-infant remains the unequivocal rule. Throughout the entire mammalian range, male involvement in parenting beyond protection and resource-sharing borders on the nonexistent. And if a male is the least bit uncertain of his paternity, his help in bringing up offspring is virtually unheard of. Not that ancient gatherers had a whole lot of time for raising children either. Only postnatal intercourse taboos and breast-feeding, nature's own birth control devices, spared a woman from another immediate pregnancy. By the time a mother's previous child was one or two years old, she was often forced to turn her attention to a new infant.

Today's single mother seems just as harried. For starters, absent fathers mean absent dollars, which often results in children growing up in impoverished neighborhoods where family instability and crime are more prevalent. In addition to resource deficiencies, many studies report a significant correlation between an absent father and a child's poor scholastic performance, higher drop-out rates, a doubling of emotional and psychological disturbances, and big increases in drug use, teen pregnancy and violent crime by boys.

Fatherless children make up the vast majority of young suicides and 90 percent of runaways and homeless youth. Daughters living only with their mothers are nearly twice as likely to give birth out of wedlock and to experience divorce in their own marriages, according to the National Longitudinal Survey of Youth and other studies. The U.S. Department of Justice reports that almost two-thirds of juveniles and young adults in state-run institutions are from fatherless homes, as are most of the nation's rapists, nearly three-quarters of adolescent murderers and long-term prisoners of both sexes. The presence of a surrogate male does not help. In fact, it points up another big problem about an absent dad, one that is a real killer: it invites the presence of the mother's boyfriend or a stepfather.

In the animal kingdom a new adult male hanging around with your mother can make it a dangerous place if you were sired by her previous mate. Combing through crime data, researchers at McMasters University in Canada found that a young child is sixty to one hundred times more likely to be killed by a stepfather, or his mother's new mate, than by his or her biological father. Sexual abuse is committed eight times more often by a stepfather and is much more likely to happen to a child from any source if mom is single.

Stepmothers are no angels either. While they are less likely to inflict physical harm, they can get pretty nasty about the time, attention, and resources their husband devotes to the children he shares with a previous wife. About half of American children will find themselves in these potentially volatile situations. Despite the added pressures, however, many step-families work just fine and some intact households are a disaster. Admittedly, the world is filled with normal, thriving adults who have endured broken homes, absent fathers, and all manner of unorthodox families.

Spoiled Kids

One way or another, our hopes for the future are handed off to our children. In the broad view, they have never been in worse shape. Since kids still arrive with the same basic equipment kids have always had, it doesn't take a PhD to figure out that today's unprecedented levels of childhood dysfunction are more likely a result of recent alterations in the family unit as well as the absence of other social and cultural supports that used to surround them. The most painful price society pays for the breakdown of family is the sordid legacy we leave to the future. Disturbed, broken-home children often become dysfunctional parents, crippling the promise of youth for generations to come. Barely four in ten children can now expect to have both of their parents around until they leave home—half the rate of the 1950s.

Destabilizing children can take more subtle forms than the absence of a parent. Outsourcing them to childcare has grown at a dramatic pace. Studies by the National Institute of Child Health and Human Development report that up to 80 percent of American children are cared for by someone other than their mother on a regular basis, a process that can begin before an infant is a year old and averages about thirty hours a week. In a series of releases, the institute reported on the largest long-term study of childcare in U.S. history, which found a direct correlation between time spent in daycare and aggressive, disobedient behavior by children. This disturbing finding was true for both boys and girls no matter the socioeconomic standing of their parents. Other studies have focused on the poor quality and high staff turnover at many daycare facilities.

"Latchkey kids" are also an American commonplace as about one out of every five children between the ages of six and twelve is without regular adult supervision during after-school hours. Teenagers now park themselves in front of a monitor for about four-and-a-half hours a day. Although one study suggests matters started to improve in the 1990s, today's mother and father, on average, spend about twenty-two fewer hours each week with their children compared to parents in the 1960s. No wonder, in survey after survey, many children report feeling that their parents are just not there for them. In many cases, they aren't.

As for what they are doing in school, despite what looks like a tough work load, American children rarely rank higher than the middle ranges in most international educational comparisons. Barely 70 percent of students entering high school these days manage to graduate. Even after an adjustment in the 1990s making the tests easier, SAT scores are twenty-seven points lower compared with scores in the early 1970s. Children from broken or single parent homes do the worst.

Despite the threat of AIDS and other STDs, youthful promiscuity remains high, even as teen pregnancy rates have stabilized. From the end of the 1960s until the beginning of the 1990s, the proportion of fifteen-year-old girls who reported having had intercourse soared from 5 to 25 percent. Although rates of early sexual experience are topping off, there is little evidence that the trends will be reversed and today's sexual activity rates remain far above those in the 1960s.

Meanwhile, despite all the inspiring self-esteem classes, the Centers for Disease Control reports a threefold increase in childhood depression since 1970. We are experiencing something of an epidemic of behavioral and learning problems in our schools. Widespread reports from teachers suggest many school age children lack focus, a desire to learn, or an ability to conform to rules and regulations.

Children are also increasingly the victims of violence and, perhaps more disturbing, more often the perpetrators, too. From Columbine-type schoolyard slaughter to petty larceny, youngsters under eighteen are involved in a huge and growing number of crimes each year. Ten times more likely than their parents to be the victim of violent crime, they also accounted for roughly one in six arrests for crimes of violence, according to a 1999 report by the National Youth Violence Prevention Resource Center. Cheating is rampant in school, widely considered to be "no big deal." In all, about half of our adolescents are at risk for early pregnancy, school failure, or serious drug abuse.

A millennium study reported by the American Psychological Association declared that anxiety levels among children aged nine to seventeen are way up from the 1950s. It concluded that what we now think of as normal standards of childhood anxiety would have qualified as psychiatric disorders just a few decades ago. The report cited the isolation caused by divorce and the breakdown in community involvement as principal causes. "Never before," intoned a national commission in the 1990s, "has one generation of American children been less healthy, less cared for, or less prepared for life than their parents were at the same age." No

American generation has spent more time on its own. Two-thirds of Americans now tell pollsters that youngsters are generally rude, irresponsible, and wild.

Assuming that divorce or single parenting is the standard and cut off from the ballast of extended family, ill-prepared and undisciplined children grow up to vote, buy goods and services, and work for the IRS. Tomorrow's young citizens will be a big part of determining what is delivered to us in the media, how safe our streets will be, and whether the clerk on the other side of the counter knows what they're talking about. In many ways, modern society is contoured around its lower common denominators. For the foreseeable future, the equation looks grim.

The Urge to Merge

We are a slow-moving species struggling to adapt to a fast-moving world. The last few thousand years of civilization are but a thin coating of refinement over millions of years of hunter-gatherer brain-molding. It's easy to forget our ancestral past, even though the high-tech wonderland we have been splashing around in is barely a few decades old. After all, it may be all we know. Still, we are born of nature, and like all animals, we are motivated to survive and provide for ourselves, our family, and the future.

Despite our sophisticated surroundings, the deep primal urges of men and women continue to call out. Parenting is the instinctive drive to be a part of the future. The desire of fertile women to realize their body's potential through pregnancy remains one of nature's most immovable forces. As it always has, this compels women to connect sexuality to something larger, like a long-lasting and meaningful relationship. They do this despite the propaganda telling them otherwise, despite the pill and forbidding divorce statistics. Bearing a legacy born with Lucy, women seek a relationship, not an encounter, a committed future in order to bring a child into the world.

No matter how much today's men treasure family, like their male ancestors most remain alert to sexual variety and are much more likely to respond to casual openings of sensual possibility. This is true across every culture no matter the male's position, status, ethnicity, race, or nationality. From construction worker to Nobel laureate, from street thug to the chairman of the board, from pumped up rocker to high-powered politician, urgent hormones propel men's primitive sex drive into every light and dark corner of masculinity.

Behind the subtle nuances of even our most sophisticated contemporary cultures lurk all these basic animal urges. It is no secret that hardcore porn sites drove the early video cassette market and seeded the Web's infancy. They still account for the lion's share of Internet pay services. It should come as no surprise that five out of six people logging on to porn sites are males, a good proportion adolescent boys. (If they can break into the Pentagon database, they can get past those filters in a double click.)

Fulfilling archaic influences, males often make a bee-line for explicit visual Web sites and detached sexual imagery, returning time and again; women may look once out of curiosity before moving on to chat rooms for emotional connection and relationship. At sports sites men outnumber women seven to one; at baby and infant sites, it is precisely the reverse.

At the end of 2005, a researcher, summarizing six years of studies by the Pew Internet and American Life Project, described the online habits of the sexes in succinct terms. "For men, it's just 'Give me the facts.' For women, it's 'Let's talk about this.'" Technology and media come and go, but the evolutionary templates that power the sexes have hardly budged in a million years. There are cavemen at the keyboards. And cavewomen.

BEEP

"I don't know. This is all happening, like, so fast.

"Every time I think about getting, y'know, married, there's like this voice of doom in the back of my head. 'You're cutting off your options' it keeps saying. 'You're taking on a load of responsibility.' 'No more strange and wonderful encounters with sparkling new hotties.'

"You heard what the new guy at tennis said the other day. By the way, between you and me, every time he serves, he footfaults. Anyway, he's married, what, three years? And already he wants a patch to a divorce lawyer? Three years!

"I mean, don't get me wrong. I think she's great . . . mostly. We're still having a good time. She'd be an excellent mother, but now she's not so sure about kids. She's worried about messing up her career.

"It's like a business doing pleasure sometimes. She doesn't think my place will work. Her place is out of the question.

"Then there's her cat. Hisses at me all day. Peed on my jeans yesterday. It's getting to the point I'm gonna tell her 'it's me or Muffin.' Except I'm not sure how that will turn out exactly.

"She's also pushing a bit about where we're going. She doesn't want to waste her time. I get this all the time.

"I mean, I don't want to lose her. It's like I say to myself, am I really going to find anybody better? Is this normal?

"What's wrong with me? I don't get it. Am I ever going to take the plunge? Are these legitimate concerns? Or am I, y'know, making excuses for myself?

"It's not like I'm getting any younger, as my mother reminds me with numbing regularity.

"Did our parents go through this? Somehow I don't think so. Y'know, they had it tough. I don't think they had the time, the luxury to screw around the way we do. Maybe we have too many choices.

"Look, this is not really about darkness or frustration or depression. That's not the issue. The issue is anxiety. It's the age of anxiety. I think that's what I'm feeling. Anxiety.

"And, now, a word on your finances. You see where Colossal Industries reported earnings a cent below the 'street' estimate? They gave it a haircut, took it down like 20 percent in an hour.

That's business for you today, my friend. Ruthless and cutthroat.
And that's when they're being nice.
  "Nobody cares how the company is actually doing anymore.
It's like betting on football. We just play the spread.
  "Later."

The world works in pairs. Marriage, or something like it, is a universal phenomenon, a public commitment by a woman and a man to collaborate in cementing the pair bond and building a family. This bond is the central, indispensable social unit, the vital hub of every society on record. Matrimony is the cradle of morality, the vehicle that launches our deepest aspirations and contains our most basic primal instincts. It is the place where women and, especially, men commit to the future.

Civic virtue is promoted and fortified through wedlock. Families take shape, and parents develop a stake in the world beyond their own horizon. There may be a lot of different ways to get to marriage, and there may be some elastic ways to keep it working. It doesn't always succeed. But there is nothing to replace matrimony. Just about every significant cross-cultural study has determined that marriage is good for both men and women; the evidence is overwhelming that married people live longer, safer, sexier, and happier lives. They are also healthier and wealthier, a finding once again confirmed in a 2005 report by the Brookings Institution and Princeton University. Yet, while unattached women can do almost as well as married ones, single males are every society's most unhealthy and dangerous segment.

Over and above the damage they may do to the rest of us, unattached men are in lousy shape compared to married men. They have fewer resources and are more often depressed. As they wander the spiritless sexual alleyways of the Global City, they have sex about half as often despite rumors to the contrary. For a lot of married men, hormonal tugs can make the grass look greener on the other side of the fence. Not for the first time, they may discover that looks can be deceiving.

We have come a long way from the savanna to cyberspace, but there are still only two genders out there and the family unit is only as strong as the couple that creates it. The principal avenues to human fulfillment remain centered on the development of emotionally intimate and enduring relationships. From animal studies and a wide range of human research, we learn that people are happiest doing nature's bidding. When we abandon nature's wisdom for the rootless social fashions of the day, we court trouble. When we stir the pot further with self-centered arrogance, trouble can turn to disaster—like shattered marriages, broken homes, traumatized children, and distressed communities.

One way or another, our children grow up. We survive the perilous task of parenting, and they survive adolescence. The next generation then sets out into an indifferent, often hostile planet to survive and hopefully prosper, to build mating partnerships and families of their own. In the end, we are shaped by both chance and circumstance. The chance is the breath of life we have all received and the genetic legacy we carry within us. The circumstances are the gifts of love, support, and guidance we get from our parents.

Except for choosing a mate wisely, there is not much we can do about the genetic medley we pass on to our children, at least not yet. But there is a lot we can do about their circumstances. The world outside our children's door may no longer hold snakes and tigers, but it contains no shortage of dangers. As ever, we must foster the next generation, help our children hone their skills and talents and see the benefits of a healthy, respectful sexual partnership in gaining the fullness of their legacy. Turning to the challenges facing our daughters, we might begin this effort by honoring their exceptional gifts.

7

DESIGNING GENDER

All That She Can Be

A withered-looking woman, pouch in hand, hurries toward a cluster of bushes. Drawing near, she hears the gentle murmuring from the circle of women and her musings are cut short. The women grow quiet. The elder has seen many summers and knows the ways of nature. Like the other wise women leaders, she prepares the clan's herbs and potions in times of sickness. She understands the seasons, gives counsel, and sometimes even tells the men where to find the place of big waters.

The girl with the swollen stomach has known only thirteen summers. This will be her first child. The medicine woman kneels before the mother-to-be. There is a special spirit between them for she is one of the elder's granddaughters. Rubbing ointment on the girl's swollen belly, offering her a medicinal bark to chew, the elder lovingly coaxes the seedling forward. Meanwhile, the men folk stand guard at a distance, telling tall tales of the hunt and teasing the young warrior who stayed close to the girl during the months her belly grew. Even now, he sneaks up to the birthing circle only to have the giggling women shoo him away.

Soon the panting comes quicker. Like a chorus of guardian sisters, the women swoon rhythmically, their sighs of encouragement containing the pregnant youth's struggles with their collective strength. She heaves back and forth. Perspiration gleams, her cries muffled against the dangers of the night. Howls of anguish and exclamation pierce the darkness! Amid a torrent of fluids, an infant is ejected into a bed of silken leaves. A girl-child! The infant is bathed, swaddled in soft animal skins, and laid upon its mother's budding breasts.

As the new mother inspects her child, the elder ponders the future of this new life. The baby will live among the other young children, watched over by older girls, in just two or three summers. A few more summers and the new girl-child will herself watch over the young. And then, but a few summers more, in her turn, this new child will bear her own infant. Such are the ways of nature.

The wise woman ponders why the newborns usually arrive at night. Surely it is a blessing as they are less vulnerable to danger. As dawn breaks, she gathers her potions and scurries to the safety of the huts, joyful at the thought of the new addition. Preparations for the great feast will soon begin in celebration of the clan's renewal.

Daughters Cast Out

GIRLS STILL REACH PUBERTY AROUND TEN, AND MOST ARE menstruating by thirteen even though today's generous life expectancies take the urgency out of getting married early and having children. As a result, young women are capable of being impregnated when they are half the age they enter wedlock, and mature women arrive at menopause with nearly half their lives in front of them. Aside from the prospect of being a conscientious mother, women will need things to do.

Until recently, daughters went directly from the shelter of their extended family circle to a protective mate. As the pair bond expanded into the modern nuclear family, young women left the hearth as teenagers only to start a family and a home of their own. Though they were doing chores from early childhood, girls never really had to fend for themselves. Women were not concerned with financing their independence—there was no independence to finance.

For better and for worse, in the long modern stretch from adolescence to the altar, young women have been cast out. The straight line from daughter-to-mother is now more like a cross-country obstacle course. To an extent unprecedented in history, a woman must carry her own economic weight, and then some, possibly throughout her entire life. According to the Census Bureau, over the last two decades of the past century, the number of women living alone mushroomed by more than 50 percent.

Reared with the notion that natural forces are only vaguely connected to life's satisfactions, and encouraged to believe there are no limitations to personal growth, today's worldly young woman may find herself detached from the protection and support of family, matrimony, and community. Without much of a choice, young women have been propelled into today's competitive, fast-paced world. Girls just wanna have fun? It's time to hit the pavement, find a job, pay the rent, and build a career. Then, *maybe*, you can have fun.

Given today's lengthy interlude from menarche to marriage, young women must also negotiate their budding sexual appetite in often tenuous encounters with men before they marry in their mid-twenties. There seems hardly any place for virginity or sexual modesty these days. It's just too long a wait, especially when everyone else is doing it. A teen counselor, commenting for a 2002 *New York Times* article, observed that, "The teenage boys I see often say the girls push them for sex . . . and will bring it up if the boys don't ask."

Two teenage boys agreed. "The girls are way more aggressive than the boys," said one. "They have more attitude. They have more power. And they overpower guys more. I mean it's scary." "There is a kind of machismo among girls now," says the other. "They have the male-conquest attitude." Most young American women now have intercourse by their middle teens, barely a year later than young men and, by twenty, less than one in five is a virgin. Since the 1980s, women have been approaching most male measures of premarital sex.

Whether Lucy, the first hominid daughter, was gathering foodstuff, skinning an animal, or keeping an eye on the children, she worked as hard as any hunter. She had to cook the bacon, but at least she didn't have to bring it home. Long anchored in natural rhythms, intuitive feminine wisdom, and the rich gender reinforcement of pregnancy, the archetype female has been the reference point of sexual equilibrium and balance. Reproductive integrity has always been a woman's evolutionary mandate. Yet ever since the time the world shifted its attention from mother earth to father sky, natural feminine values and sexual integrity have been in retreat against a techno-centric, competitive, and masculine-driven world.

Long life expectancy and deferred marriage means that today's young women must not only support themselves for the first time but must also balance intimacy, career, and, eventually, family, in ways men never have. In an otherwise noble quest for sexual equality, women often find themselves having to ape male behavior in the workplace while suppressing innate feminine impulses. When mothering enters the equation, another consequence of "equality" appears to be legions of overburdened women saddled with the unrealistic demands of modern womanhood while their central and empowering reproductive role is denigrated.

A woman investment banker tells *Fast Company*, "I realized seven years had gone by, and I had only seen [my daughter] and my five-year-old on weekends." Missing a lot of the little moments that count she wondered, "What the hell am I doing?" A few months later she quit. In the same February 2004 article, the female chancellor of the University of California at Santa Cruz had some advice for a daughter: "Remember that the assumption that one's marriage will remain intact as she moves up is a false assumption. You really have to know yourself and know it will take a toll." In a cover story for *USA Today*, a Hollywood production company executive says, "I got so totally caught up on the career track . . . I forgot to have a child."

One early-retiring female media executive told *Business 2.0*: "The more you embrace your job, the more you disconnect from your family.

Before I know it, my kids will be in college—and I'd have gotten more people watching their cable network? So what?" Another female executive told *Fortune*: "I don't cook. I don't take my children to malls and museums. And I don't have any close friends."

Our modern shift to a unisex economy, in which nearly everyone works outside the home, is the most significant change in the sexual bargain since the deal was struck on the savanna hundreds of thousands, if not millions, of years ago. Today's maturing female, freed of family oversight, liberated from the threat of unplanned pregnancy and reared in a digitized universe of sexual androgyny, has been sprung from the women's circle. Out there on her own, she has been prepared by our culture to live in a community of perfect equals.

The problem with sexual equality, however, is that it can be a demotion for women. When our daughters step out of the protective family circle into the exterior world to support themselves and make it on their own, they find themselves struggling to succeed in the domain of creatures that have always been there. They find themselves in the world of men.

Same Work

The OECD, an economic club of prosperous nations, reports that among people aged fifteen to sixty-four, there are now more than two working women for every three working men. Just a third of American women held a paying job in the 1950s, almost three quarters do now. In addition to the social and economic forces pushing women into the workplace, cultural and technical barriers to their employment have been disappearing and the nature of work itself has been changing in their favor.

Business is no longer only hunting; it's also about gathering. Advanced countries are shifting from heavy manufacturing to knowledge-based commerce. Rust-belt manufacturing industries have streamlined, transferring tough, labor-intensive work to less-developed countries and automating what's left. Technological advances have replaced muscle with a precise hand at the keyboard.

Our sleek new information and service businesses put the accent on customer relations, where patience, nurturance, and communication skills are preferred. Like their ancestral gatherers, modern women's sensitivity to interpersonal cues is keener than men's. Countless studies show that women listen better, keep track of more things simultaneously, and adapt more easily to physical prompts and emotional nuances. With their tendencies toward inclusion and networking, women are also better equipped to handle the egalitarian teamwork that today's burgeoning knowledge and service sectors require.

Except for the few jobs where muscle or math still matters, women are well-placed not only across the economic landscape but in government as well, where they now account for 60 percent of public officials. They are the majority in most institutional settings such as schools and hospitals, and their numbers in most traditional male professions are growing. Nearly half of our economists, for example, are women. In addition, the feeder lines to quality careers are filled with female entrants. Since the mid-1980s, women have accounted for the majority of college graduates and master's degree candidates. They now make up more than 40 percent of doctoral candidates, a big contingent of business school graduates, and are approaching parity at top-ranked medical and law schools.

The fact that women remain underrepresented at the top rungs of science and engineering in industry and academia was the source of an incident in 2005 which provided a sharp reminder that the excesses of doctrinaire feminism are not yesterday's news but are still very much with us. Lawrence Summers, Harvard University's brilliant and principled president, was incautious enough to suggest, at an off-the-record conclave on the subject where he had been asked to be provocative, that the dearth of women in the upper reaches of university science might, in part, be connected to innate differences between the sexes or their respective career choices. Notwithstanding a large and growing body of research supporting these speculations, his measured and qualified remarks triggered a firestorm of protest.

A female MIT biology professor managed to escape the proceedings, suffering what can only be described as a hysterical reaction, giving credence to the notion that women still do succumb to the vapors. Upon hearing Summer's ruminations, this highly trained scientist felt she "was going to be sick." Her heart was pounding, and she was having trouble breathing. If she hadn't bolted from the room, she reported breathlessly, "I would've either blacked out or thrown up." The National Organization for Women called for the president's resignation. Before being marched off to re-education camp, Summers was forced to grovel in an unseemly cascade of apologies.

Women, of course, enjoy all manner of innate capacities that are superior to those of men. The evidence is available throughout the academic community, from the literature departments to the expressive arts, the social sciences and university language labs. However, lest a budding female teenager somewhere in the nation be discouraged from pursuing a career in science, the president of a great American university—motto "Veritas," or "Truth"—shall not dare whisper his belief that innate differences between the sexes are a worthy topic of discussion.

Whatever their proclivities regarding science, women are hugely increasing their roles as entrepreneurs. At the end of the 1960s, there were only a handful of women-owned businesses, less than four hundred thousand. In just four decades, that number has exploded at twice the male rate, to more than nine million enterprises. Although typically smaller and more service-oriented, women-owned companies make up nearly 40 percent of American businesses, with annual sales approaching $4 trillion; they employ a quarter of the work force, or nearly thirty million workers.

Same Pay

For women more inclined to collect a paycheck than sign one, there is now near-complete acceptance of pay-scale parity for employed women in the American workplace. This is the result of labor supply and demand levers as well as the impact of federal legislation. Women's wages have exploded from the late 1960s, growing at several times the male rate. While this ought to be something to celebrate, we are still treated to catchy headlines proclaiming that women earn just 76 cents for every working man's dollar. These periodic pronouncements provide cannon fodder for placard carriers, but they do not stand up to analysis.

Those kinds of wage comparisons are broad averages and yesterday's news. For example, the average working woman puts in less than

85 percent of the hours clocked by a working man. More importantly these gender-wide calculations fail to account for the choices women make. A disproportionate number of them, for reasons of their own, gravitate to lower-paying careers, such as nursing, teaching, or service jobs, because they choose to put more emphasis on a flexible schedule, a safe working environment, or the possibility of working at home. According to the U.S. Department of Labor, women make up more than 75 percent of many low-paying jobs including waiters, telephone operators, childcare workers, secretaries, and beauticians.

As we might expect, women also interrupt their working lives for family or other personal reasons at several times the male rate. On average, this reduces their seniority and their on-the-job experience to about half of men's levels which, in turn, affects their pay. The General Accounting Office reports that men put in more time at work than women in virtually every field, an average exceeding 2,100 hours annually compared to less than 1,700 hours for women. Recent surveys of women MBAs report that a third are not working full-time, and one study suggests their failure to negotiate, or simply ask, for a higher salary may account for the modest gender differences in starting pay.

Almost all studies that adjust for education, training, work experience, hours, seniority, age, and public-versus-private employment consistently report that women and men are paid just about equally under the same circumstances. Late in the 1990s, the Congressional Budget Office confirmed that American women had achieved near parity with men when overall job conditions were about equal. "Among women and men aged twenty-seven to thirty-three who have never had a child, the earnings of women in the National Longitudinal Survey of Youth are close to 98 percent of men's." Comparing apples to apples, men and women earn almost the same. As it happens, in more than 30 percent of married households with a working wife, the husband earns less.

A subtle and typical example of hype versus fact was a well-publicized study proclaiming that female physicians earned about 70 percent of the income of their male counterparts. On closer examination, it turned out that women doctors were seeing 20 to 40 percent fewer patients, depending on the survey. This was partly for the commendable reason that they spent more time with each of them and partly because they chose to work 10 to 20 percent fewer hours. The disparity was eliminated when physicians of either sex, with comparable training, worked the same schedule.

The relatively recent bulge in the entry of women into the workforce also meant that some time would have to pass before they began accumulating seniority and filling managerial pipelines. Surveys report that women are hugely increasing their presence in higher-paying middle management positions, rising from around 3.5 percent of these slots in 1960 to about 40 percent by the late 1990s. It is only near the top of the big corporations and within a few professions that women are not yet earning at male rates or working in proportionate numbers. Among Fortune 500 companies, there were barely a half-dozen female CEOs by 2006. Just one in six senior corporate officers or directors is a woman, a near doubling in the past decade. Women also remain scarce at the top of many cutting-edge, high-tech, new economy industries that you'd think would be unburdened by historical gender bias. Only 7 percent of working women pursue careers in quantitative fields, less than a sixth of the male rate.

Although their reduced visibility in the upper reaches is partly because women have not been in the workforce long enough, career women also frequently decline to make the kinds of sacrifices needed to get up there. Unlike many competitive men, they are often unwilling to descend into cut-throat competition and corporate politics, put in eighty-hour weeks, or take a key promotion that means a move away from family and friends.

Consider a wave of resignations by high-profile women in 2002. Governor Jane Swift of Massachusetts gave birth to twins and dropped out of the race for reelection because "something had to give." "Being a CEO is hell," commented the head of a major Web portal company as she quit corporate life to get married, take her husband's name, and become a stay-at-home mother. Cokie Roberts departed her top network perch saying, "I want a life." The managing editor of *People* resigned, determined not to "drop dead in my job." "Men never leave jobs," she observed. Men in senior positions "die or get forced out. They are addicted to the power and the status and the games."

Women also regularly decline ulcer-generating line positions, the ones that most often lead to upper managerial reaches. Although they are edging up, women hold a low percentage of these slots. Surveys suggest that few women regard the stresses and strains that come with the fiercely aggressive territory at the top as worth the payoff. Yet another disengaging female CEO had this to say to *Fast Company*: "The reason a lot of women aren't shooting for the corner office is that they've seen it up close, and it's not a pretty scene."

Yet the thing that really slows women down the most, in both pay and the scramble to the organizational heights, is deciding to be a mother. Getting pregnant may be good for your health, but it can be damaging to your wealth. As late as that decision may come these days, it disrupts women's careers, often at critical junctures, and it frequently shifts their priorities. Studies suggest that having a child will reduce a woman's lifetime earnings by more than an eighth; two kids will cost her close to 20 percent. Overall, women without children bring home about 90 percent of men's earnings, but mothers make less than three-quarters of their male counterparts.

This used to not matter a whole lot. In 1960, fewer than one in five women living with her husband and children under six even held a job. Two generations later, this proportion had more than tripled to over three in five. Despite a small reversal near the millennium, *two-thirds* of married women with young children work outside the home. Many report feeling that they are short-changing something. "Having it all" these days for a woman can mean that, when marriage and family finally roll around, she gets to be someone's wife, someone's mother, and someone's employee. And while she's duking it out with the guys at work, she still gets to do most traditional household chores.

This juggling act is only too familiar to legions of sleep-deprived career women. "I don't know a single female executive with a family who's comfortable making the kind of compromises she has to make in her personal life," the president of Twentieth Century Fox Television tells *U.S. News & World Report*. "You have to sacrifice what your male counterparts don't." Another retiring female CEO adds, "You leave a lot of things behind—friends, family, the whole deal. You have to understand you can't be all things to all people." Resigning from a partnership in a prestigious law firm, another woman tells *The New York Times*: "I wish it had been possible to be the kind of parent I want to be and continue with my legal career but I wore myself out trying to do both jobs well."

That the sent-out women of today should be able to pursue a career is undeniable. But for the many who see this situation as more of a bind than a victory, three culprits share the blame. One is the health-science triumph of our long modern lives and the deferment of marriage. Another is the harsh slimming down of American industry over the last few decades. And last but not least is the influence of a cabal of gender engineers who decided to come to women's rescue.

Designs on Society

Post-World War II America was a Norman Rockwell kind of honeymoon era, an oasis of social and political calm in an otherwise frenetic, can-do American century. Contemporary observers have been accused of turning a dreamy lens on this period; the reality is that racial segregation, rural poverty, and ecological indifference were exacting a silent price. Still, it seems a relatively uncomplicated and tranquil time.

With a boost from the steady post-war economy, the ballooning Western middle classes begat the baby boom generation, record numbers of whom progressed to college. Raised by the newly prosperous bourgeoisie who wanted their children to have all the things they never had, and stroked by permissive child-rearing philosophies, boomers were often encouraged to believe there were no limits to their bright future. As the energetic Sixties generation flowered into young adulthood, their rebellious, counter-culture notions hardened into a vocal and powerful movement under the spotlight of America's rapidly expanding and influential media.

Galvanized by revulsion to the war in Vietnam, their irreverence and impatience drew inspiration from the romantic ideals popularized during the Enlightenment: skepticism of the establishment, subversion of authority and the hopeful belief that we are born a clean and impressionable slate, open to society's design. Adrift in cosmopolitan playgrounds and detached from instinctive guides, many of Western society's bright young lights concluded that the obstacles to progressive awareness and illumination were all in our head. Nature and the intellect confronted each other and, for this generation, intellect won.

The assumption that we can reconstruct the world to our liking, that what we are taught will triumph over our innate tendencies, opens a huge arena for social manipulation. If you believe we have been freed from our natural origins and that society is a cultural construct, you can justify breaking every rule and refusing any limitation. This rejection of human nature, the intense focus on individual and class rights, the energetic certainty that "regressive" tendencies can be redirected—all of this intellectual conceit takes shape in the scourge of our age: the social engineer.

Social engineers wear many cloaks. In a fundamental sense, they share the goal of trying to manage a specific social or political outcome. Fans of "progressive" social engineering view the past, if they think of it at all, as something primitive, something we need to get over. As with socialism, individual or collective compromises are imposed upon society in order to bring about some desired result. Freedom yields to manipulation, and the end comes to justify the means. Not content with fostering a modern savanna based on equal opportunity, the social engineer seeks equal results. Not happy with a fair shake, social designers want a mathematical shakeout. A level playing field is not enough. You need to have a tie score.

The problem with trying to redirect the flow of human nature is that it hardly ever works. For example, the busing of schoolchildren in order to achieve racial balancing has been an abject failure. Parents, including many minority parents, perceived it as a threat to their children's education and well-being. At the end the 1960s, Boston's public schools were made up of 40 percent minority students. Designed and implemented at great expense and social disruption in order to reduce this number, its busing program managed instead to *double* minority presence by the time it was abandoned at the end of the century.

Affirmative action, despite its laudable intention of correcting real and damaging past injustice, ends up visiting the sins of parents on their innocent children. It means the best qualified people sometimes don't get the job, triggering new animosities among deserving candidates who lose out to less qualified competitors. Affirmative action also demeans the truly proficient people in the favored minority whose legitimate achievements are questioned because others assume they had the rules bent for them, too. In the end just about everybody loses because the community's overall standards are lowered. If we want to help the traditionally deprived segments of our society—and we should—we need more push from below and less pull from above. Rather than quotas at the upper end of the academy, we need more head start programs in the impoverished, inner city depths.

In most societies, the great masses are rarely heard from, especially between elections. For better or worse, political change is often the playpen of the community's committed and organized partisans, agitators with an agenda, whether left or right. An activist minority can overwhelm a broad, unorganized, or disinterested public, especially if the people with the passionate program enjoy privileged access to a wide range of media.

When this is compounded by an immobilized and silent majority out of touch with the basic truths of nature, social designers relentlessly pushing their activist policies fail to encounter any sustained resistance. These conditions formed the favorable backdrop for the brand of social engineering that would turn gender, the most basic element of our identity, on its head.

In the Men's Room

When women open the doorway leading from the reproductive hearth to the exterior world, joining an army of men laboring in the trenches, the first thing they may notice is that scant few of these men are generals and most are ordinary grunts. If they did not already know it, women also discover that a lot of the men at the top of the various heaps in our technologically facilitated world are, in fact, having a good time.

At the upper reaches of wealthy societies, in the elegant offices, animated trading floors, and university research labs, at all the institutional, professional, and political perches and mountain tops, some men really are doing things that would look more interesting to just about anyone. Mind you, even at these heights a career can appear to be a lot more exciting than it really is since men are rarely more creative than when they are describing the size of their jobs. Still, there's no doubt about it: in the wide-open, media-saturated Global City, alpha male heroics are visible and exalted.

The life of the *average* American man, however, is no joy ride and it is anything but glamorous. It may have its satisfying moments but, generally speaking, today's man is writing boilerplate software, arguing with the auditors, or selling insurance to people who don't want to buy any. It is true that hardly any women make it to the dizzying corporate heights, but most men don't get there either. In fact, what the regular working Joe is doing usually is not any more appealing and may be a lot less interesting than what Jane Doe is doing at home: caring for children, allocating much of the family's disposable income, and building social capital through a variety of merchant, teacher, and neighborhood relationships.

When women are forced, or choose, to venture outside these realms— if they become hunters as well as gatherers—many will discover that it's not enough to merely do men's work. You also have to internalize a lot of masculine traits. You have to think like a man. Responding to an article about women and business schools in *The Economist*, a female MBA writes the editors with some cogent observations. "Business schools and the careers to which they lead mold one to be self-promoting, analytical, decisive, and ambitious. Motherhood requires that one be self-deprecating, intuitive, patient, and tied down. I have had to develop hastily the skills for motherhood that I had repressed in order to succeed in the business world and now resent having spent so much time and energy developing exactly the opposite of the talents I need to do what I consider the most important job of my life."

Some advocates for women acknowledge that much of industry and politics will run on men's rhythms and that entering this world means being directed toward male pace and patterns. In one typical book, a female CNN executive argues that women haven't made it big at the top because they haven't learned how to play the game. For this author, winning is the only objective; to get there, women are advised to toughen up, be aggressive self-promoters, and play power games. Is this what women want?

Other spokespersons for women believe the "revolution" stopped too soon, that the wave of working women should have persisted and "womanized" these traditionally masculine spheres. To some extent they have, especially within expanding service sectors, many institutional environments, and the rapidly growing satellites of smaller, women-owned businesses. But heavyweight international geo-politics, global commerce, and big business are driven by aggressive, multinational males who will not

WOMEN ARE OBTAINING MORE AND MORE GRADUATE AND DOCTORATE DEGREES EACH YEAR. THEY'RE BECOMING LAWYERS AT RECORD RATES.

THEY'RE TAKING CONTROL OF AREAS PREVIOUSLY DOMINATED BY MEN: FINANCE, ENGINEERING, MEDICINE AND POLITICS.

THEY'RE ADVANCING MUCH FASTER THAN MEN. IN SHORT, IT LOOKS LIKE WOMEN WILL SOON BE RUNNING THE DAY-TO-DAY BUSINESS OF AMERICA.

MEN WIN AGAIN!

bow before America's social progressives. Pace-setting and influential commercial sectors, powered by the fierce international competition of twenty-first century globalization, define the temper and tone of industry and world statecraft. American companies compete in these leagues. They will be propelled by male energy well into the foreseeable future.

The small proportion of Western women who want to claw their way to the top of these corporate ladders will often find they are alone and besieged. Enmeshed in a combative corporate culture, often without the mentors who guide male executives, they continue to confront gender resentment from both female and male subordinates. According to a 2001 Gallup Poll, women who had a preference would choose a male boss by a two-to-one ratio. Executive women also suffer outright attempts at sabotage from their female predecessors and competitors, a circumstance reported by three out of four women in the workplace.

"It is not men with power who behave generally, in individualistic, defensive ways," notes feminist author Naomi Wolf, "it's the few women with power who tend to do so." A lot of competitive older women have made it to the upper ranks, and, as one female executive told *Forbes* magazine, they "don't want to share their role as the only woman." And even if they manage to maneuver around the unique impediments facing them, career women generally find that the hard-driving men who have reached the heights by fending off other ambitious and aggressive males are not about to hand their hard-won trophies to women.

The Second Wave

Ever since humanity's center of gravity began tilting from country to town, the prospects for men and women have had more to do with economic station than gender. Still, at almost every strata women have been hemmed in by motherhood, domesticity, and diminished rights. In 1792, a woman named Mary Wollstonecraft managed to get her book, *A Vindication of the Rights of Women*, published in England. Her treatise is widely regarded as the first modern feminist document. Although others before her had appealed for an expansion of women's opportunities, Wollstonecraft's essay broadly challenged existing restrictions on women in the realms of education, the workplace, and politics.

The American feminist movement dates to 1848, when activists convened at Seneca Falls, New York, on a steamy July day. They issued a declaration of independence: complete equality under the law, the right to vote, full access to education, equal pay, and commercial opportunity. It was a colorful gathering, witness, even then, to heated differences of opinion about goals and methods. One powerful faction wanted to emphasize the moral power and vital importance of historic female interests and traditional roles, arguing for a woman's right *not* to work. Viewing the home as the cradle of advanced civilization, they wanted women to be able to stay there, care for their children, and help weave the social fabric. They contended that the foundation of democracy and free enterprise was built on these domestic efforts. On the other side were factions supporting an assertive foray by women into every corner of the modern community.

By the end of the nineteenth century, the attempt in Western society to elevate women's status had turned toward obtaining the right to vote. Urged on by trailblazers such as Susan B. Anthony and Elizabeth Cady Stanton, working class women rallied to suffrage as a way to help them surmount their humble circumstances. For their middle-class counterparts, the goal was to win a formal role in the political decision-making process. Women's suffrage was first achieved in New Zealand in 1893, in Scandinavia during the first decade of the twentieth century, and in England and Canada in 1918.

George Washington and Thomas Jefferson resisted female emancipation pressures in the founding Constitution, but the significant homefront support of women during the First World War erased any lingering opposition and the Nineteenth Amendment was passed in 1920. Shortly after World War II, the United Nations established its Commission on the Status of Women, which would become a powerful impetus dedicated to securing women's educational, economic, and political rights throughout the world.

Early feminist efforts helped focus society's attention on social and political restrictions as well as the other legitimate concerns of women, and succeeded in relieving some of their more oppressive working conditions. Rather than attempting to correct these inequities within the context of the family unit, however, the Second Wave of feminism that emerged in the 1960s focused on making women a separate class of victimized citizens. As women's issues were refined and segregated in order to form a discrete, comprehensive political platform, their circumstances were uncoupled from the larger context of family. In effect, women's interests were divorced from those of husband, children, and parents.

Instead, the emphasis was on clearing the path for women, or "women's interests," not elevating natural or classic feminine strengths. There was no significant effort to introduce feminine qualities into men's lives, to resurrect the centrality of the family unit, or even to settle for creating some wiggle room for the truly exceptional woman desiring to make her way to the top of the outside world.

To many observers it seemed that, caught up in the nature-defying distractions of cosmopolitan life, Second Wave feminism did just about everything it could to deny, diminish, and discard femininity in a mad dash out of the house. As it happened, a long overdue drive to right the wrongs inflicted on America's racial minorities provided these gender activists with a golden opportunity to advance their cause.

Who Stole the Civil Rights Movement?

Ensuring the full equal rights, opportunities, and obligations of every citizen is precisely the opposite of social engineering. Equal rights are achieved through the creation of a level playing field so that unfettered potential may take its course; it is equal opportunity instead of a predetermined outcome. By the outset of the 1960s, the substantial remnants of racial prejudice in America's body politic had become the object of an organized and popular effort to remove them. The civil rights movement had matured into an effective social and political enterprise applauded by a wide cross-section of society.

Racial distinctions are modest and largely superficial. The same can hardly be said for the differences between men and women, although that is just what the Second Wave argued. Its texts and political positions often contain language such as "feminists object to females and males being held to different standards of behavior." They admit to no significant, inherent differences between men and women. Our unique bodies, hormonal engines, and specialized minds have no discernible impact on our motives or our conduct.

Ruth Bader Ginsberg, the second woman to ascend to America's Supreme Court, professed to discern no unique patterns of behavior between the sexes. She would "accept no generalizations about the way women are." The notion that sex is a social construct detached from biological and evolutionary forces makes it easy to equate the differing treatment of women with ethnic and racial discrimination.

The Second Wave agitated for a place in the civil rights mosaic and for the inclusion of gender in the Civil Rights Act of 1964. One of the most sweeping pieces of legislation in American history, it was designed to put an end to legal discrimination. Some "good ole boy" conservative legislators, believing the legislation could never see the light of day and looking to ridicule the notion of legislating social behavior, whimsically added "sex" to race, ethnicity, religion, and national origin as civil rights categories for inclusion. Against expectations, the act passed. Whether because of confusion regarding the uniqueness of sex differences, public indifference, or intimidation by organized pressure groups, hardly anyone argued for making sex-based issues an exception.

The consequences have been no joke as gender became another constituency for aggressive legislators to protect and activist judges to defend. If separate is not fair for Jews or blacks, how could it be fair for women? In the dispassionate ordinances, statute books, and legal rulings of the nation, "equal to" became "the same as." Setting women up as another victimized class under the civil rights umbrella also meant dragging in all the political machinery of "balance." Quotas and numerical parity came crashing into our most intimate relationships, the pair bond partnership, and the family.

To a disheartening degree the long overdue effort of racial redress was hijacked by gender activists who drew off much of its vital energy and momentum. Having usurped the original debate about how to champion an equitable place for women, the Second Wave proceeded to ransack the means and rhetoric of the civil rights movement. "Women and minorities" became the chant. By the 1970s, the effort to redress racial prejudice in America had petered out. The focus of political attention shifted from abused minorities to the oppressed people making up a majority of the population.

Blind Justice

The eighteenth century essayist, Samuel Johnson, surely had the biological supremacy of the female in mind when he observed that "nature has given women so much power . . . the law has very wisely given them little." How surprised he would be if he were around today to witness a society in which, if anything, laws often favor women. Although legislators and jurists have scrupulously ferreted out any trace of male privilege in the civil and criminal codes, they have let stand many historical laws, statutes, and legal biases that were less favorable to men. They have also added many new ones.

Concerning children, the single most important issue in an adult couple's lives, family law and administrative procedures now provide married women with more power than their husbands. A lot more. Aside from a woman's ability to control conception to begin with, a 1992 Supreme Court decision, which generated almost no public response, removed a husband's legal say in the termination of his wife's pregnancy, even his right to consultation, without altering his obligation to support the child.

In 2006, a Supreme Court nominee was taken to task for having had the temerity to agree, in a measured appeals court dissent, that a married woman be required to report she had notified her husband before undergoing an abortion. The 1991 law in question, designed to promote the state's "interest in the integrity of the marital relationship," had passed with the majority support of both parties in the Pennsylvania Legislature and was signed by its Democratic governor. It included all manner of exceptions for medical emergencies or a potentially abusive response by the father. A *New York Times* editorial described this requirement—not spousal consent, mind you, or even participation in the decision, merely notification—as "extreme" and "outrageous." Although surveys regularly report that spousal notification of abortion enjoys majority support among Americans, the Supreme Court found this limited notification law to be a repugnant insult to married women and deemed it unconstitutional.

It seems women have the reproductive rights; men get the responsibilities. This applies as well to unmarried men who can easily be tricked into fatherhood—and an eighteen-year obligation for child-support payments. Put another way, a women's "right to control her own body" has been translated into: "If I don't want the baby, you have no say; if I decide to have it, you pay."

Matrimony is a public announcement of procreative intent. Marriage *assumes* children. A married woman undertakes to incubate the couple's child; a married man agrees to support the enterprise in every way he can, which used to mean devoting his body and mind to the perils of resource accumulation. In this sense, a wife arbitrarily aborting a couple's mutually conceived project is like her husband declining to go to work because he does not want the stresses and strains. And since it takes both of them to get the embryo rolling, should just one of them have the right to stop it?

When marriage flounders and divorce involves custody issues, men have another interesting encounter with gender justice. That's when a lot of them discover that not only does the marriage bargain fail to apply to having children in the first place, it may not apply to holding onto them either. Once they enter the netherworld of "family courts," legal precedent and social tradition heavily penalize men. Mothers gain child custody four out of five times when it is contested, according to a Stanford University study. The courts also can assert economic authority over balky non-custodial fathers, some of whom may find their assets controlled, their wages attached, their private lives monitored, and their names listed ominously on government registers. Their children may even be used as pawns and informers.

Divorced fathers can be called upon to finance expensive court filings in order to sustain their visitation rights; their movements may be controlled; they may face restraining orders. They may even confront uncorroborated allegations of abuse, a tactic used with increasing effectiveness against them. How bad can this anti-male bias get? Although some states are cutting back on the "dad by default" legal assumption, courts in half a dozen states impose child support obligations on men even when DNA samples prove they are not the father. In one notorious case in Texas, genetic testing revealed that three of a couple's four children had been sired by other men; the district judge refused to lift the husband's child support obligations—but cut off his visitation rights.

Much is also made of deadbeat dads, even though four-fifths of fathers with custody or visitation rights pay child support, according to the Census Bureau. Men should certainly shoulder their responsibilities, but those who falter these days may face prison without a trial, even if they do not have the means to pay. On any given day, it is estimated that fifteen thousand American men are in prison for missing child-support payments with as many as one hundred thousand doing time each year.

Women also bear much lighter burdens throughout the entire criminal justice system. They are less likely to be arrested for any type of offense in the first place and more likely to get bail. They enjoy widespread jury bias; their sentences for the same crimes are often much less severe and so are their prison conditions. Though women are charged with 20 percent of all crimes, they make up barely 6 percent of the inmate population. A typical study in Florida reported that men were about 25 percent more likely than women to serve time in prison when convicted of exactly the same felony.

Employee relations law also now slants against men. An anonymous insurance industry CEO, commenting for *Esquire* on the modern etiquette of firing someone, noted that "all people are not provided equal protection under the law. It is relatively easy to fire a white male under fifty. Other race/gender/age combos are generally protected, and their termination must be handled delicately." Regarding retirement benefits, women's greater life expectancy means they remain on pension programs longer; women make 38 percent of Social Security contributions and collect 53 percent of the benefits.

By now, just about every legal disadvantage previously endured by women has been balanced, and then some. But, of course, there has been little to diminish the offsetting sexual powers of women that were so obvious to Samuel Johnson. Justice may be rendered blind to gender; nature is not. The feeble ordinances of men are easily rearranged; biology is immutable.

Pair Bondage

The belief that human capacities have been liberated from inherent sex-based differences is now embodied throughout our culture and the laws of Western nations. Nevertheless, the fetish for imposing exact balance between the sexes, the gender havoc of precise proportionality, represents only a part of the current confusion and damage. Not content to champion the prospects of our sent-out daughters and achieve gender-blind legal status, the supposed advocates of women felt compelled to denigrate just about everything that had come before.

When we let slide the idea that men and women work in pairs, that we are two indispensable components of one reproductive partnership, we open the door to endless narrow, one-sided examinations of the sexual bargain. When we lose sight of this larger intimate compact between a man and a woman and focus only on specific angles of a complex relationship, we are capable of seeing much victimhood and many wrongs. It may not be fair that women have a tougher time outside the home. Then again, they live a lot longer than men and, until their self-appointed representatives began agitating for exact equality, they did not have to do things like go to war (which is one good reason why they lived longer).

If men are unable or unwilling to enter traditional female domains, then women's equality had to be gained in the men's room. Cut loose from the anchors of instinct and intuition, dazzled by the privilege and power of uber-alpha males, and devout in their faith that intellect can overwhelm the inconveniences of nature, the aggressive activists who commandeered modern feminism set their considerable energies to work depressing classical forms of femininity in order to turn the masculine parts of the world into safe places for women. That this would result in diminishing the role of motherhood and the pivotal place of matrimony was a near certainty.

When we come to think of marriage and children as confining, we may think that we can balance the sexual equation by devaluing the mating bond and untying women from their family roles rather than reinforcing the links between men, women, and family. When we fail to understand or acknowledge that men need unique masculine outlets, or compensating inducements and ceremonies, it seems only fair to do away with their "prerogatives" or encourage women to do the exact same things. When we deny the sovereignty of nature, we see no reason not to abandon the workings of instinct and our evolutionary legacy in favor of the rosy prospect of perfectly designed equality.

Yet if there is anything at our regenerative heart and soul, it is surely the female. In this sense and many others, the further we get from nature, the further we get from the feminine. Since Lucy's days, if not before, women have commanded the heights of intimacy. Females are the sexual guardians. Giving rein to their knowing inner compass, women have evolved unique motives and capacities for encouraging intimate relationship, fostering children, and developing community networks. But a society that discourages and diminishes feminine strengths pays a painful price. It begins to forfeit the sturdy building block of the committed pair bond. Childrearing falters and is compromised, and the standards of intimacy are cheapened. The culture hardens, becoming coarser.

Men are devalued in a unisex environment that asks so little of them, but women bear the real cost. Again. Overburdened by the need to also become a hunter, the contemporary woman is often pushed into competitive domains where, in addition to everything else she has to do, she must continually subdue her feminine sides. Deadening out the vibrant feminine may serve women who have to struggle in male domains, but the reality is that, whether women elect or are forced by modern economic realities to embrace premarital independence, when they go to work they carry a lot more with them than a briefcase or a lunch pail.

Hard to Swallow

There is no better example of female divorce from nature than a handy male invention that was supposed to be their ticket to freedom: the birth control pill. Like so many technological wonders, there is a shadow side. The pill can free women, and their partners, to manage their reproductive lives and explore the bounds of intimacy, or it can distance women from their instincts and disconnect sexuality from its consequences. The pill can give a woman sexual opportunities she did not have, but it also can subvert her feminine agenda, directing it to the more casual male version.

Although its popularity is declining, 80 percent of American women will use oral contraceptives at some point during their reproductive years. At any given time, about sixteen million American women are taking birth control pills. It is hard to beat for convenience and confidence. Whether all the accompanying menstruation management and diddling around with hormones is such a great idea remains to be seen. The evidence is mixed. According to a study released in 2004, long-term pill use may lower the risk of heart disease and stroke, but earlier surveys suggest it may be a net risk factor for certain types of cancers. Some evidence suggests that offspring conceived through missed doses may experience increased cancer rates later in life due to exposure to the pill's estrogen imitators. Less apparent but perhaps more important is the pill's psychological impact.

There is increasing scientific evidence that the pill numbs the senses. Literally. In tests designed to measure the ability to pick up the scent of genetically incompatible mates, women on the pill are severely impaired. Women who are not on oral contraceptives experience subtle changes in the kind of male face they prefer as they move through their menstrual cycle. When they are ovulating, they go for a more rugged, angular countenance, while the rest of the time, they indicate a preference for softer, more-rounded male faces. Women on the pill never vary; deprived of this nuance, they almost always opt for the less masculine face.

In a report released by the Kinsey Institute, nearly a third of first-time users of oral contraception stopped using it because of reduced interest in, and enjoyment of, lovemaking, which may persist for months after they stop until suppressed testosterone reserves are revived. Some observers go further and assert that the numbed-out insensitivity induced by oral contraception is fueling a broader cultural phenomenon, suppressing both a vibrant femininity and its masculine complement in favor of a dulled-out androgyny.

If and when a woman got past all this and became a mother during the last few decades, the advice she got from our hip culture often came down to outsourcing the child to paid specialists so that she could grab her laptop and jump back into the boys' room. A burgeoning media, hyper-sensitized by the civil rights movement and just as out of touch with nature as so many of the culture mavens, proved an easy target for the activists' pushy diatribes and skin-deep math. As a result, so that an elite strata of women might enjoy an unobstructed universe of personal options, legions of ordinary women who honored their deep-rooted instincts and made traditional choices were vilified. Inevitably, males would become the sexist enemy.

NOW and Forever?

Whatever nobility may have propelled the 1960s counterculture feminists to improve the position of women, the movement they fostered has gone way past sensible protections for all women and expanded options for the exceptional ones. By urging women to compete with men for toe-to-toe equality, the activist chorus has cheapened the deep, healthy, and natural desires of those many women who seek a traditional, intimate relationship with their husbands. As marriage threatened to ensnare the newly emancipated woman, limiting her freedom and seeding doubts about her choices, early feminist positions on matrimony boiled down to delay it, denigrate it, toy with calling it slavery—and make sure you can get out of it in an hour. This has instilled a distressing sense of guilt in tens of millions of women who did not want, or could not achieve, a glamorous career.

Strident feminist literature makes persistent and continuing attempts to deny the maternal instinct and sings a constant refrain subordinating family and reproduction; the steadfast emphasis on competing with men means femininity is often repressed rather than celebrated. For the National Organization for Women the sexes are not partners but competitors. It has pushed members to oppose joint child custody, oppose the mediation of disputes over parental rights, and even oppose penalties for false charges of abuse. Despite overwhelming evidence to the contrary, NOW claims family courts are "wrought with gender bias" against women. This preference for gender confrontation, rather than reinforcing the pair bond, long ago gained the upper hand as Second Wave policies continue to attack the family while exhorting women to invade every last masculine hold-out.

Late in 1999, the Fathers Count Act emerged in the United States Congress. It was a modest, lightly funded, and belated attempt to stem the flood of out-of-wedlock births. Directed toward the poorer parts of the country, where more than two-thirds of all children are born to single mothers, the legislation was designed to prompt parental involvement by helping unwed fathers find work and support their children. Its provisions ever-so-gently encouraged the idea of stable relationships and marriage. NOW was not amused. "Promoting marriage as a goal in and of itself is misguided," explained the group's executive vice president.

Whether they have someone helping them or not, it will always be women who get pregnant and bear the consequences, including the obvious burdens of single motherhood. Yet apparently NOW's constituency would be better off if men were discouraged from supporting their children and marrying their partners. It is difficult to interpret this as anything but upper-class women instructing lower-class women that they don't need a husband to help them raise their kids. In a rare defeat, the act passed, over the loud objections of the advocates for women.

The stark reality is that radical feminism, at least the strident Second Wave brand familiar to much of the general public, is not about things feminine—it is about things masculine. It is about *suppressing* feminine values so that women can freely enter masculine domains. Although there can hardly be a true feminism that fails to connect with nature-based rhythms, it seems to be the last thing the agenda feminists are interested in. Like so many men, they see nature as something to overcome. Rather than projecting a healthy, nurturing feminization for the benefit of women, men, and children, their philosophy comes down to putting female bottoms in men's chairs—from the bedroom to the boardroom. Instead of anchoring men to the reproductive core of society, women have been encouraged to rid themselves of femininity's "disadvantages."

Since 1985, a growing majority of married women have told the Roper Starch poll they would prefer to stay at home with their children, and a 1999 *Los Angeles Times* poll reported that more than two-thirds of women and men think it is "much better for the family if the father works outside the home and the mother takes care of the children." In its June 2000 issue, *Cosmopolitan* reported on a survey by Youth Intelligence, a New York market research firm, which found "two-thirds of married *and* single young women would ditch their jobs and careers in a heartbeat for motherhood and homemaker." In 2002, *Time* reported that more than three-quarters of mothers working full-time would prefer to stay home if they could.

A 2005 *New York Times* article cited Yale University alumni studies, which found that, by the time they reached their forties, just 56 percent of women graduates were still working, compared to 90 percent of men. A survey at the Harvard Business School, looking back at women who graduated ten to twenty years earlier, found almost a third working part time and nearly a third not working at all. Of the many bright young women quoted in the article, one said, "I've seen the difference between kids who did have their mother stay at home and kids who didn't, and it's kind of like an obvious difference when you look at it."

The article went on to point out that, for many freshmen women, staying home is hardly a shocking idea as many are happy to assume a traditional female role, with motherhood as their main commitment. All of this seemed to come as a big surprise to a professor of women's and gender studies at Yale: "I really believed twenty-five years ago," she opined, "that this would be solved by now." Apparently it's going to take more than one generation to beat the nesting and mothering instincts out of women—instincts that have been building up in female genes for millions of years.

Increasingly, teenage girls are turned off by work and business, which they see as dull and sexless; a recent survey reported that less than 10 percent have any interest in a business career. By the dawn of the 1990s, just a third of college women were defining themselves as feminists; a Time/CNN poll of women near the end of the decade pegged it at barely a quarter. Even though many young women, especially mothers-to-be, seem more content to seek their rewards in the nurturing, multifaceted universe of modern domesticity—rather than in the tedious labors of ordinary men—few will get the chance.

According to the Census Bureau, over the last quarter of the twentieth century the percentage of women with infants under a year old who held a job doubled to 59 percent. This trend began to reverse, pulling back to 53 percent by 2002, which is a good thing since a recent study at Columbia University reports that, among other things, a mother working full-time during an infant's first nine months diminishes its overall intellectual development.

Despite decades of propaganda and much hurtful confusion, the harder edges of feminism have failed. Women are turning away from it in droves. That's because feminism took on the toughest opponent in the world. It challenged nature. And in the end, nature always wins.

To: HotShotWriter@writersbloc.net
Subject: hiccups

Just a little hiccup on the way to a grand fortune for the erotic gel, ok? No point getting steemed. Some very minor problems, a little 'commotion with the lotion' and it's under control.

The FDA wants them to rerun the trials. IMHO it's no big deal. Stay with me on this.

BTW talking about hiccups, we're having a little, like tension in the relationship. Not quite seeing eye 2 eye on a couple of things.

Actually, not seeing eye 2 eye on quite a few things. More like going toe 2 toe.

She says you have to work on the relationship every day. Why is that? Where is that written? I go to work every day. Making your money grow. That's what I work at. Puhlease!!!!

Hit me back.

YBTIA

The Sovereign Womb

No amount of psycho-babble can hold a candle to nature. Coquettish by five, females reach puberty before their teens and enter a nubile, reproductive maturity that runs for two or three decades. They will then often become the object of vigorous, even unrelenting attention from a cross-section of men, young and not so young. Despite the androgynous curriculum imposed upon them, nubile girls figure out in a hurry that boys are very different—about sex and a lot of other things. Early on, they come to sense the reciprocal but quite uneven sexual agenda and, sooner or later, realize the power that sexual discrimination grants them. That's when they discover that, in a civilized world, they really command nature's reproductive throne.

The fertile young woman is biology's reigning princess. For better or worse, she may not have to do much more than show up. Because her youthful features represent a genetic promise sought after by many males, she may get to dispense with a parade of petitioners. Attempting to negotiate the decade or so between the onset of sexual desire and deferred matrimony, she will be invited to use oral contraceptives in order to avoid pregnancy and test the hallowed career track while being free to diddle around in the bedroom like the guys. Writing in *The Washington Post*, a high school sex educator reports being dismayed by a response to her classroom suggestion to explore the meaning that sex should have in people's lives. "Meaning?" a teenage girl asked looking nonplussed. "Sex is supposed to have meaning? What do you mean by that?"

As her twenties fly by, however, the potential embodied in a young woman's womb will begin to whisper about the future and the meaning of sex may come more clearly into focus. Surveys like the Rutgers report on the state of marriage suggest that most women begin taking a sharp turn toward things mothering by their mid-twenties, around a decade before today's men get serious about starting a family.

Although there is, of course, a wide variety of female sexual tendencies and strategies, most women will not easily deny their intensifying sexual urges as they mature; however, they will usually be able to contain these hormonal blushes in favor of pursuing a sustained intimate relationship, one that supports their growing interest in motherhood. Sex can wait on love. A *Mademoiselle* magazine survey of sexual attitudes in the1990s summarized the majority response of its youthful female readers: "If there's no love, there's no point."

As young women glide through these early years, with men sublime to ridiculous on every corner, their thirties will arrive too soon. The built-up cravings for maternity may still not be as urgently dictatorial as the testosterone spikes that drive some of the men around them to acts of folly, but they can give rise to a deep, persistent ache in many childless women. Motherhood is a yearning that gets the near-undivided attention of a lot of single women as the years go by.

Mindful of the prospects of raising children, the maturing female may then dismiss the glitzy peacocks in search of character, ambition, and strength in a man. In time, maternal urges can start to cut like a knife through the competitive, stressful world of work and business, arenas a woman may increasingly find emotionally deadening and without compelling purpose. Informed since childhood that she can have it all, many adult women start to want just one or two very precious things: the deep, abiding love of a worthy and responsible partner and the biological fulfillment of pregnancy and motherhood.

So potent is this biological imperative that many women, in despair of making a dream match, eventually settle for "good enough" in a man—if they can find one. Many elect to bear a child on their own, despite family objections, pockets of lingering cultural antagonism, legal awkwardness, and other hostile forces. Most unwed mothers would love nothing more than to share the joys and responsibilities of parenthood with a caring partner, but the power of their hormonal countdown may simply overwhelm these formidable obstacles. The ancient, biological charge to reproduce is more powerful than the recent overlay of marriage. As one woman approaching forty informed *Time* magazine, "I could imagine going through life without a man, but I couldn't imagine going through life without a child."

Between a third and one-half of surveyed women say they would consider having a child on their own if they are without a partner in their later childbearing years. With no acceptable men in sight and a couple of decades of unrelieved ovulation behind them, a lot of women who have led an active social life may find themselves flipping their sexual interests upside down: as they seek out a suitable sperm donor, sex without the consequences turns into consequences without the sex. The number of single women electing motherhood has skyrocketed. According to the U.S. census, by 2000, about a quarter of never-married women were choosing to become mothers, a whopping 60 percent increase in the last decade.

Society's alienation from the central themes of motherhood also shows up in attitudes like our squeamishness around breast-feeding. Medical science has long extolled the benefits of this simple, natural activity for infant, mother and society. Cheap, warm, and always ready, mother's milk is available to all but a tiny fraction of women, yet one in three American mothers do not even attempt it and a lot who do quit early. Among other considerations, having to work more than a few hours per day means new mothers have to regularly pump their breasts and store the milk. So far adrift are we from nature's call that "lactation consultants" are now in demand to guide some mothers through this mysterious process.

How discomforting all this ancient pregnancy and motherhood business has turned out to be for the social engineers so intent on designing gender. It's messy, inconvenient—and unshakably female. Nature, it seems, will not listen to reason. It keeps barging into all those neat little genderless constructs.

Feminist vs. Feminine

In the mid-1990s, a book called *The Rules: Time Tested Secrets for Capturing the Heart of Mr. Right* gained some notice on America's bookstore shelves. A blunt instrument, with often simplistic advice and a manipulative, no-nonsense approach to ferreting out a husband, it nevertheless resonated with many women anxious to reassert a bit of feminine control over today's casual unisex dating scene by demanding a minimal show of male initiative. Nearly two million copies have been sold. Ellen Goodman, a widely syndicated "moderate feminist," took the authors to task for their "retro tract on how to catch the man of your grandmother's dreams by acting like your grandmother." This flippant put-down manages to capture in one sentence the heroic blend of scientific ignorance and intellectual arrogance that is the essence of establishment feminist commentary.

The notion that the things that worked between men and women all the way back there in ancient history—two whole generations ago—just might have some current relevance in our bustling, trendy lives never enters their minds. Human evolution throws up a pimple-sized change every hundred thousand years but, to our gender progressives, there is no way that eons of genetic encoding could conceivably bear on our behavior today. After all, we're so much smarter now. When it comes to hip encounters between the sexes, what on Earth could granny know?

Well, for starters, we can probably talk it over with her because, unlike grandpa, she is more likely to still be alive and kicking. That may be because she never had to do battle in a crude, stressful business environment or be a cop on the firing line. Comfortable with a husband who handled much of the exterior world, she ran the house, enjoyed her kids, and dealt with a challenging array of people and neighborhood institutions. Grandma almost certainly controlled the bulk of the family's spending, and, of course, she wound up with the nest egg when grandpa passed away early with heart disease. Savvy enough to let her husband enjoy the reality, or the myth, that he was doing something important, she now enjoys a vibrant golden era with her friends, a bunch of lively, henna-haired widows who wonder why their world-busting granddaughters don't have the time for them.

Grandma knew a few other things that the aging wunderkind of the Second Wave still haven't figured out. She knew that feminine power appears in many disguises. She had it in her head that what's good for a man may not necessarily be terrific for a woman. Without doctors having to tell her, she knew that pregnancy was a natural and healthy thing and that older, childless women can get wrapped up in no one but themselves. She somehow figured out that a man should take the romantic lead, even if she had to tease him forward once in awhile and that he ought to bring something to the party other than his good looks. She felt in her bones that if a man was not part of the solution, he was a waste of time. Grandma also knew how to handle boors without harassment sensitivity trainers. She believed that marriage meant getting joined at the hip for the long haul and that new-fangled notions like "no fault" divorce meant her husband could check out on her and the kids after a bad day.

When you get down to it, granny was a right-on gal who brought a demure smile to the dance instead of her lawyer and a calculator. She somehow figured out that men and women are as different as people get and that this was something to enjoy rather than deny. And if circumstances were sometimes a little better on one side of the sexual equation, she understood that, over time, things kind of evened out. Catch the man of your grandmother's dreams? You should be so lucky.

Unlike their grandmothers, girls now grow up with a gender-neutral world view and get massaged toward a single standard of sexual behavior—the male one. This is the inevitable result of feminism's "we can do anything they can do" propaganda. It features an unceremonious bolt from virginity, male-type sexual histories, the triumph of loveless sex, unprecedented rates of illegitimacy, smoking, alcohol and drug use at rates equivalent to boys.

In a *New York Times* op-ed column, early in 2006, David Brooks reviewed teen and college social networking sites and concluded that "girls are the peacocks in this social universe. The boys' pages tend to be passive . . . in a world in which the girls have been schooled in sexual aggressiveness, the boys sit back and let the action come to them." A University of Chicago National Health and Social Life Survey in the 1990s, describing what it termed one of the greatest changes ever in American sexual patterns, found that young women now share almost all male patterns of early and extensive experimentation with sex. Sex is such a kick in the city.

Summarizing its annual survey of first-year students in the three decades starting from the mid-1960s, UCLA found a similar pattern of strong gender convergence, attributing this trend to clear shifts by young women toward male values. Other reports confirm, even celebrate, these patterns. Despite its greater impact on female bodies, binge drinking by young women is now rampant on college campuses.

"I know it's juvenile," a Syracuse University senior told *Time* for an April 2002 cover story, "but I've had boys comment how impressed they are at the amount of alcohol I've consumed. To be able to drink like a guy is a kind of badge of honor. For me, it's a feminism thing." The article goes on to point out that girls are now four times as likely as their mothers to begin consuming alcohol by age sixteen. A prevention consultant blames this trend on the messages we send girls: "Yes, you can do math. Yes, you can play football. And yes, you can drink."

Tellingly, although most women in developed nations tell pollsters they are generally in a better situation than their grandmothers, according to a survey carried out for *The Economist*, less than 30 percent believe they are happier. Whatever their level of happiness, today's women, like the thousands of mothering generations before them, will persist in seeking out a comfortable nest to bring infants into the world and supportive male partners worthy of their gifts. It is no thanks to their strident spokespeople that today's women are having an easy time finding sex—and a tough time finding men with whom they care to become a grandparent.

Closer to Nature, Closer to Women

To women in touch with their inner drives and feminine sexual wisdom, sex, pregnancy, and child-rearing are not problems to overcome, they are opportunities to nurture. The pair bond and marriage are not tickets to submission; they are an invitation to the dance of intimate partnership. Radical feminism is a failure of sexual composure, a loss of feminine trust. It is a revolt against nature. Men, as always, may be chaotic energy in search of completion. But if males are coital accidents waiting to happen, women, everywhere and for all time, have been the rock-solid sexual anchors of society, the unshakable foundation of intimate health and integrity.

Eyes set on the building block of relationship, women remain amazingly adaptive to the immense range of male sexual rhythm and eccentricity. They demonstrate an enormous capacity for sexual pacing, effortlessly harmonizing with masculinity's one-note sexual drone. Women have forever been the calm eye of the male sexual hurricane; the steady, healthy reference point; the gold standard of a secure and rooted sexuality. But that was before the modern feminist movement abandoned sexual superiority and started demanding a tie.

Humanity faces some daunting challenges. Modern technology has armed boy toys with some horrifying possibilities. As never before, we need the feminine capacities for peace, inclusion, and wisdom. We need to acknowledge the many things the sexes share and, at the same time, venerate classic female qualities instead of abandoning them. We need to celebrate femininity and dump the feminists.

Men are capable of integrating powerful nurturing qualities into their lives and into our societies. The irony, the hitch, is that they need to be comfortable as men before they open to their inclusive, feminine side. Left insecure, uncertain of their role, and regularly undermined, they will ignore this huge gift of nurturance, even fight it. Drawn into family and bonded with their children, at ease with the mature and responsible side of masculinity, men can draw deeply from the loving and healing ways of women. Well-adjusted, grown-up men do not fear strong women. They want to find one.

Pacifying and socializing males is every society's challenge. As men stumble along the untested tracks of today's runaway technologies without the moorings of a composed femininity to steady them, they may lose their way. And if we fail to negotiate the dangerous, man-made passages that lie before us, the consequences will be devastating. No less than our survival is at stake. In this crucial effort, modern societies need to summon the truest in women—because we are going to need the very best in men.

8

THE DISPOSABLE MALE

A Few Good Men

Endless rows of competitors jockey for position at the starting gate.

The faint sound of music can be heard in the pre-dawn darkness but no one is listening—the runners are too anxious, tense, keyed up. You can hardly blame them. They have been through a lot to get here. The big race at last.

Stretching out, some run wind sprints; others conserve their energies. The tension builds.

The starting pistol is raised. A few overeager competitors spill out early and are disqualified.

BANG! They're off! Like a rocket!

Surging forward in a frantic fight for the lead, racers jostle one another on the crowded track. Skirmishes flare up. Some are roughly bumped aside. Others fall and are nearly trampled by the herd of charging marathoners behind them. The strongest and most clever bolt to the front. Pacing themselves, the focused leaders dash along the obstacle course toward their goal.

By the final lap, the contenders are reduced to a

handful—just the hardiest, best-prepared specimens with the most robust builds and the sleekest lines.

As they dash for home, the racers in the lead pack dig for every last drop of strength, pushing themselves beyond all measure, pulsating with exertion. Second place won't cut it. It's winner take all.

Suddenly, a scintillating ball of light a million miles high illuminates the horizon. The finish line is just a tantalizing sprint away. Diving like Superguppy, the exhausted winner hangs on for dear life.

The egg is joined!

Outperforming a few hundred million competitors, one triumphant microscopic sperm has won the seminal race of its life.

A S IT IS WITH SEMEN, SO IT IS WITH MEN. YET IN A FUNDAMENTAL sense, newborn males are all winners. Bred and reinforced by earlier generations, they have survived an eternity of qualifying rounds to win a place in today's reproductive contest. Lining up at life's starting gate, human males will jostle for position, the sleek and healthy pinnedup against the bumbling and the infirm. Like their sperm, men set off in a scramble. Sometimes it is a relay, usually it is a marathon.

The stakes are high. On one level or another, the challenge is survival. Along the way to maturity, males will be pushed, bruised, and tripped up. They will get into skirmishes; some will fall by the wayside, even get trampled. The clever, the strong, the healthy will pace themselves, stay focused, and keep their eye on the prize. Sprinting now and then for advantage, falling back sometimes to gather their strength, men will kick into high gear when they smell a win. To the victor goes much of the spoils. If it includes sexual consummation with a woman, the triumphant man contributes half the DNA in the creation of a new life and also gets to determine its sex.

If the result is a male embryo, it will be a fragile, unfinished piece of business. It is here in the womb that the delicate steeplechase to masculine wholeness begins. Confidence is not standard male equipment.

Combining two different kinds of chromosomes, males are nature's mutational playground. Drenched by testosterone rushes that can hit like a brick, males are an act of becoming. Beneath the bravado, they have to get somewhere. Girls begin as solid XX consolidations and move in a more or less straight line to motherhood, or at least they used to, but young boys need to cut the psychological cord and break away. It is not sufficient to simply be. Males must become.

Sending our daughters out on the hunt is something new, but we have always sent out our sons. They leave or are pushed out of the hearth in every culture, on the lookout for resources and new bloodlines, seeking allies and the respect of their peers and enemies. Masculine initiative, fueled by edgy hormonal drives, is then tempered by civilization. On their anxious quest, males profit from direction, defined goals, hurdles to overcome, and rewards for getting over them. Otherwise, they can stray outside their lanes.

Most men persevere. They have to. They are on the hero's journey. Their trophy, as for sperm, is progeny, a lottery ticket on tomorrow. In the end, there are many ways for a man to become a hero. A couple of well-brought up children, the love and respect of a devoted spouse, a worthy vocation, good friends and family—these are just a few of the valiant male outcomes. What can easily be forgotten, however, is that men usually do not get there on their own.

The energy and resources that society devotes to the chore of shaping masculinity can be immense but the payoffs are even greater: social stability, economic productivity, and cultural vibrancy, to name but a few. The price of failure, on the other hand, may be society's destruction. In our assessment of modern masculinity, we will focus the evolutionary lens on the crucial stages of a male's life—education, athletics, initiation, military responsibilities, work, and sex—the crucial passages that help mold males into men. They begin this journey as boys.

Nurturing Nature

The elders among ancient hunter-gatherer tribes knew that life could be brutal and short. There was no food or energy to spare in these formative eons. Diseased or injured babies, even frail young children, were abandoned. Those who survived were put to work at the earliest possible age. Every advantage and strength of the tiny band was exploited in the struggle to survive.

From the millions of years of mammalian and primate evolution through countless generations to *Homo sapiens*, the distinct capacities, motivations, and job descriptions of the sexes have been soaked into our genetic archives. As far as anyone can tell, every society has framed the sexes in distinctive, specialized roles, and, while neither sex had it easy, nearly all cultures have recognized that males needed special handling from the beginning.

Beyond the unique male perils during embryonic development, in infancy and throughout early childhood boys are more at risk, dying off at a rate nearly 30 percent greater than girls. Before they are a year old, boys manage to poison themselves more often. They suffer all kinds of developmental disturbances, from bed wetting to stuttering, several times more frequently than females. Boys are diagnosed as emotionally disturbed at four times the rate, get hurt, killed, and commit suicide much more often.

Even if the leaders of ancient tribes did not understand the unique nuances of boys' psychology, they knew that their bodies would harden into brawn and that a male child must be drawn out for special handling. Not more than three or four years would pass before boys were pulled away from their mothers, treated more brusquely than girls, and allotted tasks requiring increasing strength and fortitude. Older males, mostly indifferent, would encircle them. Fearful, exquisitely vulnerable, and often in tears, young males would topple over, get up and teeter forward, fall and get up again. Slowly boys stumbled into manhood.

Studies in developmental psychology suggest that at kindergarten, girls are well ahead developmentally and that boys still enter a particularly difficult transition between the ages of five and seven. Compounding their problems, a wide array of cross-cultural studies confirm that boys pull away from their mothers much sooner in an attempt to establish their own sexual identity, echoing the ancestral tug of young males away from the comforts of home. Girls, these studies suggest, do not feel the need to disengage from maternal influence until much later, when their own fertility comes into view.

This early struggle for a separate male identity, the need for a boy to cross over from motherly embrace to become the other kind of gender, looms most ominously just as the contemporary schoolroom beckons. Attempting to detach themselves from the maternal bond and mark out a young masculine ego, boys are instead propelled into an institutional world dominated by women. From preschool, in kindergarten, and throughout his primary education, the young male student is surrounded by female teachers who make up 70 to 85 percent of the staff in most school districts. He also finds himself in the presence of more emotionally mature students: girls.

The evidence, while not unassailable, continues to suggest that girls as well as boys do better when schooled apart. Girls are freer in all-female classes where they do not have to compete with boys or defer to them. Surveys have found that single sex schools generally improve girls' academic performance, reinforce their sense of self-worth, and enhance their future ability to relate to males.

In a late 1990s article tracking the novel idea of same-sex school experiments, *The New York Times* talked to the experts. "If boys and girls are together, they keep talking and get interrupted," offered an eleven-year-old boy. "Girls get you in trouble and make fun of you if you get the answer wrong." The girls were just as happy. "This class is real good because you can talk about girl things and boys won't bother you." Appreciation and respect develops at a distance; there is something special when coming together is something special.

Many successful cultures implicitly understood that keeping the sexes apart during childhood, in youthful training and through adolescence, helped forge an independent sexual identity in tender, unformed genders. Early separation minimizes premature tensions and accentuates the useful specialties of each sex. As maturity approaches, the young male grasps the purpose behind the sexual pairing as he begins to crave female company. The budding young male learns that he must prepare himself, develop the strengths and crafts of masculinity, earn his place in the community, and win a female's devotion. Although sentiment in favor of same-sex schools is building, there remained just a handful of them among the ninety-three thousand coed public schools by 2006. Including the greater number of such private institutions, no less than

95 percent of primary and secondary schools have the young sexes sharing the same classroom.

School Daze

If the goal of our educational system is to build responsible, confident, and caring adults—surely every healthy society tries to do this—we need to begin by helping our children find their sexual balance on the unsteady legs of youth. Yet, according to government-sponsored pamphlets, our children need to "grow beyond gender." By refusing to accept innate sex differences as significant, we are then forced into a single, coed standard. At the primary school stage, the appealing, politically correct model for this compromise is the more settled and cooperative one: the female model.

This bias emerges early. Consider the premium placed on penmanship and verbal skills. Boys favor visual processing and do not have the hand-motor control that girls achieve in the early grades. Girls read faster, control their emotions better, and "make nice." The emphasis is on cooperative study and feelings rather than the action, competition, and structure that appeal to boys. U.S. Department of Education guides actually encourage unisex doll play for boys, while some school districts ban running and jumping at recess. Boys, it seems, are to be rescued from masculinity. "Bullying" behavior, which can include "verbal intimidation," things like name-calling, starting rumors, dirty looks and simple exclusion—all the normal ebbs and flows of growing up—are to be stamped out.

By contrast, the physicality and modest visual and spatial advantages of boys are less valued in early school settings. Boys tend to ignore instructions and generate sloppy work. Disinclined to talk about feelings, every primary school teacher knows that boys are sometimes restless, rowdy, competitive, and aggressive. With pre-installed instincts and testosterone rushes driving them toward physical outbursts, many get punished, controlled, and medicated simply for behaving like boys.

When our little boys enter school, they are not the forward pincer movement of a diabolical patriarchy, they're just frightened little kids. Barely more than toddlers, they are forced into coping with a lot of things, like just getting through a disciplined school day, not to mention sorting out the chaos of their budding sexual identity. Should these befuddled little boys use the dolls that are forced on them to whack each other with, tear a button off a girls' uniform, or get a little restless during self-esteem classes, they can be marched off for sensitivity training or get a prescription rammed down their throats. Depending on the age group and the survey you consult, attention deficit hyperactivity is diagnosed in boys at three to ten times the rate of girls. Though some observers believe it's much higher, at least one in five Caucasian school boys spends time on Ritalin.

While some children have real problems paying attention, it is beginning to look like we're turning the boisterous tendencies of boyhood into a disease. Boys today are softened, controlled, and massaged toward passivity. Pushed into "sit still" schooling too early, many get off to a poor start. Boys compose two-thirds of the "learning disabled" and 80 percent of high school drop-outs. Their unique needs ignored, they grow up to consume more alcohol and drugs and engage in much more risky and violent behavior. On the receiving end of aggression two to three times as often, boys account for four out of five juvenile court crimes. They commit suicide at five times the female rate.

You Go Girl

An extensive, late 1990s survey by Metropolitan Life, a leading American insurance company, concluded that "contrary to the commonly held view that boys have an advantage over girls in school, girls appear to have an edge in terms of their future plans, teachers' expectations, everyday experiences at school, and interactions in the classroom." Both boys *and* girls report that teachers favor girls in class, in some ways heavily. Teachers discipline boys much more often the survey found and compliment them a fraction of the time. Many observers echo the pithy conclusion of an MTV executive who told *Rolling Stone*: "Right now we are totally in the age of the female. Girl power is huge. Teen boys feel disenfranchised."

Boys used to catch up to girls scholastically around adolescence. No longer. In America and throughout much of the West, boys are now testing, on average, well below girls at every grade level. They are falling behind at almost everything, sometimes way behind. They drop out of school at two to four times the female rate and are held back a grade much more often. While girls go online to do homework and chat, for example, boys are looking for amusements. Young minority males fare worst of all.

According to recent studies, male high school seniors are now barely ahead of eighth grade girls when it comes to writing skills. They outnumber females in remedial classes by three-to-one while girls are a significant majority in almost all advance placement courses. Although boys still make up the top performers in several math and science subjects, boys are also thick as thieves at the bottom. Girls substantially outnumber boys in honor societies and in student government, in debating societies and among school journalists. And in the few places where girls are still behind, they're gaining ground in a hurry.

The Gender Equity in Education Act of 1993 made sure of that. Together with other government programs, the legislation provides big breaks for what it defines as an "underserved population," in other words, all females. As a result, we have countless interventions and remedial classes to coach girls in math and hard science, yet hardly any organized attempts are made to bolster boys' weaknesses in reading and writing, among other disciplines. Instead, the activists who often dominate our educational establishment continue to write articles about how girls are getting the wrong end of the stick. Apparently they make up only 49 percent of automobile repair classes (actually, it's much less).

In effect, we have ceased preparing boys and girls to be the different people they are. As reproduction escapes from the center of our lives, nature fades to the edge of our sophisticated urban thinking. The hard won specialized partnership of male and female is devalued. The relationship between the sexes at every age turns into a civil rights issue seeking exact parity. We have withdrawn from the consciousness of gender. In fact, we have gone the other way. Against every impetus of nature, we are *de*specializing the sexes.

Medium Is the Message

Perhaps the only thing worse than the mindless, unisex scrambling of boys and girls in school is the gender messages these students are exposed to once they get there. In the pedagogical amusement park of American public education, political correctness has managed to delouse the curriculum of any meaningful sexual differences. From algebra to zoology, strident propaganda infiltrates the nation's textbooks and lesson plans. Much of the educational establishment—teacher organizations, administrators, textbook writers, and public officials—is enthralled with the idea that gender is something that is designed. In their hands, children often become instruments of social experimentation.

When our boys and girls head off to class, they enter an academic wonderland where "masculinity" and "femininity" are often viewed as learned roles that are essentially interchangeable. Graphic illustrations in contemporary textbooks are delicately balanced to show females and males doing all the same things with equal interest and efficiency. Nature is a blunted force. Conventional marriage and the good old nuclear family may be portrayed as something out of the dark ages. One study of twenty textbooks by the Council on Families found that nearly "half of the meager space devoted to marriage effects is taken up with discussions of how marriage hurts women."

In a morally ambiguous academic world divorced from nature, there appears to be nothing particularly special or valuable about the family unit in many of these texts. The traditional household may be denigrated, parents presented as but two voices in a chorus of potential guides and children's interests even set against their parents. Divorce is viewed as ordinary, which it is for today's kids, and essentially harmless, which it isn't. The collapse of the family may be described as a neutral event, even socially transforming. According to many of these accounts, successful cultures and genders become successful only by oppressing others. Lesson plans often twist through verbal gymnastics in order to present a "fair" multicultural world. Males can move around academia under clouds of guilt.

Then there's sex education. It is being ignored entirely in roughly a third of our school districts through abstinence-only programs. This will induce widespread and potentially dangerous ignorance of a subject that will nevertheless keep popping up insistently for hormone-addled youth through the decade from puberty to wedlock. Although programs vary widely, even within districts, and abstinence may be presented in more measured ways, by philosophy and design, sexuality is often separated from the larger consequences of relationship and love is a word rarely spoken in sex-ed classes. Discussions are usually clinical and technical. While pregnancy imposes the uncomfortable necessity of acknowledging some biological differences between the sexes, the distinctive rhythms and the varying intimate interests of males and females are minimized or absent.

Since the agenda appears to be about equating males and females, there is hardly any attempt to acknowledge, never mind venerate, the pivotal position of women at the center of reproductive life. Aside from abstinence-only programs, virginity may be nothing to celebrate while females are usually depicted as having the same sexual interests as males. As girls practice stretching condoms over boys' fingers, the socially engineered curriculum emphasizes the rights of women and an unfettered claim to control their bodies.

This willful attempt to avoid differentiating the sexual agendas or to explore the more complex emotional aspects of intimacy in most of these programs essentially sets girls up to view sex on boys' terms—as a kind of discretionary activity equally available and of more or less similar cost and emotional content. This is one of the Second Wave's gifts to its daughters: take charge and play at sex like boys.

All this meddling with our youth's educational and training regimens might be excused if it was leading to well-educated and enlightened students. By the mid-1980s a report by the U.S. Department of Education, "A Nation at Risk," famously concluded that "for the first time in the history of our country, the educational skills of one generation will not surpass, will not equal, will not even approach those of their parents." California State University, with more than twenty campuses, reports that more than half of its entering first-year students require remedial assistance in English and math. We are now sending youngsters to college better equipped to explore their feelings than to write a coherent paragraph. Barely a third will have been required to take a single high school course in the natural sciences.

At the end of the century an educational assessment test sponsored by Congress reported that only a quarter of high school seniors were considered sufficiently versed in civics to be able to make informed and reasonable voting choices. A recent international study of educational levels in more than twenty nations found America's high school seniors ranked near the bottom in math and science.

ACT, which produces a leading college admissions test, reported that fewer than one in four of the 1.2 million students taking its 2005 exams met college-readiness benchmarks in all of the tested subjects: English, reading comprehension, science, and math. Barely a quarter of incoming freshmen are deemed prepared for college-level biology. The director of the Center on Education Policy explained: "If you know of any kids who've come from Europe for a high school exchange program, they think American high schools are a lark." Another study, by the OECD, has the U.S. in the middle of thirty-seven industrialized nations on reading skills, with girls outperforming boys in every country. But we rack up big numbers on self-esteem.

Free Speech

Women now make up 57 percent of first-year college entrants, and their proportion is rising. They comprise well over half the student body in every higher educational category: two-year, four-year, public, private, or religious. Except for science and engineering, women are a visible majority in almost all undergraduate classrooms. In many academic disciplines and departments, they are an overwhelming presence.

For every one hundred diplomas conferred on men in America and Europe, roughly 125 are now obtained by women. The divide is even higher for some minorities, two-to-one among African-Americans, with more black men in prison than in college. Overall, by around 2010, college women are expected to exceed men by almost sixty to forty, or nearly 2.5 million students. This is a threshold many analysts believe threatens any semblance of university-level gender balance, an age when the maturing sexes really do belong together.

As it happens, the academic universe that most of today's first year college students enter is politically correct and feminist-slanted from orientation week to graduate school. The rules and regulations of student conduct, with their often hypersensitive politically correct codes, assume that contemporary males are privileged agents of an exploitive class and females are its victims. One University of Wisconsin graduate student put it this way in a letter to the editors at *U.S. News & World Report*: "I've endured four-plus years of mandatory feminism and 'sensitivity training' designed to brainwash me into thinking I am a socially constructed masculine relic . . ."

University orientation literature often goes out of its way to prompt confrontational attitudes. It may well define a sexual offense as any behavior "*experienced by others* as harassing [italics added]," possibly even any voluntary action the woman later regrets. Inappropriate glances, even laughter, can get a guy in trouble on some campuses. So can certain kinds of eye contact, or "*lack* of eye contact" (whatever that means) as well as "provocative" eating habits, or saying, "you look nice" the wrong way. Use the word "wife" in some classes and you may be attacked as sexist. And if the harassed "victim" objects to your behavior, watch out: attributing her response to "hypersensitivity" can be another form of harassment.

Socially engineered contamination can also seep into general course content as well. Consider a set of guidelines for academic writers published in the mid-1990s. Authors wishing to publish their work at America's university presses are informed that "sensitive writers seek to avoid terms and statements implying or assuming that heterosexuality is the norm for sexual attraction." Seekers after truth in our academic shrines are further advised that "sexist characterizations of animal traits and behaviors are inappropriate." We are warned against saying things like, "a stallion guards his brood of mares." Stallions, those fearless lowlifes, will persist in guarding their broods even in the teeth of the activists' objections, but this scientific truth is not acceptable in our university publications.

In fact, at the "progressive" American college, gender is mostly what we choose to make of it, morality is how we elect to see things and the future is any way we care to design it. As a result, when a young woman emerges from today's American educational system, she will almost certainly underestimate the importance of pregnancy in her future, as well as the impact that children will have on her life, or the odds she's facing of raising children on her own. She may someday even be confused by the power of her urgent maternal instincts when they finally awake from the anesthesia administered by our public institutions. The emotional and hormonal intensity of these urges may, in fact, induce real personal turmoil since they may get in the way of her becoming the airline pilot or TV anchorperson she just knew she wanted to be in high school.

While girls and young women may be set up for confusion, disappointment, and emotional turmoil by a curriculum bleached of sexual differences, many boys and young men seem to be losing all sense of unique function and self-worth. Their masculine energies discouraged at every turn, youthful males learn that women can do it all, that they are not needed for anything special. At best, our young men end up confused or maybe just enfeebled. At worst, they become dangerously alienated. The price we pay for this is male apathy and opportunism and, as ever, it will be women who pick up the pieces.

> Times were good for the clan. The great rains had ended; animal skins, meat, and roots were plentiful. There was time for a break, a moment for other things. The fine youth of ten summers had worked hard and learned his lessons well. He longed to take part in the upcoming contests.
>
> Using every spare moment from his many chores, he had strengthened his body and honed his skills. This time he knew the games would be different. This time he would not be confined to the sidelines, having to mimic the older youth and the big men. No, this time he would join in their contests.
>
> He yearned for the tournaments. Bold new energies surged within him, inspiring him for the challenges ahead.
>
> When at last the day of the competitions arrived, everyone in the clan gathered about the open grounds.

There would be many events to decide the quickest and strongest—who could throw the farthest, jump the highest, and find the target most often. The young contestant knew that the elders would be watching, judging the winners; noting the losers; marking those who led, those who followed, those who were most clever, bold, and fearless.

How the youth ached to excel, to have the clan admire him, his friends look up to him, the elders invoke his name in appreciation. He knew that a fine performance would gain him the attention of the clan's big men, the skilled hunters and warriors. His mother and aunts would be there to cheer, and, of course, the girls would be watching and giggling and calling out. He wanted them to see his athletic body, and he longed to show off the skills he had learned.

On the day of the contests the youngster did indeed excel! Often the quickest and the most agile, he threw his spear the farthest and sent many arrows to the target. For the final event, a relay race, the men were divided into teams with the fleet youth of ten summers running in the last position. Through forest and bush, across streams, over hills and fallen trees, the long run would call for speed, endurance, and cleverness.

By the time he took the branch from his teammate, the youth was fifty paces behind. Calculating the path to shorten the distance, bounding high over obstacles and sure of foot, he gained ground steadily. Though his legs ached and his strength ebbed, he pushed himself harder.

At last the trees give way to the open grounds and the last lap. As the runners come into sight, clan members burst into cheers. Just ten steps behind the leader, the young racer gleams with perspiration. Battling exhaustion, he somehow kicks the pace higher. Faces flash before him in a whirl of screaming images.

Leaping over the last boulders, pain wracks his body,

his lungs are on fire. Unable to endure, he is about to falter. Then he hears the voice of the big man, the one who helped him prepare. He catches a glimpse of the pretty young women. His spirits soar.

Numb to the pain now, pushing his every cell harder, he closes the gap to five paces!

With the finish line in sight, the roar of the crowd drowns out his panting exertions. Oblivious to the strain, floating in a timeless trance, willing himself forward with his last ounce of energy, he sets his head down and dashes as fast as his legs can carry him.

Neck and neck at the end, he bolts for the line, heaving his body ahead—gasping for breath, collapsing in agony.

Later, as the sun hides behind distant mountains, the clan gathers to honor the participants. Animal teeth are awarded. The youth has gained many, and he swells with pride. In two more summers, he knows he will face the final trials, the special test of entry to earn his place among the big men.

For now, a young hero, he glows in the acclaim of his people.

Good Sports

Sport was serious business for hunter-gatherers. They did not have a lot of spare time, and their work was physically challenging to begin with. When they could free up an afternoon, they needed to use it to assess and prepare the future hunters and warriors, the youth and men who would help feed and defend the clan. They needed to test their young males. Perhaps they understood, even then, that nothing is better designed to turn boys into responsible clan members than athletic competition. Sport is a place where many of the raw male instincts for action, aggression, competition, hierarchy, and bonding are channeled into healthy, constructive outlets.

The earliest athletic contests, archery and boxing, track and field, were drawn directly from the stalking, hunting, and battleground pre-occupations of early man. Even today in our sophisticated endeavors, many of the same qualities are needed to succeed: strength, accuracy, endurance, obedience to the rules, respect for legitimate authority, team-work, and consideration for your opponent. No wonder numerous studies confirm that youthful male participation in organized sports translates into less crime and violence. A disproportionately large percentage of imprisoned men did not participate in athletics during their youth.

Sport is the hunt, the chase; it is war by proxy. It's blowing off steam, defending the clan, making sacrifices for the home team, and learning to lose with dignity. Athletics are a critical right of passage for males, an opportunity to join a larger family, a precious chance to display attributes and skills before the clan. A noble pageant, athletic competition is con-ducted on a level playing field; a glorious place to mark, measure, and celebrate physical splendor and achievement. And there's another thing about sports and men—it's their chance to be a hero.

The Olympics dramatically represent the universal celebration of athletics. Just as the Greeks originally intended, its contests showcase the power, stamina, and grace of the human form. At the same time, it serves to channel fervent clan loyalties into entertaining, world-stage competitions. As a spectator at public sporting events, the ardent fan of any age gets to belong to something bigger while escaping the burdens of everyday life. Projecting into the athlete's world, the fan cheers his team's skirmishes, experiences hormonal ebbs and flows and gets caught up in the tumult of surrogate combat. Happily, he can do this without inflicting damage on himself and society.

Women follow and attend a lot of male sporting events, in some cases at rates close to men, and they experience some of the same physical and emotional surges. According to surveys, however, women's interest typically reflects classical female perspectives: while men go for competition and stats, women seek to know more about the athletes' lives, placing greater emphasis on the relational aspects of the games.

At its best, athletic competition can be a joyous celebration of hu-man achievement and a delicious foretaste of evolution's potential for breaking new ground. Athletic competition also draws our attention to racial preponderance in some sports as subtle human adaptations come into play, shadings that have evolved over hundreds of thousands of years in response to unique global domains. At the highest levels of professional or international competition, when performance is measured in millimeters or fractions of a second, otherwise inconsequential racial and ethnic differences and faint evolutionary traces may provide a critical edge in some sports.

Yet the human family is wondrously diverse, individual capacities are elastic, and brilliance can flower anywhere on level athletic playing fields. For all practical purposes, microscopic racial and geographic disparities are irrelevant in day-to-day life. But the same can't be said about the physical differences between the sexes. Here the playing field is not level. Tiny nuances within the same sex expand to a deep divide when we compare the athleticism of men and women, distinctions that have an enormous impact in many sports. Even more important is the significance of athletics in men's and women's daily lives.

Entitled to a Tie

Women, of course, share men's inclination toward physical activity and movement. There is no shortage of superb female athletes and performers, many of whom have widened stereotypical definitions of women's capabilities. In some events, including track and swimming, they have noticeably narrowed the gap between the sexes. Women also dominate several forms of physical and gymnastic competition.

We ought to be able to appreciate the particular physical talents and abilities of both men and women. But if we persist in seeing the sexes as essentially the same, with the exact same interests, we risk forgetting that sports have a special, compensating role for males. At its universal core, athletics are crucially important to most males, channeling masculine energies toward healthy and productive forms of competition. But instead of honoring this vital male domain, while at the same time accommodating those women who wish to pursue sports, we now find ourselves in the athletic wonderland of gender mathematics.

Title IX of the Educational Amendments Act of 1972 is what happens when the social engineers develop a plan to fix something that isn't broken. Conceived for the laudable purpose of balancing educational resources between the sexes, it reaches way past the equitable sharing of *overall* funds by dictating that athletic opportunity and resources be near-exactly matched between the sexes. Instead of fostering the expenditure of approximately equal dollars on male and female students according to their interests, an enforcement bureaucracy now mandates sexual parity in athletics—category by category, program by program. "Equal to" becomes "identical with."

While schools, colleges, and universities can show compliance if it looks like they are really trying, and the Bush administration eased the rules further, anyone—even a single student—can do a lot more than complain. They can sue. After all, it is a civil right. Court-wary institutions not already smitten by the fetish of political correctness have anticipated this litigation by adopting legally defensive policies. The result, earnestly encouraged by the Department of Education's Office of Civil Rights, is "proportionality." You know this as a quota system.

Since far fewer women than men are interested in many types of organized, competitive athletics, simply building up women's sports programs often fails to achieve the mandated balance between the sexes. As a result, facilities for boys and young men are often cut back, sometimes hard. Sued and now monitored by the National Organization for Women, California State University was forced to make huge cuts in male athletic programs, including several nationally ranked teams, so that proportionality could be achieved on its campuses.

In the mid-1990s, at Brown University in New England, a bevy of female students took to the courts—not the athletic courts, the legal ones. Though women represented just over 50 percent of undergraduates, less than 40 percent of the university's intercollegiate athletic slots were available to them. Student questionnaires showed that fewer female students were even interested in trying out for a team—30 percent versus half the men—and the university's take-all-comers intramural sports programs were attracting men at eight times the rate of women. In fact, surveys at female-only colleges regularly report that just 10 to 15 percent of their students play sports. Nevertheless, the Brown suit was victorious—not the gym suit, the law suit. The Supreme Court declined to review it, thereby enshrining the quota system.

Title IX's enforcement bureaucracy, blissfully ignorant of the sexes' differing interest in sports and ever ready to view any kind of gender distinction as another form of bias, warned schools in 1998 that even a 1 percent sex difference in the granting of athletic scholarships would be intolerable and went on to admonish institutions for encouraging too much media attention on their male

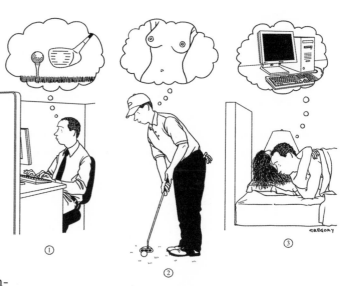

sports teams. Coaching salaries must be balanced; cheerleading can't favor the boys; transportation to and from games must be the same.

Between the mid-1980s and mid-1990s, when Title IX gender parity was aggressively enforced, NCAA Division I colleges jettisoned numerous men's sports programs. For example, in order to comply, UCLA dropped its men's swimming team, winner of sixteen Olympic gold medals, in the mid-1990s. In just the five years to 1998, more than two hundred male NCAA teams were cut, removing in excess of twenty thousand positions in order to create six thousand slots for women. Since not as many women are interested in playing sports, determined female athletes now face far less competition and have a much better chance of making an NCAA varsity team than a male.

It is true that most big men's collegiate sports programs—the ones so visible to the public on national television—remain untouched. In fact, the rich proceeds of the men's top football and basketball games now often finance female sports activities. College football, in particular, maintains its lucrative alumni and commercial roles, providing about 40 percent of the revenues for many big college athletic departments. It is the less popular everyday male programs that are dropped to achieve balance.

The compromise of male athletics has worked its way down to the nation's public schools. Entire states may be denied funding or face the wholesale reworking of their athletic programs because of sexual "imbalance." In addition to this federal push for gender-neutral sports programs, progressive public school administrators regularly attempt to downplay male interest in competition, even on informal pick-up teams, so as not to stigmatize children who are selected last. Is this the way to prepare our kids, especially boys, for real life?

Playing Games

We should strive to celebrate the full range of human performance. Gymnastics and figure skating, for example, favor the grace, suppleness, and endurance of female athletes, echoing the unique traits of ancestral gatherers. But competing in many male-dominated sports, such as the shot-put or boxing, which so heavily favor upper-body strength, means a female may be working against her body. In these circumstances, women's finest athletic achievements may serve only to advertise female limitations rather than their strengths.

Sports injuries are way up for women. Their knee bone and pelvic structures, for example, are different than those of men. They suffer serious knee ligament injuries and stress fractures at eight times the male rate, according to the National Institute of Health.

In some sports, physical disparities between the genders are so wide that top-ranked women might lose to an intermediate male pick-up team. Women on the professional tennis circuit play fewer matches, fewer sets, and get beaten regularly by their older, unranked male coaches. With the possible exception of basketball, female sports teams simply cannot build a commercial audience.

Opening its tenth season in 2006, the WNBA, the longest lasting league in the history of team sports for women, survives at the whim of a handful of sponsors, the NBA owners, and content-hungry cable networks. Its champion team would struggle against a good boy's high school squad. Attendance averages barely eight thousand per game, a figure spiked by big numbers in the progressive nerve centers of Washington, D.C. and New York. Ratings are barely holding their own despite aggressive niche marketing—more than half the teams actively seek out a lesbian audience—and no one has a clue when it will turn a profit. The payroll, for more than two hundred women, is less than half the salary of just one of the NBA's big stars.

Forcing exact parity on the sexes when the interest and capacity simply aren't there creates few winners and a lot of losers. Under the self-righteous cover of overcoming discrimination, federal programs like Title IX are actually inflicting it on males. Women are heavily over-represented in a wide range of college departments and extracurricular activities. English, social studies, communications, and many other university disciplines are predominantly female. Women are huge majorities in most artistic, dance, and drama departments as well as student government. The thought that we might set up a civil rights bureaucracy to ensure "proportionality" for men in these areas never occurs to us. We readily accept the notion that most men are not as attracted to these kinds of activities. But we punish them because they are more interested in sports. There, it has to be 50–50.

Confusion about the natural place of athletics in society is not the exclusive preserve of America's social activists. The shameless mavens of the modern Olympics movement recently declared that only those newly proposed sports that include identical events for women will be eligible for future consideration. No male rugby teams, no football, weight-lifting, or sumo wrestling unless there are female equivalents. Even established sports like boxing and classic wrestling may introduce female categories. The gender mathematicians can rest easy. The planet has been made safe for female pugilists. The world is a fairer place.

Responsible manhood is a state of mind, and young males must be introduced to it. Wise societies help them gain this confident maturity through controlled, constructive, and entertaining outlets. They know this has a big payoff, not only for individual men but for the entire community. In our techno-facilitated economies where brawn is fast disappearing behind brains, competitive sport remains one of the last preserves of masculinity, a universal male passion replete with setbacks and disappointments, spills and chills.

Athletics is training for life itself. Turning boys into men requires more than the passage of time or the onset of puberty. Males must act. They must cross over. Sports and athletic competition help them get there.

It would be dark again soon, the time that scared him most. Long forgotten was the glory of his athletic triumphs. All that he felt now was aching loneliness. And fear. The youth was frightened of the strange night sounds, terrified that a big animal would eat him. He longed to be back at the camp with its warm fire pits, the big men, the women, and shelter.

He had set out alone four sunrises past with nothing but his bow, a few arrows, and a crude knife. He had to provide for himself, survive on his own. Those were the rules. This was a test for all males before they saw their twelfth summer, and things had been this way for as long as anyone remembered.

He knew he must kill a deer before he could return. Along the way he would catch small animals to eat, find the place of water, and suck the juice of the plants. Twice the hyenas had followed after him, laughing their hideous laugh. But he screamed, stamped his feet, and scared them away.

As the sun settled behind the mountains, he crawled up onto the limb of a tall tree and fell into fitful sleep.

He was dreaming of the joyous celebration awaiting his return when he woke with a start.

The gold, piercing eyes of a big ferocious cat were measuring him from the ground below. His heart pounded; fear grabbed deep inside him. Breathless, he somehow found the composure to lift his bow. He knew that he would need an exact hit if it attacked.

They gazed at one another without a sound, sizing

each other up, two hungry creatures in survival's cold embrace. After what seemed an eternity the big cat looked away, then pawed the ground.

Then it slinked off silently into the night.

When the sun announced the new day, the youth refreshed himself by a small stream. It was then that he saw her, a young fawn, alone and thirsty, separated from its mother.

Instantly he began stalking it, engaging all the stealth and agility, the tricks he had learned from the big men and practiced in his games. Circling closer, then closer still, he raises his bow and aims for her heart.

Sensing danger, the doe looks up. Pulling the arrow back with all his strength, the boy steadies his eye—and fires!

The fawn stumbles when the arrow finds its mark, then begins to run in panic. The young hunter races after it, summoning all his reserves of speed, strength, endurance, and calculation.

Bounding across the land, through tall grasses into the woods, he keeps the animal in sight until at last it stumbles. Struggling to gain its feet, the fawn is stunned and disoriented. Breathless, too, the hunter cocks another arrow and fires.

Jolted again, the doe heaves her head up and down. In the throes of death, she falls back and succumbs.

As he approaches the home camp with the kill strung around his neck, the young hunter's chest is filled with pride, gladness, and hope. As he gets closer, the young women look up from their gathering. They laugh and wave playfully to him much as they always have, but something about their gaze tells him they are looking upon him in a different way.

He knows this will be a special day. The sacred ceremony will begin as the sun hides from the night. The big men and the elders will welcome him among them and teach him their secrets. He knows that after this night he will wear the special sign upon his chest, that he will join the men as they gather to speak of serious things. He knows that he must now fight to defend the clan. He knows that he could lie with a woman.

He knows that manhood is upon him.

The Initiated Male

Young males of every mammalian species must depart the cozy nest. Sometimes they do it on their own; other times they are forced out, often by an older male. They have to break new ground, embark on odysseys of tedium and fear, mystery and ceremony. Along this path to adulthood, human males have always been given signposts, way stations to reassure them, and rewards to point them forward. Men are contoured toward maturity and initiated into manhood by society. There they join the company of other responsible men.

Sigmund Freud, surely a brilliant and innovative thinker, seems to contemporary observers wildly wrong about some of his concepts, as pioneers so often are. For example, there is scant evidence of "penis envy" in nature. Curiosity, perhaps, but not envy. As Karen Horney, one of his prominent female successors, pointed out, it is more like the other way around: as in womb envy. Women's elaborate physiology; their internal, protected genitals; the rhythmic female cycles; the privilege of dispensing sexual favor; the sensual unfolding of pregnancy and birth— all of this sexual complexity and sophistication is in sharp contrast to the humdrum simplicity of the male sexual function: penetration, ejaculation, and hanging around, sort of. Men know this, if only at a primal, semi-conscious level.

For millions of years our ancestors venerated the towering female role in reproduction and were only vaguely aware of how males contributed to the enterprise. When our ancestors finally figured it out, they could not help but see what we know now: males are merely the starting pistol triggering the creation pageant's reproductive marathon. Anthropologists long ago suggested that male initiation rites are but a faint attempt to imitate female birthing capacities. In many primitive cultures these male ceremonies include mimicking pregnancy—right down to simulating labor.

Women may yield life but, through these formalities, adult males turn boys into men. Just as birth rituals in most indigenous cultures are attended exclusively by women, male initiation rites are rigorously masculine. Elaborate taboos give it an air of mystery and elevate its importance. Women are excluded, if only to prevent them from discovering just how limp the aping of their powers can be.

Females may giggle at the strutting heroics, but these rites of passage are anything but trivial to young males. The ordeal of initiation, begetting reward and respect from your peers, is a fervently coveted entry into manhood. This initiatory challenge focuses young male attention. It helps enforce discipline, establishes an authority structure, earns the youth eventual acceptance, and confers responsibility upon him. It is a big help in harnessing, socializing, and civilizing young men and channeling the undisciplined energies of fledgling masculinity into something productive for the entire community.

The initiated male values his place in society because he has earned it. He gains an acknowledged entrance into adulthood and is elegantly yoked into accountable manliness. Bowing to those who came before him, he expects the deference of those yet to arrive. Brought in from the cold, he joins his peers and gains a stake in preserving and advancing the community. The initiated male becomes an agent of peace, a saddled unit of production, beneficial to women and other men alike.

Male initiation emerged to compensate them for the innate reproductive power of females, as a way to balance the scales of sexual confidence. Admittedly the gender reinforcement of pregnancy comes late these days but its potential emerges early in the voluptuous promise of female adolescence. If girls also have the same initiation ceremonies, it is not special to boys. There is no uniquely masculine rite if girls and young women do the same thing. The passage carries no gender-specific value or compensating qualities. For women to mimic these male ceremonies is a piece of cake. The problem is that men will not be giving birth anytime soon.

Rights of Passage

When we lose touch with nature, we may see no wonder in reproduction. If giving birth is no big deal, there is no need to compensate for it. If women are just people who squat down and expel an infant once in awhile, then what are men missing? In other words, if there is nothing special about femininity, there's no need to make masculinity special either. This denial or denigration of female reproductive power makes the male ceremonies of compensation look unnecessary at best and sexist at worst. Unique male preserves then become archaic barriers to overcome, injustices to be eliminated, or ceremonies to be aped.

Until a few minutes ago on the evolutionary clock, females were pregnant by eleven and boys were turned into men by their teens. No doubt this math accounts for the bar mitzvah, a classic male initiation rite. The Hebrew sages well understood the power of a woman's reproductive sovereignty; to this day Jewish identity is traced along the maternal line since that is something we can keep track of. During the recent social activist era, superficial gender equations trumped nature and tradition became something to overturn. Initiation rites only for boys seemed unfair so the nonorthodox wings of Judaism introduced a similar rite for girls. Thus a storied rite of male passage morphs into something that happens when you are Jewish and turn thirteen.

By now almost all unique forms of male initiation have been neutered across Western culture. Even the more casual masculine sexual passages have become standard for both genders—as girls lose their virginity within a year of boys and, despite its emotional significance, do so with equal lack of ceremony. There is now next to nothing in school, the educational curriculum, or even sports that marks a gender distinction. Boy scouts and little league offer some male compensation, but female equivalents are available. Driver's licenses and gun rights arrive for both sexes on the same birthday. We all get starter credit cards in the mail, open our first bank account, move away from home, and head off to work.

Boys still get to shave or grow a beard, maybe go hunting with dad, or wear different clothes, kind of. This is thin gruel for a big male hunger. There are now hardly any special tests for young men, few unique challenges, distinct passages, or formal transitions. Just young people, with rights, coming of age. The result is that females have most of the same ceremonies yet continue to graduate eventually to sexual wholeness through pregnancy and maternity; young males are left with few unique places to cross over.

Another tried-and-true halfway house on the way to male maturity used to be college, but fewer men are going now and it is hardly a place where maleness is celebrated. Distinctly masculine initiation rites on campus are an endangered species, and fraternities, with their crude rushes, hazing, and rituals, have proven easy targets. They are largely subdued or are fast disappearing.

In 1999, Dartmouth College decided to turn its fraternities and sororities into coed residential facilities to foster, in the words of its president, "respectful relations between women and men." University administrators may not understand that respect is more likely to emerge from a distance, but their presumed beneficiaries know better. Calling it "the dumbest idea I ever heard," one female student told a reporter: "No woman in her right mind is going to move into a fraternity house." A male student put it another way. "Guys are slobs. Girls are meticulous. It'll be a nightmare." Six months before this grand experiment was set to begin, Dartmouth officials acknowledged they had no idea how to make it work. This would not, however, deter the trustees who were prepared to spend "tens of millions of dollars" to overthrow 158 years of tradition and make the changes. Almost everything is coed at college these days, quite possibly the dorm, maybe even the bathroom; apparently some university authorities think separate toilets for females is the same as separate water fountains for blacks.

If society fails to encourage healthy pathways to masculinity; if there are no unique initiatory outlets for male youth, no preparation, signposts, or special acknowledgments, legions of young men will be deposited into adulthood confused and unsteady. They will persist in behaving like uninitiated adolescents. Too many will wilt into their thirties and forties, amiable but weak, subdued by the shallow math of gender sameness and the persistent attacks on a patriarchy they never knew. They will struggle with the confusing urges and signals thrown up by potent hormones, fumble along bewildered, barely attentive to the demands of masculinity. Or they will rebel, reaching out in exaggerated behavior and macho crudity. Either way they will have failed the hero's journey.

Perhaps it is because we have abandoned formal attempts to differentiate the sexes that young men concoct their own initiation rites. Male athletic hazing remains rampant, and binge drinking goes on in heroic proportions among college-age males. Drugs are everywhere, an embedded part of their transformative rituals. Bereft of positive signals from the culture, youthful male-oriented music is often violent, acutely macho, homophobic, and frequently barbaric in its attitudes toward females. Groping desperately for any sort of male affirmation, it is enough to send a young man off to join the Army.

The men of the clan gather quickly when the young look-outs arrive with the news: a long line of fierce enemy warriors is moving toward their encampment. The elders form in the center around the headman, with the big men behind them. After some brief animated chatter, the leader's instructions are relayed outward.

The men and older boys prepare to defend the compound, while the women and children are sent off to a secret shelter. Traps are set; ambushes made ready; perches mounted. The young warrior, just two years past his initiation, works feverishly through the night. Not an ounce of energy is wasted.

A few moments before dawn. The compound looks undisturbed. Animals bleat and the last of the night fires waft lazy curls of smoke into the air. Approaching with stealth, deceived by the quiet, the enemy circles the huts, before setting fire to their arrows.

Then a thunderous scream rises up! The invaders are set upon from all sides!

The sky is filled with arrows, and the ground shudders as the battle is joined by charging warriors. The young men are pushed out in front of the big men to fight hand-to-hand.

Blades flash, blood gushes. Fighters from both sides are struck down. Some cry out maniacally. Others are hacked to death.

The young warrior is terrified, but his courage rises with the knowledge that he stands with his people. He jousts bravely. Deaf to the shouts and screams and the mayhem around him, he battles fiercely to defend the clan's territory.

In the fury of all the mayhem, he fails to see a blade flashing at his side. It cuts deeply into his upper leg. Felled by the crash of the blade against bone, he collapses, blood pouring from his wound.

Most of the attackers are soon surrounded, bewildered, and critically weakened. In disarray and retreat, they drop their weapons and fall to their knees in surrender. Resistance meets with immediate death.

Later, as steam rises above the carnage, the captured invaders are herded together. Their leaders are butchered on the spot. The young and strong among them are lucky; they will be enslaved, but they will survive. Their lands will be claimed along with their women and children. The invaders' infants that are too young to work are put to death.

With the women and children returning, there would be time to mourn, to heal the wounds, assess the losses, and honor the brave. Rollicking in fermented juices and the swoon of victory, the warriors appraise the value of the enemy's enchained young men and the female concubines they have rounded up. The clan has survived.

For now.

Warrior Classes

What soldiers do is aggressive, ugly, and brutish. Then there's the hard part. Sometimes they get killed. Or maybe captured, which can make getting killed start to look attractive. Without apparently ever doing any deep thinking on the subject, nearly every known society has entrusted this sordid task to their men. The reason this happens everywhere on the planet is that everything about war, from start to finish, moves to assertive male rhythms. While the counsel of women may be useful, even critical, in determining whether or not to fight in the first place, once the talking stops and the shooting starts it's men who do the killing.

Territoriality, displays of physical strength, competitive tension, the chase, sudden violent eruptions—these are patterns that float on a sea of testosterone. Energized from primal kill-or-be-killed survival instincts and directed by biological dictates to guard their mate and protect their progeny, the inclination to hold ground is seared into every fiber of masculinity. Territory may be all a male's got, and it brings him most everything he cares about. The effort to take and defend territory also invokes, among many other things, male pecking orders, bonding, trust, and teamwork. Men have been shaped by countless eons of natural and human hostility. They are designed by and for combat. Which is why they love action in everything from movies to video games to modern wrestling mayhem.

Women are no less interested in the survival of the clan. Through every generation and in every society, females have supported their tribe's battles—whether sewing uniforms or sewing up broken warriors. It was on the heels of a massive industrial contribution from women during World War II that President Harry Truman ushered them through a wider doorway into the military by signing the Armed Services Integration Act in 1948.

By the 1970s, women accounted for 5 percent of the two million Americans in the armed services. This was an unruffled accommodation consisting largely of women taking on a variety of non-combative roles. A few military-minded female officers may have longed to get closer to the action, but the waiting line for women interested in hand-to-hand combat was short.

By the end of the sixties, the environment in and around the armed forces began to change. Young women were pursuing higher education in record numbers and were moving into most employment sectors both before and after marriage. Meanwhile, the social engineers, poking their calculators into every nook and cranny of America's private and public sectors, were honing in like scud missiles on all the traditional male bailiwicks.

While its effort to achieve racial integration has been less than perfect, the American military takes justifiable pride in the relatively seamless blending in of minorities, who now make up more than a quarter of the armed services. Sheathed in the camouflage of the civil rights movement, however, activists pressed for opening the full range of defense and military positions to women. If sex is no different than race or ethnicity, then unequal access in the military means civil rights are compromised. The military had also switched to all-volunteer status in 1973 and was anxious about maintaining staffing levels. Marching in step with the progressive times the barracks were flung open. From grunt to general, from boot camp to battlefield tent, America would have a coed military.

Today, women make up about 15 percent of military personnel, a little more in the Air Force where about a quarter of new recruits are female and just 6 percent in the Marines. By the latter half of the seventies, men and women had also begun to take basic training together in coed boot camps, except in the Marine Corps, which resisted the civil rights argument and pleas for "fairness."

By 1982 the Army had petitioned for a temporary cease fire in its five-year, mixed-sex boot camp trial. Apparently things were not working as planned. Equal standards for the sexes in training and performance meant that women were failing and getting injured a lot, as well as being sexually harassed. Something more than cloddish prejudice seemed to be at work. Gender, the military had discovered, is not the same as race and ethnicity.

Warrior Women

In addition to being five inches shorter than men, on average, mature women have just over half the upper body strength and about two-thirds of male physical endurance levels. Today's combat soldier may carry as much as 80–110 pounds of equipment on his or her back. Under physical strains like this, many more women suffer upper body ailments, knee problems, and stress fractures. Overall, military women are injured twice as often as males and are out of commission about five times as long with each injury. Nearly a third of female colonels in the army suffer chronic orthopedic problems, more than four times the rate of their male counterparts. Eating disorders among military women run three times the civilian rate.

You would think someone would try to put a stop to this coed military madness. In 1997, a bipartisan presidential commission headed by a respected former senator, Nancy Kassebaum Baker, found coed training resulted in "less discipline, less unit cohesion, and more distraction." The commission unanimously recommended shutting down gender-integrated basic training and offered some modest proposals for separating the sexes. Nothing as dramatic as actually dismembering unisex units, mind you, merely a recommendation to separate the sexes during those first few raw weeks of boot camp.

Before the ink dried, howls from the strident feminist chorus reverberated through the nation's capital. "A slap in the face to women," snapped one congresswoman in a swift reaction. "It sends the wrong message about the direction we need to take in the military," fumed Senator Olympia Snowe. "Boot camp segregation was a giant leap backward," intoned the congressional women's caucus. And, from a vice president of the National Organization for Women, a sharp retort containing a dire warning for the nation: "Creating a two-tiered training system will focus on the symptom rather than the problem—a military culture (you need to sit down for this one) that values women less than men."

Apparently the commander-in-chief could not fathom such a thing either. Describing himself as "very reluctant" to accept a recommendation that might diminish women's opportunities in the armed services by separating the sexes during basic training, President Bill Clinton declined the panel's recommendation. Damning the torpedoes, the defense secretary instead authorized a step-up in military funds for separate . . . latrines.

Nature, however, is unimpressed with political expediency and even the heated response of ardent activists. Declining to draw any distinctions between the sexes on paper does not change the facts on the ground. To accommodate the inconvenient fact that females do not perform at the physical level of men, military tasks are redefined in a kind of corporeal dumbing down of the species.

Two women can't carry an injured man on a stretcher? Simple. Re-define it as a job for four "sailors." Half the women in the army can't throw a grenade far enough to get out of its way? Piece of cake. Get lighter, weaker grenades, thereby endangering everybody. Things getting a bit rough in boot camp? Give inductees little blue cards to hold up if their egos are bruised and they need time to get in touch with their inner selves. One army manual cautions: "Stress created by physical or verbal abuse is not productive and is prohibited." No stress in the military. No sir. Er, no ma'am. Not fair.

When this silliness fails to bridge the unbridgeable physical gender gap, we finally abandon the word games, scrap the "equal" and "fair" stuff so dear to the gender mathematicians, and simply apply lower standards for women. An old Marxist idea called "comparable effort" is invoked in order to transform one of the last places on Earth where male physical strength counts for something into a safe place for women: we simply lower the bar for them. They get to run slower, do fewer push-ups, and stop climbing those funky training walls at the yellow line.

In the long trek to responsible masculinity, today's young male is propelled through a neutered, coed education; he gets browbeaten with a grade school curriculum discouraging even a whisper of sexual distinction; he is denied unique outlets in athletics and other rites of passage; and, in the increasingly unlikely event he goes to college, he is forced to endure the great leveler of the politically correct academy. When at last he goes belly-to-belly with women at boot camp, the fantasy of gender equality comes face-to-face with raw truth. That's when he learns that "equality" means women get higher scores for doing less.

Then again, he should have known about the military double standard. Every eighteen-year-old male has to register for the draft under threat of a $250,000 fine, up to five years imprisonment, and student loan denial. If it is reauthorized, twenty-year-old men who lose the lottery will have to report for duty in six months. No ifs, ands, or buts, soldier.

Rank Desires

Aside from the obvious impact that reduced and variable standards have on military preparedness and morale, the quick-step to a unisex military has triggered an engagement of another kind: good old-fashioned sex to, uh, help meld the troops together. Whether or not it's a great idea to shoehorn libido-ravaged nineteen-year-olds into coed barracks during periods of intense emotional strain and adrenaline rushes depends on how you feel about the morale-building potential for sexual intimacy in the ranks.

There is also the complication of romantic jealousy among tight-knit troops to consider, the possibility of sexual abuse by superiors, and the implications of pregnancy in the unit, to name just a few concerns. The Army has admitted to a "high frequency" of sexual relations between recruits at just about all of its training bases. Add to this combustible mix the military's rigorous, unwavering rules of deference to higher rank and all sorts of sexual hi-jinks and misdemeanors can pop up among the warrior classes.

By May 2000, a report in *The Wall Street Journal* noted that "Ten years into its vision of a 'gender-neutral' gender-blind force, the U.S. military is more preoccupied with sex than ever." One civilian review panel found that drill instructors were so caught up with sensitivity training and preventing sexual harassment that some will not permit men and women recruits in the same unit to talk to each other without a witness present. Just the ticket for building a strong, united, and coordinated military.

The military's own studies confirm rampant sexual harassment "crossing gender, rank, and racial lines." Although it can be loosely defined, between half and three-quarters of military women report some form of sexual harassment during their careers; more than 20 percent do every year, with many assaults unreported. Affairs between officers and enlisted soldiers are, in fact, widespread in Iraq as they were during Desert Storm, America's first coed war. In Afghanistan and Iraq, many female soldiers have been attacked or raped—by their own side.

Not surprisingly, armed service surveys report extensive problems in overall morale. Over and above the distressing reports of sexual profligacy and harassment, one study noted that two-thirds of junior male noncommissioned officers and more than half of their *female* counterparts did not believe that the women they knew in the services would carry their share of the burden in tough military situations.

"This idea of female marines? It's a bunch of bull, man. They cause trouble, and they can't do the work. It's why we call recruits 'girls'. You ever see a woman try to change a tire on one of those big trucks? Or hike thirty miles with all that gear? With my black buddy it's different. He can carry that one hundred-pound backpack, and when I wake up next to him in the field, I don't want to sleep with the dude." These are the observations of a young marine to a *New York Times* reporter.

When there is even a single female soldier in the unit, field deployment means special arrangements, added work for others, and extra costs. In addition to their distinct battlefield needs, women are more injury prone and often have to be evacuated. At any given time, 10 to 15 percent of females in the armed services are pregnant, including a fifth of the women on ship duty. Maternity leave is disruptive and expensive. The American military administers the largest daycare service in the world.

Military experts are about as unanimous as you can get that the presence of females in war zones goes against every male instinct of chivalry. Men will die; in fact, men have already died, trying to protect women who now qualify for roughly 70 percent of combat roles. Maybe you believe in the tooth fairy and assume that mortal enemies will respect our female POWs in their heroic resolve to achieve "equality" and will, therefore, decline to harass a woman prisoner.

On the other hand, you might be inclined to credit the testimony of former POWs, who informed a presidential commission that women prisoners could count on being sexually abused and tortured in excruciating ways. As an extra added attraction, this molestation could be employed to break male prisoners who would likely be forced to watch it despite the military's current efforts to steel them against it. Then again, the whole nation might get to look in on the evening news as a pregnant American soldier is mutilated and dragged through the streets of some godforsaken hellhole.

Old Women's Wars

Women soldiers are now fully engaged in the kind of support functions that get close to the front. In Iraq, where women have participated more extensively than in any previous American war, they made up approximately eleven thousand of the 140,000 U.S. troops at full deployment. Females have served as everything from drivers to aviators, medics to military police, occasionally commanding male-heavy units and drawing disbelieving glances from Iraqi locals when heavily armed on patrol. In a war without clear front lines, women soldiers are inevitably exposed to lethal encounters. By 2006, forty had been killed in combat together with more than two thousand men.

During the invasion of Iraq, a navigational error drew the 507th Maintenance Company into an ambush. Among those captured was nineteen-year-old Pfc. Jessica Lynch. Despite the military's concerted attempts to paint her as a hero who went down in a blaze of glory, Pfc. Lynch was injured as she crashed her vehicle; her weapon jammed before she could fire it. Fortunately, she was treated well by Iraqi medical personnel and, notwithstanding the night-light dramatization of her rescue, the hospital was already in friendly hands. Much less attention was focused on the eleven soldiers who died in the conflagration, including Pfc. Lori Ann Piestewa. Most captured female soldiers are likely to meet a less hospitable fate than Private Lynch. Only two were taken by the enemy in Desert Storm; both were tortured and sexually molested.

The Abu Ghraib prisoner scandal brought us yet another unpleasant reminder of the military's overzealous attempt to integrate women. Being blind to gender distinctions means employing female guards in men's prisons. As a result, the world was treated to lurid images of a smirking, female soldier pointing her gun-shaped hand at the genitals of naked male Muslim prisoners—when she wasn't holding one on a dog's leash. Impregnated by a senior officer in her division, she informed a military hearing that they did it "just for fun." Apparently there were all sorts of sexual shenanigans going on since a captain at the prison had been relieved of his command for photographing his women subordinates while they were showering.

The abuse of Iraqi prisoners was bad enough, but the insensitive and inflammatory involvement of a female in these images will no doubt encourage the recruitment of violent, anti-American terrorists for decades to come. Reports regularly circulate of attempts by radical elements and terrorists to capture female American soldiers for torture and abuse as payback for Abu Ghraib and to further alienate the American public.

Despite the obvious difficulties, feminist military strategists cannot comprehend why our nation's warrior function requires a masculine tone. They are out to build a fuzzy, feel good army, a gentler and kinder military. Unable to get around female physical limits, not content with softer training standards, in the end we are encouraged to emasculate the military and reduce preparedness to the lowest common denominator in order to maintain the fiction of a genderless society. Sexual equality is achieved by compromising military superiority and sending young women into the trenches to die with men. With friends like these, women don't need enemies.

Before coed military madness set in, a woman who wanted to help out the nation's defense effort did not have to go to boot camp or join a unisex field unit in order to work in procurement, heal wounded soldiers, and even earn promotion to high-level staff positions. But rather than admit to the slightest sexual specialization between men and women, we are forced to diddle with words and numbers, and press deeply unnatural arrangements on boisterous young warriors. When, predictably, they misbehave, we must not question the faulty intent or design of the policy. Instead, we "sensitize" our fighters, subject them to harassment awareness training and lecture them on the nuances of sexual misconduct.

Men, for insensible reasons embedded deeply in warrior archives and hormonal compulsion, are still ready to fight and die for women and their families. But the advocates for women won't let them do it. Women, it seems, will only achieve equality when they are dying in combat like men.

And while we're making it easier for the handful of women who seek to get close to the action with men, what about the women back home? Does the insistence on cramming nubile, young women into the next cot in adrenaline pumping warfare conditions help the many wives and lovers of the six out of seven military personnel who are male? When you send your man off to war halfway around the world, it must warm your heart to know he will be in close personal quarters over several lonely months with some bouncy young females. Do women's "advocates" speak for *these* women?

This effort to build an "ungendered vision for our army" is not how you prepare warriors. This is how you administer an enormous social experiment. When you give way to the dogmatic feminists' feverish compulsion for sexual symmetry, the end result is that young women get sent off to fight old women's wars. Nearly everyone involved is damaged, and the entire country compromised.

Even before the September 11 attacks on America, the Bush administration had begun scaling back some of this madness. Ground combat units in Afghanistan and Iraq did not involve women, and the military's feminist-heavy advisory committees were being marginalized. Talk of shoehorning women into submarines has come to a halt. For those interested in a strong and disciplined American military, it's not a moment too soon.

They had been on the move for days searching for food. The elders knew the lay of the land, the ways of the animals, the grounds of their enemies. They also knew the skills of each hunter, those who could run fast and long and throw spears with a fine eye. But game had been scarce along the way. The roots, nuts, and berries the women had prepared for them had long been devoured. Gnawing hunger claimed all their thoughts.

The big man who kept an eye on the young hunter of fourteen summers had given him leaves to chew, dulling his hunger, lifting his spirits, and easing the pain from his near fatal battlefield wound—the flash of blade to the bone of his leg.

Some of the men had become fearful on the hunt; many were weak. The younger ones, new to the hunt, grew restless with hunger. One had gone berserk and was killed by the big men. An elder had been injured and fell too far behind; he was abandoned, with poison from the arrows and a lion's tooth for luck. The men had to find food—and soon.

The next day they came upon the hoof prints. The big men knew where these animals would seek water. This shored up their hopes, but they grew weaker by the hour. The starving young hunter's mouth watered and his stomach ached.

Moving with all the speed and stealth their wracked frames could summon, making sure the wind would not betray them, they at last spot the herd!

Their hunger is soon forgotten. Concentrating intensely, they crouch low and form a half-circle. Inching forward carefully, they watch the leader. Closer and closer they come.

Then closer still.

At last the headman gives the signal! The young hunter rises from the tall grass with his mates and throws his long spear.

The herd panics and stampedes. Arrows shoot out. The hunters chase after the wounded animals. Singling out the young, the weak, and the most vulnerable creatures among the fallen and trampled beasts, the hunters slash at them furiously, laying waste every animal they can reach.

When the slaughter is finally over, the killing grounds are littered with carcasses and stained in blood. A huge fire is built, and a mammoth beast is hoisted above the flames. The men laugh and clap each other in joyous celebration. Ravenous, they tear off strips of meat and eat until they can eat no more. With hungry wolves howling jealously in the distance, they fall into a stupor.

The next day the hunters set off with their bounty. Big cats lurked beside their column trying to pick off their hard-won spoils. The young hunter, his stomach full, thought about his first long hunt. He saw that the elders and the big men stayed in the center, near the front of the group; the weaker and younger men were exposed at the edges of the pack. He saw how the ones who grew frightened or selfish were shunned. He knew, despite his limp, that he had been strong and brave, that the big men had noticed. He would receive more meat and hides, more food than he alone could eat.

On the long trek home he dreamed about giving some away to others in the camp, to younger boys who would admire him. And to a girl—the captured one that he thought about sometimes—so that she might lie with him and take his seed. By the time he saw the wisps of smoke from the home fires curling lazily into the sky, he was swooning with pride and joy.

Job Prospects

Bringing home the bacon is what men used to do. Resource providers, they were supposed to put something on the table. "In every known human society, everywhere in the world the young male learns that when he grows up, one of the things which he must do in order to be a full member of society is to provide food for some female and her young," Margaret Mead once observed. The rounding up of resources is the most important aspect of a man's daily life. It's in his genes. No job, no money; no money, no honey.

Over our long evolutionary haul, males have adapted to the hunt and honed their provider skills in order to earn mates, support offspring, and gain an unchallenged place in the clan. This "learned nurturing" of the male is the foundation of every prospering society. It focuses vibrant male energies giving men purpose and meaning, helping women launch the next generation. Just as important, this male nurturing responsibility stabilizes the entire community and helps mold men out of boys.

Elaborate male hierarchies, like modern organizational charts, are a feature of every human and primate society. They reduce tension, help assure a man's place, and determine his share of the enterprise's proceeds. It is his bit of vertical territory. Will he be expendable, exposed to risk or downsizing at the perimeter of the organization? Or will he be on the inside, among the leaders, protected from assault, helping to direct the hunt? Does he feast at the heart of the captured prize or wait, uncomplaining, for scraps?

To succeed in the chase and defend against predators and rivals, single-minded concentration and cooperative bonding were critical attributes for the hunter. Trust and harmony in the field were pivotal. Diversion could be costly and distraction deadly. This agitation between the needs and ambitions of individual men and the cooperation with others so vital to achieving group goals is the root of men's vocational bargain. In return for a share of the spoils, the solitary hunter inside the modern male settles into hard work. He obeys the rules, acknowledges authority, and gets his piece of the pie.

Maneuvering gently, or not so gently, within modern companies or organizations, men build alliances, fend off competitors, and trade IOUs. Like his ancient forefather, modern man is both a lone hunter calculating his personal advancement and a team player trying to enlarge the overall pie. He needs his fellow hunters as protectors against competition, as allies in landing the big deal, and for support when resources turn thin. Gaining entry into the upper ranks through initiatory challenges, he is expected to maintain standards of performance and conduct under the close watch of his peers and superiors. The modern hunter secures his position today by the very traits that were so valuable during ancestral pursuits: speed, agility, strength, endurance, mental cunning, and intelligence. Having earned a perch, he defends it and strategizes for advancement.

In contemporary societies, the ability to provide derives from money, power, and status. Work is the modern hunt. It is the means of survival, the way to garner resources, and the avenue through which men successfully propagate and achieve community recognition. Work is where a man finds his purpose, his identity, his place. So pivotal is career to their survival and sense of self-worth that men are capable of monumental sacrifices in order to succeed at it. Even if it means eighty-hour weeks, constant travel, compromised health, and the deterioration of some treasured relationships.

The Digital Hunt

Not always up to the physical demands of the hunt, females could also be a distraction on the savanna. A potential source of dissension among the males, women slowed things down and increased the danger. Clinging infants were a hindrance. And even after most of the world's people abandoned the hunter-gatherer model and settled into agricultural and pastoral encampments, muscle still counted.

With the advance of technology into our digitized modern workplace, the ancient hunting domain has been radically and irreversibly altered. Just a tiny fraction of people in developed societies farm the land. Brawn is out, brains are in. High rise and high tech, we've gone from javelins to laptops, from smoke signals to cell phones, from crude barter to high finance. The hunt has become industrialized, civilized and computerized. But it's still the hunt.

The contemporary world of commerce remains competitive and aggressive. Initiates are still tested. Risk is still rewarded or punished. The industrial chase still draws to fierce, competitive climaxes, and corporate hierarchies continue to provide a clan structure through which big men and industrial elders do battle. What's new is that the digital domain is a place where a delicate hand on the keyboard and refined communication skills may be best at getting the job done. More than four-out-of-five American jobs are in some way service-oriented.

As muscle yields to mental, work tasks and career success become mostly unrelated to sex. Together with the growing preponderance of women in higher education, this means our service and knowledge-based industrial future will employ ever increasing numbers of women. Meanwhile, America's manufacturing industries have gone lean, mean, and nearly extinct through merging, down-sizing, outsourcing, computerizing, and exporting labor-intensive work to other countries. Despite a mostly favorable economy during the 1980s and especially the 1990s, blue collar, rust-belt, and lower-level management jobs have disappeared. These are the male-heavy places.

U.S. government reports paint these national trends in the kind of harsh colors that translate into millions of displaced men. The impact was especially ferocious in the 1980s, when American business trimmed something like three million middle-management positions and a similar number of blue collar slots. Among men who do not have a college degree—nearly 75 percent of working males—disposable income has actually trailed off since the end of the 1970s. A third of young employed men take home less pay than is required to sustain a family of four above the poverty line.

Career Interests

With women moving into the workforce, a change in the economic and social landscape was clearly necessary. If women, for whatever reason, are propelled into employment, they have every right to expect equitable treatment and appropriate opportunities. As it happens, except perhaps for the exceptionally ambitious woman, new economic realities and legal pressures for equal job access tend to work themselves out in the real world.

Traditional careers of interest, such as teaching, healthcare, and other services, continue to appeal to large numbers of women. Many also gravitate to jobs featuring public interaction, flexible scheduling, and part-time employment. Favoring steadier, less aggressive slots, women, including female MBAs, often avoid engineering, computer, or other technical careers, or positions with acutely competitive "on-the-firing-line" elements. Even in Scandinavian countries, which have aggressively attempted to redirect traditional gender attitudes and enforce strict codes of equality, youthful male and female career choices remain starkly different. Young men overwhelmingly favor technical jobs, and large majorities of women apply for service and healthcare employment.

Consider how these differences play out in an everyday business such as administering a commercial real estate portfolio where the two principal tasks are securing leases and managing the properties. New tenant possibilities are often pursued aggressively by landlords and their agents in a one-shot, sign-them-or-lose-them kind of initiative. Prospects are wined and dined, crudely or artfully wooed. All kinds of promises are made. Competitive suitors lurk on every corner anxious to attract the new tenant's favor. Proposals rifle across monitors and fax machines.

Things get a bit frantic as the decision nears. The pace quickens. Everyone holds their breath. The deal closes!

It's over. Things sort of go limp. But never say die. Tomorrow's another day. Another hot candidate is spotted, and the game begins again.

After a tenant is successfully signed, the baton is passed into the hands of the property manager. A relationship begins, potentially a long one. The tenant is eased into occupancy, transitional move-in needs soothingly accommodated. The buildings are the property managers' "babies," and they keep them running smoothly, cultivating networks of subcontractors who work around the property. The tenant relationship is nurtured in order to minimize problems and encourage an extended commitment through future renewals.

No prize for figuring out that the leasing agents will be mostly men and the property managers mostly women. No grand authority dictates this division of labor; the sexes come to them by nature. For the men, chasing tenants every day is hunting, war and conquest. For the women, managing property every day is peace and tenderness. The men battle external competitors, try to out-do each other, build mutually beneficial alliances, seek out mentors, and take on apprentices. Working on commission, they may earn next to nothing and get fired—or make out like bandits if they're good. The women managing the buildings work on the inside; they are inclusive, nurturing, and protective. They put a high premium on being liked and are content to take home a lower, but steadier, paycheck, one based on long-term results instead of racking up big numbers.

The medical profession is another good example of how things can work out between the sexes if we just create a little space for natural inclinations. More than half of entering medical students are now women. It may be no surprise to discover that they gravitate heavily to family practice, pediatrics, gynecology, and dermatology. That's not all. Men and women function differently as doctors even if they were taught at the same medical school and have the same specialty. Videotaped studies find women physicians more nurturing; they talk to their patients more than male doctors do and they make their patients talk more, too. Visits with female doctors also last longer, no matter the patient's sex.

"Male doctors tend to be puzzle solvers, whereas women tend to be healers," one male physician told *The New York Times*. Men will gravitate to challenging specialties; women will take over general medicine. Patients also mimic their ancestors. Women overwhelmingly report that they want a relationship with their doctor. Men mostly treat visits like a car repair job—they just want the problem fixed.

Woman's Work

Whether or not we allow a free-flowing marketplace to sort out gender specialties, the modern hunting domain—the contemporary workplace— is no longer exclusively or even predominantly a male preserve. The notion of a job and the provision of resources as the offsetting male contribution to the matrimonial pair bond has been lost. A generation or two ago, just yesterday in evo-speak, a man without a family was considered odd. It may have even restricted his promotions at the office.

Today, work and career are things that all men and women are expected to undertake. Although many women shy away from the danger professions, the physical sciences and engineering careers, most male domains have been breached and the salary scales nearly balanced. A man's career may still have a little more importance attached to it, but not much, and not necessarily.

Yet cries of inequity continue apace. The European Union's high court, which sets legal precedents for its member countries, recently upheld hiring and promotional preferences for women, finding that "where a promotion is involved, men tend to be chosen in preference to women *since they benefit from deep-rooted prejudices and from stereotypes* [italics added]." Priority in favor of women with equal qualifications, the court argued, would be a legitimate method to "restore the balance" and correct earlier discrimination. So much for the amused European attitude that Americans have taken feminism far too seriously as Europe's most eminent jurists don't see anything unique about males or females either. For these venerable minds, only prejudice, discrimination, and stereotyping can explain why men are the predominate force in industry.

There are places where men are holding out, of course. Notably in the action-oriented, risk-prone line positions often found at the core of competitive industries. Men also continue to prevail at the top. Whether they get to these heights by hook or by crook, or just plain hard work and brainpower, men will not easily relinquish the powerful high ground. Not to other men, not to women. Not where it counts, not if they can help it. But beneath the top rungs and high-tension wires, men now dominate only in extreme high-tech playgrounds where gigabyte and gadgetry keep an adolescent boy culture alive, as well as those few places where acute hunter instincts and muscle still count.

Ninety percent of workers in the nation's ten most dangerous professions are men. Each year nearly 2.5 million American workers are seriously injured or afflicted with a job-related disease. Sixty thousand of them are permanently disabled, and while things are improving, more than five thousand die at work according to the Centers for Disease Control and Prevention. The great majority are male. At 55 percent of the workforce, men account for 93 percent of job mortalities, a yearly average approaching annual battlefield deaths during the Vietnam War.

Until women were pushed past the workplace periphery and pulled into the industrial mainstream by social and economic necessity, those relatively few men who actually did wield control over other people wielded it over men. No longer. As career comes to be as big a deal for women, they have as much at stake as men in the decisions of their superiors. The more you need your job or desperately want that promotion, the greater is the power of the person who controls it.

Labors of Love

As we head off to our jobs, we are usually encouraged to leave our personal lives at home. In reality, we bring just about all of ourselves to the workplace. An undertaking that consumes a quarter to a third of our waking hours will inevitably bear witness to most of our desires, especially the more pressing ones. Like sex and relationship, for instance.

Nearly a third of our romances develop at or around work. Estimates are that between five and ten million romantic liaisons grow out of on-the-job contacts in America every year. Much of the time they turn out fine. More than a third are believed to develop into longer-term relationships while the rest end with a bang, or a whimper, or something in between. Usually it is nothing worse than some sore feelings, a little awkwardness around the water cooler, and a tattered ego or two in need of re-inflating.

As in the world at large, men at work are generally dragging testosterone around with their tool kits or laptops, which sets them out initiating most of these work-based relationships. Notwithstanding our sophisticated modern workforce, this means that men usually still ask and women usually respond. Most of the time most women can handle a man trying to get his point across. Prodded into action by hormonal urgency and masculine insecurities, however, some men don't know how to take "no" for an answer. Sexual tension and confusion in a coed workplace are as certain as death and taxes.

The unisex office serves only to further confound the confused male, who is born a bit bewildered and reared around neutered schoolrooms and playing fields. Young men often arrive at their first job with boundless energies and urgent hormonal drives. Everywhere they look there are women. Women who work with them, women who are their competitors, women who may be their superiors or, in time, their subordinates. To expect that every man will relax and make nice in otherwise charged-up and aggressive business environments is to ignore the forces that have shaped us over millions of years.

In a culture unable to detect or unwilling to admit to distinct inclinations between men and women, sexual dynamics in the workplace open up another enormous playpen for social and legal agitation. In lawyer-infested America, where the genders are but citizens with perfectly balanced rights, the sexual axis between men and women on the job can get reduced to a battleground of activists toting calculators and ever-tightening definitions of a hostile environment.

Under current interpretations, harassment can be reduced to just about anything that creates feelings of displeasure or embarrassment. Which means that today's crude remark in the elevator can become tomorrow's lawsuit. A low whistle may mean a visit to a re-education camp. Discussions about last night's TV sitcom can result in a suspension or get you fired. An army of lawyers, consultants, compliance specialists, investigators, and therapists are thus summoned to redesign a pivotal male arena so that it is made safe for supposedly delicate female sensibilities.

The U.S. Supreme Court has found that a company can be liable for an employee sexually harassing another, even if the employer was not notified of the problem and the "victim" was regularly promoted. Organizations can escape this fate only if they have forceful preventive policies, sensitivity training, and appropriate reporting procedures. The mere possibility of litigation throws corporate America into a defensive crouch. For good reason.

Dozens of people were thrown out of work in Pittsburgh because a loutish bartender gave one waitress a tough time; the resulting lawsuit, over a single sentence, closed the profitable restaurant where, incidentally, waitresses testified to regularly pulling their jerseys off their shoulders in successful attempts to goose their tips. A legal secretary in San Francisco cleared punitive damages about one hundred times the lifetime earnings of a dozen hard-grinding strippers, because her adolescent boss pulled back her arms to see which breast was bigger.

Sex Appeal

Although high profile harassment charges and big money awards make occasional headlines, in the end relatively few cases actually amount to much. In fact, complaints to government agencies rarely reach a formal stage and many are dropped for lack of evidence. Still, the sexual harassment machinery now in place means continuing tension in the workplace. It sets men and women against each other, and hands the levers of false charges to people with mercenary or retaliatory agendas. In corporate and public America, it is now the man whose reputation can be destroyed in a minute, sometimes by a completely uncorroborated accusation. According to a *Washington Post* poll, nearly 80 percent of working women acknowledge the likelihood of false charges of abuse by workplace females.

There are ugly things that some men do to women at work, not to mention a lot of other places. There is no excuse for physical or psychological badgering of women, or men, for that matter. This kind of behavior is also offensive to responsible men who have to witness it, pay for it, or experience it second hand. It's also true that many working women take full advantage of their sexual appeal. More than one in ten women has consensual sex with a supervisor during their working years; almost two-thirds report that the affair advanced their career.

Men's sexual agitation is just one of the dispositions they bring to the workplace. Their penchant for status hierarchies and peer group bonding also enter through the office door or the factory gate. Despite women's recent march onto corporate organization charts they do not infiltrate the informal all-male hierarchy that maneuvers around them. They are "whited out," free-fire zones—a no man's land. Women have their own workplace hierarchies, of course. Reflecting their evolutionary heritage, it is almost always more inclusive and less rigid. The female pecking order also may be based on criteria other than formal rank or career success.

More importantly, should a woman tire of all the competition, the politics and pressure, and discover what many men have long known— that most jobs are hard, regimented, and not all that fulfilling—they can ultimately retreat to the domain of parenthood, and if their husbands can provide it, fruitful domesticity. Women can and generally do define themselves in much broader terms, garnering a significant sense of self-worth from a wide array of personal relationships and activities. Career may be vital for those few women charging to the top of big organizations or working at jobs they love, but for most women there is usually a lot more going on in their life away from the office.

While women can withdraw from work and career to concentrate on family and other things, men have almost nowhere else to go. The hunt is their specialty. It is what they do best, their natural counterbalance to what women do best. It is more than a job for a man; it's an identity, a position, a purpose. That's why losing it can be so devastating.

Men, it appears, have hardly any unique, indispensable functions left. Enabled by modern technology, women have entered all their domains, eminent or otherwise, but biology forecloses men from experiencing the female ones. Degendered in school, aped at sport, denied unique rites, competing in a sex-neutered workplace, there are few arenas left where a man can define himself.

When the young hunter comes upon her, she is moving effortlessly, gathering branches, roots, and berries. She has seen twelve summers, and her young breasts are filling to womanhood. His blood rises as he spies her. She is healthy, young and strong, athletic and finely featured. He is attracted by her easy and confident movements, aroused by her pleasing frame, the ample size of her mid-section—the place where she might carry his baby.

They had often exchanged shy, curious glances. She thought this young warrior, injured in the attack by her people, was handsome and strong.

Now, sensing his eyes upon her, she moves effortlessly, showing her agile limbs and figure as she reaches high for berries, delicately balancing her load. She is a vision of youthful vigor and allure.

He shows himself. Tentative conversation gives way to bashful banter. He holds out his hand, and after a moment, she grasps it. Soon they are running together, laughing, joyous, grasping playfully at each other.

This is her ground, and she knows every inch of it. In time she leads him to a bed of soft ferns where the sweet scent of flowers engulfs the air and fresh water is cradled in large leaves nearby. But the young male hardly notices.

In a flash he's beside her. She does not flinch or move away. He hands her a brilliant stone he found on the hunt. She turns the sparkling pebble in her hands, as he begins to fondle her. She remembers the stories the women tell about the men. She is frightened . . . but excited.

He embraces her more forcefully. Slowly she opens her body and lets him explore her. He is neither tender nor rough. She senses him feeling her as if he were testing an animal, to see the ways of its body, to calculate its strength and capacities. She loves his firm hands, begins to nip at him, teasing him on. Their touches become more intense.

Lost in pleasure and exertion, still they muffle their cries against the dangers of the night. As a wet sheen of exertion shines on their skin, she senses the end is near, as he turns her in front of him.

Thrusting deep within her, his control shatters, his seed explodes! Then, he falls away, exhausted.

His breath is heavy as he slumbers beside her.

Laying quietly at his side, her eyes are wide open. Listening to his contented breathing, to the familiar sounds around them, she feels safe, dreamy but alert. She will remember this night: the feel of the grass, his scent, the ways he touched her, how the night was lit up with stars so brilliant.

She wonders if her belly will swell up like the older females. She wonders if a child will come. She wonders if he will bring her away from the long hut of the concubines to stay at his side.

Sex and the Joker

We may not be able to make out the modern hunter behind his PC or his cell phone. We may not detect the dominance struggles and status competitions that hide in sophisticated organization charts. We may even find it tough to spot the warrior in a high-tech, demasculinzed army. But it is impossible not to see the primitive origins of the modern man on the hunt for sex.

Throughout the mammalian, primate, and hominid eons, during the millions of years of human evolution, the deeply entrenched genetic program for a male has been to plant his seed wide, plant it often, and plant it quickly. Until recently life on earth was a brutal, competitive struggle, a place where feeble infants were slaughtered, weak children fell by the wayside, and relatively few offspring lived to maturity. Quantity, not quality, won the genetic future. Place a lot of bets so that a few survive—and hurry, because you may not be around tomorrow. Natural selection made shoot-from-between-the-hips a sexual winner for males. Besides, it wasn't *you* getting pregnant.

The resulting sensitivity among men toward shallower sexual arousal and a bent for immediate gratification is a universal phenomenon. In every culture males demonstrate more compulsion, more aggression, and less discrimination when it has anything to do with sex. Nature did not favor the sensitive male. If he dallied, a man's potency might falter, or maybe he got killed. Numerous fleeting, nimble-footed forays were the way to genetic immortality—or at least to a good time.

Ever on the lookout for young healthy females, ancestral males developed a sexual approach designed for breadth, not depth. Rapid visuals were in; long interviews were out. The "quickie" was born before the savanna. These dynamics help explain the persistent male interest in pornography. Crude, in-your-face, anonymous female nudity sends male blood rushing. Pornography may be failed imagination, or just brute instinct given shape. Either way, it appeals directly to the testosterone-addled hunter who is alive and often pumped in today's man.

Skin-deep male arousal is the force that propels a million girlie magazines, a thousand strip joints, and pervasive sexual imagery throughout most cultures. It is why more than $20 billion is spent annually on "adult" videos, and more than $10 billion on escort services. It is why prostitution and the sex trade claim staggering amounts of our gross national product. Adult Video News, the industry "bible," reports eleven thousand new porn titles in 2000, versus four hundred out of Hollywood. Who rents them? About 70 percent are lone males and 20 percent are men with women. Gay men together rent 7 percent. One percent is rented by women with women, and just 2 percent by women alone.

According to Nielsen NetRatings, about a quarter of the Web-connected population checks out porn sites at home, one in six do at the office. The superficial sexual trigger, honed in the forest and out on the savanna, is why men still duck out of chat rooms and keep going back to the superbabes and vixens. Commenting on the dot-com shakeout, Hustler's marketing director told *The Los Angeles Times*: "The sex industry really isn't affected by the markets. Sex always sells." The male modem is always online.

While we are on the subject of babes and vixens, picture a half dozen strapping teenage boys forming a circle to masturbate. Assume it's all over in five frantic minutes (there may be time to spare) and their ejaculate is collected in a shot glass. These few grams will hold enough semen to impregnate every fertile female on the planet. What then, you might ask, are the other three billion males here for? It is an equation to shake any man's confidence, even before we consider his design flaws.

Males are the all-terrain vehicles of sexual insecurity. It is a standard deficiency built into masculinity's frame, engine, and dashboard. Men are not grounded by a womb and its responsibilities; they are not tied to lunar cycles. Scratching itches a lot of the time, they are more like motorized erections looking for a dark, damp receptacle. An erect penis has no I.Q. Logic may be its enemy.

Also lying in wait in most males is a sexual eccentric. The homeless male drifter and the Nobel laureate are equally at risk to succumb to overcharged or misplaced testosterone bolts. Archbishop to rock star, through sexual deviance they risk the loss of exalted position. They may even risk their lives. Unable to control themselves, deviant males of high station endure wide public shame. We are unlikely to read of female movie stars buying sex at three in the morning in a sleazy red light district. No British baroness will be asphyxiated in a masturbatory frenzy by hanging herself in male leggings and an athletic supporter. Men, it seems, are the sexual jokers. The problem is that they make up half the deck.

They do, however, come by it honestly. Males of many species have a lot in common, including an amazing range of sexual dysfunction. Everywhere in the animal kingdom, hyper sexuality is male sexuality, strange sex is male sex. Male animals are widely known to go in for aggressive sexual cajoling and whining, not to mention incest, kidnapping, and sadomasochism. Bondage is not uncommon in the animal kingdom. But whether it is an insect, a bird, or a primate, you can be sure a male will be orchestrating the proceedings.

All these strange animal crackers may come as news to people who think the fuzzy little critters out in nature spend their days nibbling roughage, building nests, and cooing. Given the amazing range of human creativity and invention, these male eccentricities are easily translated into whips, enema bags, obscene phone calls, inter-species sex, and getting it on with a corpse. In some species, the females do get to even the score—mostly with cannibalism. They just eat the bastard, especially after he's made his sexual deposit. That's when he starts to look better as protein than he did as a lover.

While females also have been known to wander into exotica and even enjoy themselves immensely, especially if they trust what's going on, almost every form of sexual aberration—animal and human—is a male proclivity. Men account for 95 percent of all psychiatric sexual disorders. Extreme forms of masochism, for example, are twenty times more likely to show up in males. In mild forms, many of these inclinations may be harmless and might even enhance an intimate relationship between consenting adults.

In fact, just about anything that works its way toward intercourse can be sexy. Most of us are aroused by scents and body odors. Lots of people like to nip their partner playfully without resorting to knife-and-fork cannibalism. Many lovers enjoy some physical tussle and feigned resistance in the course of lovemaking. In all this, mutual consent is a must. Still, someone has to get it started.

BEEP

"Coming to you live on the cell phone, from the bank. The sperm bank, that is.

"I swore if this relationship didn't work out, I'd freeze my sperm. Did you know it starts to fall off by the millions when you're, like, twenty? Who thought that one up?

"Anyway, with my razor-sharp mind, I knew something was wrong when she showed up for 'the talk' wearing a burqa. Y'know the cloak that's like a black cloud and there's a mesh thing where her face is supposed to be? Just kidding.

"Actually, she showed up in four-inch heels 'cause she knew it would mess me up.

"Let's pick this up in a few minutes—I'm just about to walk through the door and check out the inspirational technician babes in their hot med scrubs."

Perhaps the average male maturing in today's degendered world does not sense the power of the reproductive matriarchy during much of his boyhood. Quite possibly he is not aware enough to fathom the complex, internal, and highly elaborated body that a woman lives in. Maybe he isn't in touch with the earthy sexual confidence that has been massaged into place by a female's rhythmic, gender-reinforcing cycles or the feminine confirmations of pregnancy.

But if today's testosterone-propelled youth is not thinking about the grand female preserves of womb, marriage, and family, the adolescent dude is most definitely thinking often, long, and hard about sex. Raw, repetitive sexual interest is where boys and young men encounter the introductory notes of the reproductive symphony. That's when they come belly-to-belly with a woman's sexual sovereignty—each and every day of their post-adolescent lives.

From an early age males come to understand that sex is a female grant. If nowhere else, sexuality is the place where "fair" and all the neat symmetrical constructs of gender math come down to zero. Males petition for sex. They ask, wheedle, cajole, negotiate, seduce, or apply pressure. But at least in most parts of the world, it is her call. The woman chooses. This uneven sexual equation, anchored deep in basic biology and reinforced by ancient reproductive strategies, is there for all to see.

Women pay the price for sex, and it's made them choosy. Men are copulatory pile drivers in comparison, often devoid of nuance or cyclical shading. Responsive and flexible, women can adapt to almost any male sexual tempo; males, on the other hand, often have a tough time managing their sex drive. Men can be compulsive; female desire rises from context and occasion. If her committed mate wants a lot of hot sex she can go there. If he's content with an occasional quickie, she can get comfortable with that, too.

When it comes to sexual intensity, a woman is, in the best sense, a blank check for the right man. How much does he dare write in? But whatever the tally, when the hero's ejaculatory sprint is over, it is the female's nurturing marathon that kicks in. For women, sex is hugely more than a five-minute thunderclap. This sensual female wisdom and sexual discipline helps make civilization possible. If not for women's reproductive serenity, societies run the risk of male chaos.

Less urgently compelled, mindful of extended horizons and the responsibilities of the womb, women seek trust, stability, prospects, and relationship. If there is no future, or at least the prospect of it, there's no point. Women are sexual cohesion, the benchmark of intimate constancy, the steady drumbeat of an enduring future. Closer to nature, the regenerative female is imperial.

Other aspects of the lives of men and women may be finely balanced in the utopian fantasyland of social engineering but not sex, not reproduction. Hard as the activists try to relinquish feminine sexual power, women still dispense men's pleasures and incubate their genetic future. Seduction is not a symmetrical exercise. Sexual confidence reposes in matriarchy. We can see it there with our own eyes.

As the twenty-first century dawned, the cloning of a human embryo became a plausible experiment. Cloning can be achieved by simply implanting the nucleus of any human cell into a female egg whose cells have had their nucleus removed. The newly inserted nucleus can come from a man or woman, but only a female can incubate the embryo. Sperm is not needed, only a womb.

The real reason we need so many men around is to help support so many women and their children. And the greater the number of males, the greater the possibilities for genetic variation, especially the "brilliant" mutations that push us forward. A planet of clones would be a stagnant world without growth, only slow deterioration.

The pair bond and marriage direct men away from sexual chaos toward committed intimacy and nurturance. Sperm doll and worker machine, the becalmed man needs to know that he has a distinct role to play. Otherwise, he is pleasure without principle, energy without direction, locomotion without purpose.

He is the disposable male.

BEEP

"Okay, here we are in 'Self-Love Room #6.'

" It's . . . it's kind of like 'hospital room modern.'

"There's something positively bizarre about this. You get fifteen minutes. What? They use a timer? I bet the staff runs an office pool. Like, how long you think this dude's going to take?

"I mean, is it better to be fast or slow? What if I can't, y'know—like how you can't pee sometimes when there's a line-up behind you at the john?

"Boy, this is pressure. You want pressure? This is pressure.

"Great sign here by the sink: 'Wash your penis thoroughly before beginning to masturbate.' They're very big on romance here. Atmosphere. This place makes up for its shortage of actual babes with a complete lack of warmth.

"You should have seen the college kids in the lobby—they're sperm donors? Five of them, each one a different shade, not one under 6'6." They come in here twice a week to 'spank the monkey' at fifty bucks a pop. Is this a great country, or what?

" 'And just how did you pay your way through college, young man?'

"Pay phone. Nice touch. An ad for a 900 sex line. Very clever. 'Call now—we can do this together.' Too much. Talk about targeting your market. Y'know, point-of-purchase?

"Okay, let's kick back here, put our feet up on the La-Z-Boy.

"There are some very, uh, thumbed-over skin mags here . . . they're, like, for teenage boys with acne.

"How do they expect me to, y'know . . . a full grown adult male . . . supposed to get it up for . . . (silence) . . .

"Now . . . she's sort of awright.

"Boy, position is everything in life, isn't it?

"Later, pal . . .

"This one's for eternity."

A Look Ahead

9

BREEDING ANIMOSITY

It's a Jungle Out There

IMAGINE FOR A MOMENT PLAYING A GAME WHERE THE GOAL IS TO SABO-tage the two-parent family, imperil the pair bond, and, for good measure, discourage responsible fatherhood. It's obviously a farfetched thought experiment, but let's give it a shot.

The first thing you'd want to do is set humans apart from nature. You might do this by insisting that we come into the world as blank slates ready to be programmed. Account for all the enchanting differences between boys and girls by explaining that it's because boys are given trucks and girls are given fluffy dolls. As a general rule, champion every imaginable legal right, even for kids; encourage individualism over family, and indulgence over personal responsibility.

When it comes to sex, remove the role of reproduction from the center of intimate life. Teach young women that their maternal instinct is merely a cultural overlay, invented as a form of bondage, and exhort men to believe that they can be just as nurturing if only they would try. Be patient, speak clearly, and be prepared to repeat yourself. With any luck, women will come to view sex and intimacy as the same kind of disconnected physical activities that males so often do, giving men easy access to sex without the bothersome inconvenience of making a commitment. While you're at it, characterize nonreproductive forms of sexuality as optional lifestyles on a par with reproductive sex. If anyone complains, call them a bigot.

You will want to mix the sexes indiscriminately at the earliest possible age, making sure to discourage compensating outlets for budding masculinity. Eliminate any hint of extra male facilities for anything, even sports. Trash male rites and encourage girls to ape any boy ceremonies that manage to survive. While you're at it, take every opportunity to associate all males with a diabolic patriarchy and don't forget to run down their historical achievements. You can never start too early on this.

Dropping the kid gloves, attack marriage directly. Make it okay to have kids out of wedlock. Celebrate the single parent and tell young women that marriage is the way men control them. Be sure that divorce is available at any time, for any reason, by anybody. You can weaken the fragile paternal connection even further by encouraging wives not to take their husbands' names. In fact, you can go for the jugular on this fatherhood business by ensuring that a husband has no say if his wife wants to abort their fetus but be sure to stick him with the bill if she decides to keep their child. As an added sweetener, just about always grant child custody to the wife when divorce rolls around. Limit the father's visitation rights but hound the rascal for support!

Closing in for the kill, neuter men altogether by making sure they do not have the slightest advantage when it comes to resource provision. Eliminate any trace of job function by sex and always demand exact gender balance. If you can't completely shake up or destroy a male institution, label it "misogynist," or scream "sexist!" This way you get to set up some funky gender quotas in all the male domains regardless of whether or not females are even interested or qualified.

You will know you've done a bang-up job when the everyday man starts to fade away, tuning out, or turning inward. You've hit a home run when males descend into apathy, licking their wounds on the sidelines. Watch with well-earned satisfaction as gender hostilities sharpen and lawyers split ever finer hairs. Notice, too, how a blunt, macho backlash—angry music and crude male "entertainment"—surge onto the social landscape.

When, at last, the legions of undereducated, underskilled, unmotivated men abandon the matrimonial bargain of civility for a life of perpetual adolescence, or worse—relax. Game's over.

Bad Boys

One way or another, the everyday man has begun to disappear, and the everyday woman is getting bombarded from all sides. The society we inhabit becomes a cruder place with each passing day, and the bargain between the sexes has been reduced to a zero-sum game that we are all losing.

Hardly anyone would disagree that women needed and deserved greater opportunities and fairer treatment. Economic realities, extended life expectancy, and deferred marriage—among other powerful forces—pushed young women into the workforce, and they were entitled to advocates. Carrying a worthy enterprise to damaging extremes, the activists succeeded in pushing the sexual pendulum from sublime to ridiculous. On the way from success to excess, motherhood and family were denigrated, men were assaulted, and our child-centered culture abandoned. The result is a social and cultural landscape littered with hostile debris, and we will be picking up the pieces for generations to come.

One consequence is that masculinity has been turned into pathology. When a New England teacher printed up some T-shirts for her sons with the simple, hopeful inscription, "Boys Are Good," every one of her ten female student-teachers registered an objection. So did casual observers when her son wore it around the yard. Even more disconcerting, many adolescent boys were uncomfortable with the slogan because they had bought into the propaganda that being male means there is something wrong with you. By 2004, hot-selling T-shirts exclaimed, "Boys Are Stupid—Throw Rocks At Them."

This hostility and indifference means that boys, and the men they turn into, have become mightily confused. Contrary to some cynical observers who hail this as a good thing, in fact, it is a bad thing. The result of all the gender turmoil has not been a heartfelt, sensitive re-examination of their role by men. Most of them won't go there. The result of the offensive against masculinity has been more like a regression into apathy, hostility, or macho overcompensation.

If we fail to give boys positive signposts as they grow up, if we discourage distinct passages to mature masculinity, they will more often lose their way. If we fail to provide healthy models of mature strength, adolescent males will sink into confusion. They will tune out or take off. And if we persist in demonizing grown men, sooner or later there will be hell to pay. Healthy societies neither pull away the support structures of masculinity nor attack men for their weaknesses—they compensate them for their deficiencies.

Surveys from the late '60s found women describing men as basically kind, gentle, and thoughtful. Three decades later, they were telling the same pollsters that men were immature, self-involved, sex-obsessed, and inattentive around the house. Men probably have not changed all that much over the past few decades (do they ever?), and the reality surely falls somewhere in between. But aggressive demonizing of males does change attitudes, and there is a price to pay. Putting men down robs the sexual covenant of trust, setting a suspicious and pessimistic backdrop to the challenges of intimate partnership. Besides, behind the bravado, men are in enough trouble already.

Sick and Tired

In our era, maleness may have become a new sort of social pathology, but masculinity has always been a real killer. In addition to their more precarious position in utero, male infants and young boys die off at levels nearly 30 percent greater than girls, a higher rate of masculine mortality that holds true across every subsequent age grouping. Much of this is men's own doing. Risk takers, men eat more meat and fat, get less sleep and exercise. They drink, smoke, and carouse more than women, or at least they used to. They make up three-quarters of our alcoholics and get arrested for drug violations about twenty times more often.

Recent studies report that men are much more likely to engage in more than thirty types of high-risk behavior. Compared to women, men see their doctor less than half the time, if they have one. One in four doesn't. They die in accidents nearly three times as often. Except for

Alzheimer's, men succumb in greater numbers to all of the nation's fifteen leading causes of death. Whatever the reasons, everywhere in the world, and in most every species, males live shorter lives. As much as 10 percent shorter in America.

Adding insult to injury is the public perception that men get more of the national healthcare dollar. In most of the ways people count these things, they get less—a lot less. This is partly because women are more health conscious. Acclimatized to regular doctor visits by the need for annual pap smears, women are better connected to the nation's healthcare system. They are almost always their household's "Secretary of Health and Human Services," and, often as not, men are dragged kicking and screaming into the doctor's office by the women in their life.

Studies and extensive surveys regularly report that doctors take women's complaints as seriously as they do men's and order diagnostic work-ups that are just as complete. Where differences are reported, medical complaints by women usually get more attention when measured by the number of additional tests, prescriptions, follow-up appointments, and referrals. There's been a governmental Office on Women's Health since the early 1990s; the male equivalent is still locked up in congressional committees. As one specialist informed *U.S. News & World Report* in March 2002, "You've got a segment of the population identifiable by a certain trait—maleness—dying prematurely, and no one is paying attention."

Contrary to popular belief, medical research also favors women. We know this because the gender-bias folks demanded that the National Institutes of Health, the nation's principle sponsor of medical research, undertake a gender-oriented survey of its funding in the late 1980s. Assured as ever of their victimization, the petitioners assumed research money that was not spent on women was spent on men.

It turned out that most of the institute's research is devoted to issues of concern to everyone. When it isolated its sex-specific funding, exclusively female ailments received more than twice the money allocated to uniquely male diseases, an imbalance that actually increased in the 1990s according to N.I.H. reports. Almost the same number of men die annually from prostate cancer as women from breast cancer, but breast cancer gets five times as much research money and more than three times the number of clinical trials. Despite the fact that lung cancer claims the most victims of both sexes, the National Cancer Institute has long devoted more funding to breast cancer than any other form of tumor research.

Critics also claimed male bias in heart research funding, but they confined their comparisons to studies of middle-aged patients; coronary problems before sixty-five affect men three times more often than women. By the time heart disease impacts most women, the average man is resting in his grave. At age sixty-five, there are just seventy-seven American men for every one hundred women. Looked at in the full medical context, we spend about twice as much on women's health as we do on men's.

A painful footnote to the neglect of male medical and mental health is the abject misery of our Vietnam veterans. In addition to the fifty-six thousand men who perished during the war, along with eight women, a similar number were blinded and tens of thousands paralyzed. Post-traumatic stress disorder claims nearly a third of men directly exposed to combat. A presidential review of those serving in Vietnam discovered that in the first ten years after the war no fewer than four hundred thousand male veterans were in prison or otherwise within the criminal justice system. Suicide is estimated to have claimed another one hundred thousand Vietnam vets, and legions more are institutionalized or homeless.

Peacocks or Pigeons

There is no coordinated male conspiracy. Men don't do things for their gender. They are a lot more interested in their wives, their family, and friends (and maybe the redhead at the office) than they are in a guy across the street, let alone some male they don't know living halfway around the world. The few men who really do wield significant authority out there in the big tent aren't looking out for men and are so far removed from the daily grind of masculinity that they pay no personal price for yielding to activist demands. It isn't *them* getting stiffed.

Most ordinary men are reluctant to confront the everyday assaults on their dignity. Big boys don't cry, and they don't fight with women.

The rare article or book decrying the average man's reduced condition is immediately attacked or cynically dismissed, usually with a snide reference to the visible privileges enjoyed by alpha males, privileges the average Joe will never obtain. In fact, since the early 1970s, the position of the working stiff in America has eroded persistently, at times dramatically.

Since 1980, the average worker's pay has barely inched up over inflation while, among the top 10 percent of employed men, it has risen by more than 60 percent. Blue collar jobs and lower-level management positions have nearly disappeared. Accounting for nearly 30 percent of America's gross domestic product in 1960, manufacturing and its male-heavy jobs had almost halved by 2000. Since the late 1980s, real increases in buying power have been achieved only in upper management.

The male economic pecking order, which used to be solid and gradual like an Egyptian pyramid, is now stretched out like the Eiffel Tower. There is a cluster of alpha and beta males at the top with a long, lean swoop to a huge base of bottom feeders. The man in the middle is withering away. The "average Joe" is below average. Men are now peacocks— or they're pigeons.

In our contemporary "sweepstakes culture," a few star athletes pocket mega-millions, their rookie teammates pull down a hundred grand, the guys in the minors starve, and the ordinary fan gets mugged. Business moguls take home a few hundred million; their chauffeurs can't make the rent. While the average hold on the CEO slot has shrunk, depending on the study, from between seven and ten years in the 1980s to barely four years today, the big guys get golden parachutes and everyone else gets a pink slip. In the 1980s, the typical boss earned about forty times the wage of his average employee. By the end of the century this gap had stretched out to 419 times in America—ten times wider between the top and the bottom in just two decades—many times the ratio in most other parts of the industrialized world.

According to the Congressional Budget Office, between 1979 and 1997, average pretax income for the top 20 percent of Americans rose from $109,500 to $167,500; the bottom 20 percent saw its income fall from $11,800 to $11,400. Looked at another way, in roughly the same period the nation's median family income rose by 18 percent, while the incomes of the top 1 percent increased by 200 percent. 2004 represented the fourth straight year of increases in the nation's poverty rate: more than one in eight Americans live below the official poverty line. In 1977, the wealthiest 1 percent of Americans had as many after-tax dollars to spend as the forty-nine million people at the bottom. By the end of the century, the richest 1 percent, with nearly 40 percent of the country's riches, had as much to spend as the bottom one hundred million.

The wealthiest American now boasts a net worth roughly equal to the entire bottom half of the nation's families. The gap between rich and poor in the U.S. is now the widest of any industrialized country. The fat cats are few and bloated; the tomcats are everywhere—and hungry.

The Myth of Male Power

The diminishment of the everyday man is a phenomenon not limited to commerce or the sporting world. In our educational academies, classic male brilliance is no longer enough as dead white males need to be superstars or they are turfed from textbooks so female students will have "appropriate" role models. When Shakespeare gets sacked in favor of diversity, just how safe are Milton and Yeats? Most big-time male college sports programs have survived the activists' blitz, but the delicate balancing to kick-start female athletics under Title IX has meant the wholesale abandoning of a lot of good, ordinary male teams.

Accommodating the entry of women just about everywhere often means a male is displaced or does not get the slot to begin with. The men at the top have not vacated the heights, and the men on the bottom have always been below the radar screen. It is the man in the middle who's getting it in the chops. The growing majority of women in universities and the upper reaches of professional education means this trend will not only continue but intensify.

Most men don't get to the top, nor do they sink to the bottom. They don't excel at sports, even if they love to play. They don't paint dazzling works of art, discover breakthrough cures, or lead great corporations into battle. If they did, they probably wouldn't need athletics or the other forms of male compensation. Most men are simply struggling to survive, to support their families or secure a big enough piece of the pie to afford one.

Except in the uppermost echelons of society, what most men do not have is real power. For the most part, they are caught in the lower and middle rungs of corporate and institutional hierarchies, locked in the universal male pecking order. The heady heights of real, big-league power are gained by few men. And until women plunged into these worlds, it was power they brandished mostly over other men.

Presumably the men at the top of these modern heaps are having a good time. If they're not, it's nobody's fault but their own. Although they work hard under near constant pressure and face steady competition from somewhere—or everywhere—they do gain the opportunities, the rewards, and the challenges of leadership. But for most other males, real power is a myth, an instrument used to hold them in place. Many men find power where they can, of course, in the quiet byways of society. They achieve recognition in the athletic triumphs of youth, by landing the big sale that wows them at the office, and through mentoring a budding apprentice. Or, perhaps, they find what they can of male authority in a comfortable, balanced sexual confidence.

There is big-time male power to be sure. The myth is that all men have it. For the many who do not, the traditional, reaffirming avenues to responsible, assured masculinity have steadily been closing. Women's financial independence has devalued the everyday man's offsetting influence and pride as a resource provider, while women's control over their own fertility has reduced men to bystanders at the gates of immortality.

Educated to believe he's the problem, the average American male has been deprived of traditional social reinforcements and has watched his paycheck all but shrink. He has been ignored, if not demonized, by the media. Assaulted from youth by incessant propaganda that he's a brute, frustrated by unfair and arbitrary treatment, the everyday man has begun to leave the scene.

When men lose their role and their ability to share the right to progeny, they often lose their sense of self worth, their claim on dignity. They stop caring. One way or another, they lose interest and check out. Retreating to the edge of the pack, they nurse their uncertainties and hone their resentments. Waiting to pounce on stray opportunity, they get caught up in lifeless diversions or seek shallow outlets for their wounded ego. Abandoned in countless ways, women are then forced to carry a greater load. Meanwhile, frustrated masculinity paces impatiently, prowling on the culture's sidelines.

Job Satisfaction?

"Most women are too smart to run for a crummy job like that—too little pay, tons of stress, and there's always someone mad at you." These are the observations of a thirteen-year-old responding to a teen magazine question about whether there will be a woman president in our lifetime. This splash of virginal insight offers a sense of proportion about what seems to be important to so many women: securing a safe hearth and adequate resources, avoiding tension and stress and being liked by the people they care about. If that's how crummy the president's job looks, consider how unappetizing are the other careers men crave.

Of course, if there is one job worth applying for, the presidency of the most powerful nation on earth is probably it. It may or may not be filled by a woman in our lifetime. As it happens, less than a quarter of women tell pollsters that a female on the presidential ticket is important to them. Nevertheless, except at the very pinnacle of some industrial and political organizations, women will be deep in the ranks of every job and vocation that does not demand serious muscle or high risk. Their way paved by fingertip technology and a service-based economy, today's blue collar, business, and professional woman is discovering that, for the most part, she can do just about any job that men can do. More to the point is whether she really wants to.

For every woman enjoying a glamorous and exciting career, there are dozens if not hundreds mired deep in workdays of drudgery. Watching as their family life erodes, or fails to materialize in the first place, many women are caught up in tiresome jobs or demanding positions. Little by little, career women are forced to toughen up and internalize the male pace and attitudes that often surround them. Carrying the hunter's spear means thinking like a hunter. Winning like a man means playing like one too, from binge drinking in college to aggressive corporate competitiveness.

Some women may succeed at all this and get to swim upstream with the big male guppies. Many more will flounder, just get by, or plain fail. They will endure frustration, pain, and self-doubt because they were not as good as the next guy. And, whatever the grand possibilities for today's liberated woman, one way or another, the contemporary conceit for having it all must mean having children, a partner and a family. Otherwise, it can't mean having it all.

All in the Family

A comprehensive survey at Rutgers University on the state of marriage at the millennium painted a forbidding picture of wedlock. Although an underlying desire for matrimony lurks in the background, especially among college-aged women, today's young singles often emerge from divorced homes into a long, pre-marriage "breakup culture" of dateless hooking up, of "no rings, no strings." It is a use-and-discard world of sexual barter with lots of partner dumping.

When women get past the "quarter life crisis" so many of today's youth experience, and reach the latter half of their twenties, they begin to acutely feel the pull of long-term, committed intimacy. The incubator of survival introduces itself; the womb calls out. Meanwhile, the men close to their age simply are not there. Nowhere near thinking about marriage, boys still want to have fun.

Today men well into their thirties, or later, often pay only lip service to the idea of a long-term commitment. Browbeaten from preadolescence to shun traditional "stereotypes," many young men regard women as more or less the same as they are, and, to their way of thinking, females want the same kind of encounters they do. They think, or choose to think, that women don't want special treatment. Therefore, none is offered. Demanding the right to work means women are now expected to work. Meanwhile, the regular appearance of women operating freely in all their domains, from sports to commerce, confirms male assumptions of gender sameness, opening a hole in masculine responsibility big enough to drive an army through.

In the brave new universe of sexual parity, there are few resources required of men, hardly any funky tests of character or personal resolve to disturb their day. Hell, they may not even have to pay for dinner. It often seems that these days the only thing a man has to bring to the party is testosterone. In this way, women's liberation has freed men. They can relinquish their primary responsibilities and still get what they want out of women.

Male ambivalence and fear of commitment may be irrelevant to an attractive woman enjoying her independent twenties. But as she approaches the mothering thirties, when the insistent pull of maternal instinct finally breaks through the flimsy retaining walls erected by the gender architects, the full range of gatherer instincts emerges from her subconscious into the waking mind of the modern woman. She starts to get serious. She starts to think like a parent with potential dependents.

Perhaps this accounts for popular American novels about hip young women who, confused and a bit jaded, long not so much for empty independence but a nurturing and protective relationship with a solid man; or the plaintive books and articles by older women wondering whatever happened to their family life and why they thought work was such a terrific idea in the first place. Many women have boxed themselves in. It seems the smarter and richer women get, the smarter and richer their men have to be—and the tougher it becomes to find one. It just isn't sexy if he is not as smart as you, or makes less money.

In any event, "dead end" men, the ones who are not serious or ambitious, become a waste of time to the maturing woman with an eye on the future. The used-to-be-good-enough men are harder to find or are no longer good enough—too wrapped up in themselves, aggressive, fumbling, gay, or taken. As time passes and more unfertilized eggs descend, the fairy tale of living happily ever after begins to yield to stark realism. Pessimism, cynicism, and self-centeredness can take hold as the chances of marrying narrow. By the time a single woman crosses her mid-thirties, matrimonial possibilities and the option of raising children with a husband shrink dramatically according to several studies.

Surveys and anecdotal reports also suggest that many "have-it-all" mothers wind up feeling deeply constricted, guilt-ridden, and personally deprived. Torn between spending quality time with their children and pursuing a career, many intelligent and vibrant working women are perplexed, depressed, or, if they actually have it all, utterly drained. Since most of women's household responsibilities are still waiting for them when they get home from work, they also pay an added price when they assume the burdens of a career. Even when today's working mother has an attentive, contributing husband, as well as outside help, something is almost certainly missing: like a close daily connection to her children. Mothering-at-a-distance often means that paid professionals are there for so many of the little moments that count.

As it happens, many husbands are not especially attentive nor are they contributing much more at home despite the wholesale entry of women into the workforce. Current research suggests that in married households where wives are working, men's contribution around the house has risen from about six hours a week in the mid-1970s to a little over seven hours today—about ten more minutes a day.

According to an extensive Labor Department survey released late in 2004, working wives still put in more than double their husband's contribution around the house. They are twice as involved in their children's school and stay home with sick kids four times as often. Working women get an hour less sleep each night compared to stay-at-home mothers. Overall, when it comes to one-on-one face time with a parent, American children get barely a fifth of it with their fathers. That's when there is a father around at all.

From All Sides

Perhaps we should not be surprised that, despite decades of touting the glittering arenas outside the house, for some time now surveys have reported that sizeable majorities of women would happily forego the career part to raise their kids and run the household. Many women have come to see a career as heaping additional labors on top of their other responsibilities. Men have not been introduced to the power of the feminine. Instead, women have taken on the chores of masculinity. The perverse result is that overburdened women are diminished, and underchallenged men are demeaned. Win-win between the sexes has been turned into lose-lose.

Pushed by "you go girl" feminists from below, sidetracked by the aggressive males on top, and often abandoned by the men in the middle, today's woman is getting it from all sides. Sex over relationship, job over family, abortion on demand, outsourced motherhood, "no fault" divorce, male-type stress disorders, and females in combat—the price of freedom for a privileged few has consigned millions to bondage.

In our modern "breakup" culture of casual intimacy, commitment-shy men can take off when the chemistry drops back or the responsibilities get too heavy. Hit-and-run lovers, many men are forever escaping the scene of the accident. Through divorce or because of greater numbers of out-of-wedlock births, female-headed households have increased dramatically throughout the Western world. By and large, they are also the poorest and the most vulnerable.

Today's vast throngs of single mothers face the world alone, their social mobility and finances burdened by raising children without enough help, their chances of attracting a new partner steeply compromised by the presence of another man's offspring. The growing legions of these women can teach the gender mathematicians something. It's called "multiplication," as in having to do just about all the work at home, in addition to supporting children and holding down a job. The harsh result is millions of overworked women parking their children with "professional" overseers so they can hurry off to mostly ordinary jobs to make enough money to pay people to do the things they no longer have the time to do themselves.

The most vivid illustration of the Second Wave's failure to serve even its own constituency will be revealed in life expectancy tables during the first decades of the twenty-first century. The good news is that the gender gap will narrow; the bad news is that equality with men will be gained by diminishing women. The growing presence of women in the danger professions means youthful death for female police, fire, and military personnel while on-the-job accidents kill increasing numbers of women exposed to other hazardous or physically demanding work. According to the National Center for Health Statistics, this trend is already in evidence. Since 1970, the mortality spread between men and women continues to shrink, from 7.6 to 5.3 years.

More subtle but equally devastating over the long-term are the classic male stress killers that will accompany women pursuing demanding line jobs, executive and professional careers, and male diversions. A 2001 report from the surgeon general's office pointed to a "full blown epidemic" of tobacco-related disease among women. By 1987, lung cancer had surpassed breast cancer as the leading source of cancer deaths of American women, having increased sixfold since 1950. Is that what they meant by "you've come a long way, baby?"

InterCoarse

The bill for all the gender engineering has come due. The price is paid every day in the descent to edgy coarseness between young men and women. Popular fiction, television, movies, and much of our culture often fosters a vulgar, manipulative, and adolescent attitude toward intimate relationships. The sweetness between men and women is long gone. "Trust no one" is the current moral posture. Selfish grasping is ever-present. "Getting it"—and getting even—are obsessions. A cosmopolitan culture of crass manipulation is the rule, disconnected urban dwellers hoping to score.

It has become a business doing pleasure in a transitory society where matrimony is a dreamy half-hope in a sea of alternative and transient possibilities and the cherished notion of having children is nearly extinct. For decades now, gender-balanced casts in popular television and cable sitcoms have been hyping the single life while performing bowel movements in adjoining toilet stalls. Hip single women in the city have it all—except the things that seem to matter most to grown women. Fatherhood, especially in its positive forms, is nearly a no show in prime time where plot lines and character motives are devoid of moral consideration and dumping on men is standard fare.

Responding to another tiresome complaint about the so-called impaired status of women in Anna Quindlen's *Newsweek* column, a male reader sees it another way. "Every other sitcom, talk show, and commercial depicts women as goddesses who can do no wrong, while heterosexual males like myself are for the most part depicted as brainless, spineless, sport-obsessed, breast-ogling Neanderthals who need five gay men to dress them up. How much more emasculating can it get?" *Men's Health* put it more succinctly in the header to an article on the subject: "Every time you turn on the TV, some lard-ass dad is trying to extricate himself from a ridiculous predicament."

It used to be that only men were confused about their roles in nature's reproductive compact. The new news is that it seems a lot of women are confused now, too. Schooled in the superficial math of gender equality, encouraged to believe they should break free of regressive tradition and be empowered to do all the things men do, many young women are confronted with an acute dilemma as they mature. Compelling hormonal washes and ancient evolutionary legacies rise to consciousness and begin to color their personal and intimate calculations.

Women have never been better positioned to look after themselves but archaic gatherer instincts keep clawing through. The desire for security, to be helped, protected, and provided for, will not lie still. This leaves women informing pollsters that they are highly ambivalent about modern independence. Much as they covet male license they also wish to indulge female prerogatives. Women want to be spoiled sometimes. They don't always want to do it all, even if they can. Balancing on the fine edge of this new double standard, many women are pushed and pulled between interdependence and autonomy, intuition and intellect, submission and assertion.

Confused women further destabilize men. What can we ask for in the way of subtle romantic shadings from a male generation that has grown up seeing patriarchy demonized, male ceremony attacked, and gender differences demolished? The response is more likely to be exaggerated masculinity, immature "guy stuff," angry music, lots of game-playing, predatory males, and sexual mayhem.

Today's intimate dance is a passionless contest, an edgy competition where love's supposed to be. Sex is up and romance is down, a triumph of the crude, lowest common social denominator. In our "throwaway" culture we are moving from the extended pair bond to a ticket that is good for one night. Pay per view, pay for play.

From cleavage-filled "laddie" magazines to misogynist rap, from big-breasted babes in CD games to digitally precise porn videos, from 900 phone lines to rub-you-up lap dances—men will continue to seek outlets for their urge-driven sexuality wherever and however they can. Prostitution, which looks a lot like resources-for-sex an hour at a time, thrives despite the fear of AIDS and other STDs. Reports suggest that there are more than four million porn sites, roughly one in eight on the Web. According to some analysts they now generate revenues exceeding $12 billion a year in the U.S. alone, nearly twice the combined take of CBS, NBC, and ABC, and greater than the sum total revenues of the nation's big three professional sports.

The feminist establishment sees only female degradation in the huge commercial sex trade but, except where minors are involved or women are forced to participate against their will, the degradation is all male. To the contrary, the sex industry is a huge win for women and all of civilized society. Commercial sex is a male pacifier, and its female participants are silent heroines to other women. On the front lines of male sexual chaos, female sex workers soothe the beast of testosterone, draw off excess male sexual tension, and provide a release for inchoate urges that might otherwise be inflicted on ordinary women. Adult Web sites are portals to sexual freedom for constricted males, a place where even healthy, married men can live out the fantasy of some new, exotic sex out on the savanna.

A lot of the marginalized men who are not busy buying sex retail are digging in against women in ways that range from annoying to worrisome. Attacked, ridiculed, or ignored in the media and elsewhere, their options narrowed and demeaned, they have watched the women around them enjoy unprecedented choices. For too many of these men, women are becoming the opposition to be exploited rather than partners to be gained. The Internet, for example, is loaded with male backlash sites. Most women who have dated a cross-section of contemporary men are only too familiar with this hostility, even if it hides behind an elegant mask. Sometimes the antipathy can take on tragic proportions.

Pillage and Plunder

There may have been a time in our distant past when rape was an effective sexual strategy, particularly for a lone male wolf at the edge of the pack. Rape generates the possibility of offspring without having to provide anything in return. But aside from the brutal violation of its innocent victims, rape comes up against another crucial bio-evolutionary issue: the quest by men to certify their patriarchy. As a result, rape long ago became an act of violence against not only women but their mates and family. Just as the murder of a provider-husband victimizes a woman, the rape of his wife imperils a man.

Contrary to early radical bleatings from the Second Wave, rape is not condoned by men as a way to hold women in their protective thrall. Rape is an attack against civility and order, a breakdown of socialization. The unprovoked rapist preys on the entire community. It also does women a great deal of good when men view rape as an attack on themselves as well, since it brings them more effectively to a woman's defense. In the places of our world where rape and pillage broadly surface—during war, bloodshed, and anarchy, or in the throes of fanatical hatred—it is a sure sign that civilization is eroding. Under these extreme conditions, many women are raped. That is a terrible and ugly thing. If men manage to stay out of prison they usually don't get raped. Instead, in these violent upheavals, they get killed.

When it comes to sexual assault, nature again works backward from coitus. Western women are spared the extremes of religious cloistering or veils (thank you, *thank* you), but responsibility still rides with female power and women's grant of sexual access. The closer a woman's appearance and attitude get to sexual availability, the closer we get to impulsive male behavior. Parading in front of the guys at a construction site on a hot July day in Minneapolis in shorts, halter top, and four-inch heels may earn you more than a nine-second ogle. (If the brutes do it again, it's a misdemeanor.) Sex is a fiery thing that surely needs to be handled with responsibility on both ends.

It is only in the last few seconds before ejaculation that the rapist still lurks in men. Ordinary males do not rape under ordinary circumstances. Confused and antagonistic men, however, sensing easy sexual access in the media and elsewhere, and groping for affirmation in the few places they can find it, can become sexually aggressive. Harassing behavior, date rape, and sexual assaults have mounted over the last few years despite an overall decline in violent crime. U.S. Justice Department surveys report that a quarter of women and 7 percent of men, including gay men, say they have been raped or sexually assaulted by a current or former partner.

A 2001 report in the *Journal of the American Medical Association* suggested that one in five girls will be physically or sexually abused by a date. Stalking, a relatively new occurrence, has increased strikingly. Over their lifetime, roughly one in ten American women will be stalked, five times the male rate. In our ever more coarse society, the civilized overlay of marriage is eroding. The tried and true pair bond is in retreat. We are regressing socially, returning the sexual agenda to its raw, primitive origins. We are heading back to the jungle again, where it's every man—and woman—for themselves.

BEEP

"Yes, I saw the news on the ticker. You have every reason to be pissed . . . look, something went wrong, okay?

"One of the molecules mutated or inverted or something. The ED gel gets hard after a few seconds, instead of, y'know,

lubricating the surface it's rubbed on. It turns into, like glue. Super glue, actually.

"Well, not exactly glue. More like concrete. While people are, y'know, using it, trying to rub it on.

"And, yes, I most definitely understand that this is not a big selling point for a love oil. That it turns to cement in your hands. I get that part.

"Look, how was I supposed to know?

"Did you see where a guy got stuck committing an unnatural act with his vacuum cleaner? And I don't even want to think about what was going on at the old people's home, the way the paramedics found them.

"I know . . . it's not funny. But if I don't laugh, I'm going to cry.

"This is a disaster. I know a disaster when I see one and this, my friend, is a disaster. A soul-destroying disaster. I'm up to my eyeballs in this thing. I got everybody I know into it. My entire world!

"The stock is dropping like a stone. The Feds just cuffed the CEO and took him on a 'perp' walk for insider trading. And now, of course, my boss wants to have a word with me. Told me to hot-foot it into his office. He has that gleam in his eye.

"Lawsuits. Investigations. Job hunting . . . excuse me, 'vocational realignment'.

"Welcome to my future.

"Jesus!

"Are you there?

"How come you don't pick up anymore?

"You there?"

In the midst of all the contemporary sexual confusion and disquiet, it may be difficult to make out our indispensable personal and evolutionary responsibility: pairing up, mating, and reenergizing our genetic legacy. This fundamental enterprise is not some abstract notion concocted by social philosophers about how we ought to live our lives. Living true to our biological heritage is the meat and potatoes of individual joy. Getting hot and bothered, making a commitment, having babies, raising children, building a life together—animals are happiest doing nature's bidding. Despite the seductive blandishments and beguiling diversions of modern living, real and fulfilling pleasures accompany the reproductive enterprise. Even for those refined animals known as humans.

Nature has specialized most of the planet into two sexes, and in the service of this sexual undertaking, males have been allotted a tiny chore. Sex is something they try to perform often because they get worked up easily, because it feels good and because it only takes a few minutes.

The male inclination toward sexual breadth and promiscuous anarchy grows out of the inherent insecurity of sperm contribution. On this fragile hook of an affirmed, reinforced patriarchy hangs society's ability to draw men into a peaceful and settled community. Thriving societies learn to use what they can to harness male energy for the benefit of everyone. Tying men confidently to their children is a superb place to start.

Women can choose to duke it out with the guys, mimic masculinity, toughen up to compete, and develop a taste for risk and status hierarchies. Or they can serve as agents of calm and conservation, drawing men into the safe harbor of family and community, centering their sense of self on nurturance and relationship. Liberated women may abhor the inequity, if not the downright indignity, of having to capture commitment-shy men but the relationship between a woman and a man is a marathon that, in most respects, runs on female cadence and to a woman's overall advantage.

The relatively new idea of connecting fathers directly to their children evolved as an effective way to acculturate men and to encourage them to support their mates and offspring through the lengthy human maturation process. But unlike mothers who come to parenting by nature, fatherhood is shaped by culture. Motherhood is immutable. *Paternity* is the social construct. Amazingly, we have been doing everything we can to deconstruct it.

For all but the last few thousand years, a man's work has summoned his evolved mental and physical skills as hunter and defender. Males had a sharply defined purpose, a mission that harmonized with their abilities and held their attention. Men knew what was required of them.

More recently men have learned that being yoked ever so gently to wife and child holds profound rewards, enlarging their horizons and extending their perspective into the future. Purposeful partner rather than an optional loner, the married man is encouraged to become a responsible citizen, enriched by the connection to his children and the exclusive, enduring partnership of a woman. Nevertheless, the recent cultural overlay of fatherhood remains a fragile bit of scaffolding.

The newly won economic, political, and reproductive autonomy of women has dramatically shifted the ground, severely loosening the interdependent axis of the sexual bargain. Encouraged by the modern fetish for individual freedom and the denigration of marriage and family, the tenuous links that attach men to their families are under unprecedented strain. Instruments of androgyny, modern technologies have blunted male advantage. Across our finely balanced if not slanted legal structures and the sexless keyboards of modern commerce, male privilege has been nearly obliterated.

Equality of the sexes has been achieved, and then some, in every field but one. The most important one. In the low tech world of sexual regeneration the female continues supreme. As we pounce on every compensating male preserve, ordinary men have been reduced to second-class citizens. The everyday man is now the outsider looking in.

Paternity and emotional commitment have a tenuous hold on men. We can make it easier for them to see the payoff in relationship and responsible masculinity by acknowledging and honoring the imperial dictates of our natural legacy. Or we can abandon nature, see to it that unique male socializing institutions are demeaned, disrupted, or destroyed, and try to design the world to passing intellectual fashion.

The Men We Deserve

In response to modern gender disarray, there are increasing pleas by women to recapture classic female control over intimacy. A growing bevy of young woman authors embrace the socially defining role of femininity and often beseech women to reassert some discipline in romantic relationships. Though heartfelt and commendable, short of a really scary heterosexual plague, this call for collective female modesty will fail.

The sexual agenda gets played out one bedroom at a time. We may empathize with others of our sex, enjoying the rueful banter of the locker room or the baby shower, but people focus mostly on their own individual relationships and families. Besides, Western societies are too large, too diverse, and too sophisticated to impose this kind of mass, gender-based discipline. And as with so much else, the restraint of many is undone by the wavering of a few. It's hard for women to impose an enduring cost for intimacy on men when it's going for nothing next door. In any event, if recreational sex became unavailable to men, today's wide range of commercialized alternatives would no doubt satisfy their immediate needs.

Individual women should, and often do, take back the night, but the gender progressives who presume to speak for them have made this task especially difficult. Through misplaced attempts at sexual equality, we have come close to turning femininity from an advantage to a burden. The unwinding of the activists' handiwork, pervasive and entrenched across our entire educational system and much of our culture, will be a forbidding, multigenerational chore. Even then, a slender but significant minority of women will continue to buy into the line that they desire the same things from life and sex that men do, and behave accordingly. They will do this because they believe it, they've been told to believe it, or they want to believe it.

We need to go the other way. We need to honor and encourage the full potential of women by resurrecting the heart and soul of femininity. The best way to do this is by elevating and celebrating female strengths rather than diminishing them so that women can ape masculinity. We need to soften the rough edges of men, not masculinize women.

We can do this by returning nurturance and reproduction to the very center of our culture. Regenerating the community and conserving nature, women have been the anchors of society, the civilizing force of humanity. They are not "as good as" men. For one thing, it's not a competition but a merger enhanced by each partner's unique specialties. For another, in many of the ways that really count, women may well be superior.

Women have clearly shown they can succeed in most contemporary male domains. Yet men, as ever, are foreclosed by nature from the most significant feminine realms. Women can now play on both sides of the court and men just one. Too often this has come to mean that women work twice as hard while men do half the job.

Perhaps, then, it is not too outlandish to argue that, to a large extent, the particular male task is done. Having propelled an exquisite degree of digital convenience and technological sophistication into our world, it no longer matters to civilization whether men pull back or drop out. Muscle having been muted, men are edging to the sidelines and women will carry a load-and-a-half. So what?

The problem is that this leads to millions of beleaguered women and billions of human inefficiencies. Disposing of males offends nature's hard won triumph of sexual specialization and summons a vision of an ever cruder, more competitive world. We are happiest honoring nature's call, and women will be least happy doing a man's part of the job.

Worse, the men we do not make a part of the solution may become a big part of the problem. Many will tune out, extend their adolescence deep into adulthood, and be irresponsible, maybe irretrievable. Opportunistic lovers and perpetual players, marginalized men will avoid commitment, evade responsibility, and possibly abandon their offspring. And the longing we all have for love and intimacy will continue its descent into a battlefield of wounded souls.

The more pressing problem for us all is that the flip side of men who are apathetic, gone, or too soft is men who are too hard and only too near. For those males who refuse to be disposed of, the spears that modern innovation places in their unsteady hands become ever more terrifying. As advances in technology place the discoveries of our best minds into the clutches of our worst, the power in everyman's grasp may no longer be a myth.

10

DARWIN'S CONUNDRUM

Reclaiming the Levers of Extinction

"...a planet, newly formed, placidly revolves around its star; life slowly forms; a kaleidoscopic procession of creatures evolves; intelligence emerges which, at least up to a point, confers enormous survival value; and then technology is invented. It dawns on them that there are such things as laws of Nature, that these laws can be revealed by experiment, and that knowledge of these laws can be made both to save and to take lives, both on unprecedented scales. Science, they recognize, grants immense powers. In a flash, they create world-altering contrivances. Some planetary civilizations see their way through, place limits on what may and what must not be done, and safely pass through the time of perils. Others, not so lucky or so prudent, perish." — Astronomer Carl Sagan

S OONER OR LATER, LIFE FORMS ON A PLANET EVOLVE THE INTELLIGENCE and technical ability to extend their power beyond their individual reach. As innovation and technology compound, multiplying in impact, slingshots become cannons and cannons turn into ballistic missiles. In this way the tools of widespread destruction find their way into the precarious hands of living creatures.

No tale of human evolution or commentary on the state of masculinity and the modern sexes would be complete without peering into tomorrow's prospects. It is a future of dizzying speed, glorious possibility, and unprecedented danger.

Damocles' sword cuts two ways: every glorious invention brings devastation as its twin. From the discovery of fire, the transistor, and nuclear fission, to the science called genetics—almost every significant discovery and innovation carries the potential to enrich our lives or inflict harm, to shine a light or cast a shadow. The hand axe can be used to build a lean-to or hack an innocent to death. Radio waves that disseminate knowledge can just as easily spread hate. The microchip that places awesome computing power in the palm of our hands endows two-bit tyrants with intercontinental missiles and extends the capacity to launch cyber-wars from a home computer.

In a mere two generations, men have created vehicles of Armageddon that make the atom bomb look like a meat cleaver and anthrax merely a starter kit. Rogue states, terrorists, and even small cults can now harness the levers of mass destruction. In a kind of Starbucking of terror, we are fast approaching the time when a couple of neighborhood, Columbine-like youth—with nothing more than a PC and a chemistry set—will be able to launch biotoxic horrors from smallpox to slate-wipers we didn't know existed.

The joysticks to extinction are now "in play." As always, it will be men who mess with them. Rabid rascals and unruly renegades have always been among us, a tiny fraction of the population. Yet if the fanatical and lunatic fringes make up just one hundredth of 1 percent of the world's male population, this means there are now more than a quarter of a million desperados to keep a close eye on.

In a crowded Global City packed with six billion humans and a mushrooming list of potentially devastating technologies, anybody's problem has become everybody's problem. Consider just one example: the FBI, among others, has issued serious warnings about potentially devastating chemical and biological concoctions that can be assembled using materials easily available through the Internet or conventional mail order sources.

At the close of his term, President Bill Clinton offered a warning to a Coast Guard Academy graduating class. "The central reality of our time is that the advent of globalization and the revolution in information technology have magnified both the creative and the destructive potential of every individual, tribe, and nation on our planet." On September 11, 2001, a technological triumph of the twentieth century was turned into missiles of hate aimed at 110-story modern marvels, bearing witness to this central reality of our time.

Technology is a blessing, but it is also a curse. Like it or not, it has brought humanity to an evolutionary impasse, to the greatest puzzle of all. It has brought us to Darwin's Conundrum: we've gotten so smart we've figured out how to destroy ourselves. As the forces of light race to defend us against the perversion of science, it seems our primal job as animals and our inspiring goal as humans have now become one: if we don't get better, we're not going to survive.

It is our brains that got us into this mess, but it is going to take more than smarts to get us out. We will no doubt endure a future of nasty biohazard riffs, the odd toxic viral assault, nuclear threats and acts of terrorist sabotage, not to mention some potentially ruinous natural calamities. To forestall these ultimate world-threatening hazards we are going to need unprecedented, planet-wide discipline and the entire depth of our feminine and masculine bequest.

Otherwise, the coming time of peril may be our last.

To: HotShotWriter@writersbloc.net
Subject: YOUR SUCCESSFUL FUTURE!

We wish to inform you that your personal investment advisor is no longer associated with our firm. We are taking immediate steps to place your valued account with another of our skilled, highly trained representatives and apologize for any inconvenience.

With all the horrors lurking in the Global City, around the corner or across town, watching women and men going toe-to-toe starts to look like we're rearranging the deck chairs on the *Titanic*. Getting better and confronting the disturbing scenarios that face us will call forth the best of our talents and skills. In this effort, we are going to need all the technological smarts and sturdy fortitude of mankind working in concert with the nurturing instincts and adaptability of womankind. Once again the world confronts us with the need to work together and harmonize our sexual inheritance in order to survive.

If we accept the basic tenets of evolution and the continuing influence of ancient natural forces, what sort of guidance can we draw upon for addressing this challenge, for preparing our societies, and for improving the sexual partnership at its core? How might we apply nature's wisdom to achieving social harmony and collective strength? Can we translate our understanding of evolutionary principles into workable solutions for the problems plaguing modern societies? And what can we do about it as individuals?

Honor the Family Circle. First and foremost, before confronting external menaces we have to get our own house in order. We have to get back to basics. We can start by re-enshrining nature's imperial dictates to survive and propagate and by placing these values at the center of our lives and our society. Honoring this mandate for renewal means centering our institutions on procreation and childrearing, and drawing men closer toward the enduring pair bond, parental involvement, and the essential family circle. This will require abandoning the notion that the sexes are essentially the same. Pointing to our sexual differences is good news, not only because of the fun stuff but also because thriving partnerships are built upon mutual need and *compensating* skills.

Build Better Boys. Our future rests with the next generation. Children, especially boys, struggle with their sexual identity. Turning boisterous boys into dedicated dads means relinquishing our fetish for propelling the sexes together, at the earliest possible moment, into rigid unisex training. Boys need to find some solid footing before they are thrown indiscriminately together with girls. They need to know what they are before accommodating what they aren't. We also need to develop cultural values of positive boyhood. Boys are wondrous creatures with stunning potential and boundless energies. They cannot get too much love, discipline, support, and recognition. As we know by now, sexual confidence—the thing we need most in men in order to sustain a peaceable and productive world—is not handed to males. Incomplete promises, potential-in-waiting, masculine harmony is won through action and fulfillment.

Mold Masculinity. Evolution and biology teach us that the need for all-male institutions diminishes as men age, but their value in anchoring a comfortable masculinity is crucial during the early formative years. A healthy society seeking the best in men will encourage rather than deny male bonding outlets, support the notion of mentoring youngsters and embrace the initiation ceremonies that socialize young men. These rites of passage serve to pacify male youth, anchor their sexual identity, prepare them to approach women with respect and confidence, and give them a stake in the community worth defending. Instead of looking to wipe out these male rites, we should be actively resurrecting them.

Confident Boys = Confident Men. Confident boys turn into confident men; confident men yield to reason, welcome strong women, and seek peace through the disciplined exercise of strength. As male youth mature, their confidence and steady contribution to their families and our society can be purchased through our guidance, approval, and shows of appreciation. Encouraging competent, responsible, and vibrant masculinity does not hurt or diminish women. Precisely the opposite is true.

Celebrate the Sexes. Defining equality of the sexes in higher education and elsewhere in our institutions can and should mean spending the same *overall* resources on male and female students. The fact that men and women, on average, pursue sports and the expressive arts with differing levels of enthusiasm doesn't mean there's something wrong. To the contrary, natural and healthy inclinations are being expressed. School curricula can also celebrate sexual distinctions and still make room for the exceptional student of either sex.

The Price of Intimacy. A major component of youthful, male-oriented training and preparation should also include an introduction to corresponding adult responsibilities. In particular, young men must once again be made to understand that their ticket to the intimate rewards of love, children, and family is purchased through service to their mate, their offspring, and the community. They need to see that bringing something to the party, providing resources and support, and defending and protecting the clan are big parts of their job.

Support Fathers. Fulfilling these roles, in turn, legitimizes men's right to participate in the family circle. Fatherhood—something of a foreign concept to mammals and primates—needs all the reinforcement modern society can give it. For men ready to shoulder the responsibilities of mature manhood, we must be generous with incentives, community and government assistance, and cultural encouragement. Fatherhood initiatives deserve our support. Anything that serves to connect men to their mates and their children is worthy of our backing.

Honor Men. More important than all of the specific measures and detailed recommendations for rebuilding masculinity is the overall social awareness of the importance of preparing boys and honoring men. We must remove the excessive anti-masculine traces from our culture. The events of September 11, 2001 reminded us of men's demonic possibilities, but also of their heroic potential. Men are capable of unspeakable horror and stunning sacrifice. Which way they go may well depend upon how their masculinity is forged. Modern societies can point males toward the heights of productive achievement or abandon them to their own devices, draw them into realms of civility, or let them wander like errant vagabonds. In the end, we get the men we deserve.

The Indispensable Man

But will they be the men we need? What sort of man should society strive to promote? What forms of masculinity shall we honor?

We might begin with a man who lives in concert with nature, who has the discipline to contain unruly urges and seeks safe vessels for his instinctive compulsions. We encourage the man who approaches women with assurance and treats them with respect. The man worthy of society's acclaim will be conscious of family and devoted to the mate he gains. He will be a source of resolve, resources, and moral example to his children. The responsible man will know his history, grasp his place in society, and draw with pride to his kin and his tribe.

The mature adult male plans for the future, takes an interest in his community, and makes himself aware of the world he is preparing his children to enter. He seeks to understand different points-of-view and builds his opinions with care. He takes on responsibility in his society, registers and votes, and contributes to the community's defense and welfare. Respectful of others, the man we look up to works to bring about a thriving and becalmed culture. Though he stands up for his beliefs, he is opposed to angry discord, seeking consensus and inclusion. Physical aggression is his last resort.

The male who wins our approval is a man of his word. He pursues the brotherhood of other men, accepts the gift of mentoring from those who came before him, and extends the hand of experience to younger males on life's path. The man society celebrates is fair and productive in his labors, energetic and joyful in pursuit of his passions, and forthright in the pleasure he derives from his just accomplishments.

Without apology for the initiatives he takes, the indispensable man is big enough to acknowledge his mistakes. Flexible, open to change, the man who wins his community's respect will be unafraid to confront life's deeper questions. He will rise in time with body, mind, and spirit in balance. He will be interested and interesting, inspired and inspiring.

No matter how primitive or progressive the culture, males must still gain manhood, and in the absence of helpful signals and positive reinforcements, many will flounder. In a society that requires nothing special from men, nothing special will be offered. Which is too bad because men have some spectacular things to contribute. They have brought us a long way from the simple hearth to lives of miraculous convenience. For mankind no creative notion goes unattended, no splendid ideal unpursued. For better or worse, it will be men defending us—and driving us forward.

Family Planning

If we know anything at all, it is that the most important vessel for sustaining our individual lives and the human enterprise is the bond between men and women, and the bloodlines we build around it. The heart and soul of every successful culture that ever was and ever will be, there is no social arrangement to replace the family unit. At the core of the family is the sanctified pair bond, the partnership between the sexes. Marriage emerged as a container for our crucial reproductive mandate, a biological exercise requiring the union of female and male.

This means that however much we wish to honor the civil union of our homosexual citizens, in the end, the notion of "same-sex marriage" is an oxymoron; not only must we design our fundamental institutions for reproductive survival, we trivialize them at our peril. A return to the primary mandate to foster the next generation means venerating life and enshrining heterosexual marriage and motherhood as the fulcrum of our social arrangements.

Inevitably, and fortunately, this entails **elevating the natural feminine values of nurturance, inclusion, intuition, and deeply rooted, natural wisdom**. We must project for budding young females not only the possibility to be hard-driving CEOs but, especially, the classic options of nest-building, childrearing, and neighborhood relations. This suggests **a redefinition of modern feminism**, a holistic feminism that propagates the full range of women's potential, advancing their rights to be sure, but also serving women's wider interests within the context of marriage, childbearing, and family.

Drawing males into the family circle means **seeking ways to connect men to their wives and children**. Among other things this calls for elevating the married man, ensuring his formal role in family decisions regarding abortion, making divorce a little tougher to get, and bearing down on deadbeat dads who have the resources to pay up.

Governments should be in the business of **encouraging and reinforcing marriage at every turn**—from favorable tax provisions to the kind of post-WWII grants and incentives that afforded veterans the wherewithal to acquire a home and support a family. So far have we drifted from this central societal function that a 2002 *Time* article, commenting on modest Bush administration attempts to fortify wedlock, informs its readers that "[t]he notion of government promotion of marriage may seem odd, if not dubious."

More than feathering the pair bond nest and bolstering male participation, modern societies can **elevate and support the concept of the extended family**. Our schools and the culture at large can foster this central and stabilizing social unit, not only enshrining childrearing as society's principal function but also favoring three-generation households. Once a week the word "family" should be stenciled on the forehead of every public servant and government agent. And while there is surely room for differing opinions on how to fortify the family, all new legislation, each administrative policy, every ordinance in our communities should be initially assessed against two basic litmus tests: Does the issue, law, regulation, or policy we're contemplating reinforce the family and marriage? If not, does it compromise or weaken them?

In support of the family, **the rights of parents should be emboldened**. Parental consent—at least one—should be required by minors who seek an abortion. Period. If we're not talking to our daughters about sex and pregnancy, what are we talking to them about? The nation's textbooks should honor the role of parenting, and government—at all levels—must respect parental privilege. Hand-in-hand with the favored place of the family are some reciprocal responsibilities. Marriage is a serious commitment, not something to be taken lightly. Parenthood is a privilege but also a duty. Divorce is a right not to be abused. Community is a resource to which families must also contribute.

Humans are gregarious animals. We are honed for cooperation as working together helped ensure our survival on the savanna. We build connections to a mate, bear children, relate to parents, and stay in touch with siblings. The immediate family, in turn, connects to blood relatives and a loose but often critical tribal heritage.

Our **kinship and ethnic roots are ancient and supportive links; they should be fostered** in a society that values stability and faces threats to its security. Kinship and our ancient roots provide a natural safety net for individuals and families. It is through extended families and clans that we're led into the larger community. We must reinforce neighborhood consciousness, teach the value of a strong commonwealth, emphasize civic responsibility, even explore some forms of compulsory community service for our maturing youth.

Through all these exercises the notions of **sexual distinction and specialization are to be encouraged**. No matter what we do, we must recognize that many competitive work and social environments in contemporary societies will continue to march to ancient male rhythms—just as other parts of our culture will be predominantly feminine in tone.

These are patterns to encourage and celebrate, even as we try to make room for the many individuals, of both sexes, who choose another way.

Where Do I Begin?

Okay, okay. I've read the book. I get the picture. Now what? What are the fundamental ways I can go about applying an evolutionary perspective to my life and my immediate surroundings? Though this is not a "how-to" book (it's more like a "how come" book), nevertheless we *can* identify a few core principles. (Besides, if you know how come, you can probably figure out how to.)

To Thine Own Self Be True. Let's begin with a hard, cold, and, perhaps, unremarkable fact. You are self-centered. It's alright. So is everyone else. It's the survival instinct. Self-interest, reckoning for our own health and benefit, is at the core of our being. "I am alive, therefore I calculate." You are the star in the movie that is your life. Self-centeredness is something to be acknowledged, honored, and managed, not ignored or denied. Virtually the entire science and everyday practice of economics and nearly every act of daily commerce is predicated on the assumption of "the rational man," of citizens who conduct their lives and make decisions based upon what they deem to be in their best interest.

How fundamental is this "selfishness?" Consider the phrase, "I love you." Most of us want to hear this from somebody, or everybody. Many of us say it to somebody, or everybody. At heart, it is a self-centered sentiment, even if it's a compliment to the recipient. *I* love you. *I* miss you. *I* can't wait to see you. *I'm* worried about you. If these are not selfish sentiments, they're certainly self-centered. For whom do we mourn when someone we care about dies? The deceased? Or do we mourn for ourselves, for *our* loss?

Accepting that the people around us are, like ourselves, motivated by their own self-interest means designing our actions with this in mind. The way we get things done is to learn to detect what other people want and—most importantly—align their self-interest with our own. Show people how their goals can be achieved by advancing your goals, or that of the team, the company, or the nation. Being selfish is neither bad nor good; it is the way things are. It's a natural response.

Fly by the Seat of Your Pants. The second thing we can do as individuals is learn to listen to and trust our instincts. They are there for a reason. They're not funny feelings or leftover evolutionary traces. Instincts and intuition are an authentic form of knowledge, a big part of our genetic inheritance. They are predispositions, fundamental "ways of knowing" that rise up from powerful animal resources honed over countless epochs. What we need to learn to do in our high-tech urban environments is to clear away the sophisticated static, the "noise" that prevents us from hearing these instinctive voices of deep-rooted information.

However you return to nature—whether you share living space with another species, take a walk in the park, seek out pagan ritual, or simply find ways to listen to your body and emotions—trust your intuition. Is a person or situation making you feel uncomfortable? Does something feel "not quite right"? Our instincts may occasionally fail us. We may be told "it's nothing." Yet, more often than not, our instincts prove to be right. Open the pathways to intuition. When it is important, honor these instinctive hints. Use this powerful primal knowledge.

Embrace Your Sex. The third evolutionary lesson, if we don't already do this, is to celebrate our sex. If we do, we can't fail but honor the other one. Sex is the first step we take outward, away from the self. It is what connects us to our past, our future, our mate and family, and just about every other living thing. The universe works in pairs. We can neither serve ourselves nor survive into the future without our "other half." So natural, so hand-in-glove is the sexual equation that by simply and truly comprehending ourselves we gain a glimpse of the other side of our nature. The man who begins to understand himself begins to fathom women. Femininity is the flip side of a confident, healthy masculinity. And vice versa.

In fact, the other side of our sexuality is already within us. Before we're born the principal genes, hormones, and neurotransmitters of the opposite sex already reside within our bodies and our minds. Women have masculine instincts and impulses. Men have feminine instincts and impulses. As we age these characteristics become more evident, both because we gain a sense of sexual universals through experience and because the hormonal balances in our bodies and brains shift toward sexual balance.

Welcome the other side of your nature. It is a treat to be explored. It can enrich your life, multiply your pleasures, enlarge your appreciation for the "opposite" sex, and help you build a better bond with your intimate partner.

The Moral Evolutionist

The evolutionary lens is not some academic curiosity but an active tool. Use it. Focus it in the bedroom and in the boardroom, and everywhere in between. It is a rich trove of knowledge. You don't have to give up your other ways of looking at the world, just add this valuable new one. After examining a situation in all the ways you usually do—any situation involving people or other animals—try analyzing it from the perspectives of natural science.

Hunters and gatherers are all around you. The dynamics of sexual bonding are everywhere in view. Issues around your extended family, clan relationships and the hierarchies at the office have ancient roots and can all be viewed through the useful "filter" of evolution. If you look closely, there is a lot more to it than identifying the alpha male.

Finally, as we move outward from our own self-interest to become involved with other people and the world at large, we should honor the morality and ethical dimensions of evolution. Many people think of evolution as a harsh master. But our spectacular emergence from the primate pack is an achievement to celebrate, not a link to deny. And within evolution's principles and processes we may also distill some crucial and appealing human values.

Mutation, nature's change agent, can arise from anywhere in a population. Genius emerges from everyday quarters, and dunces are born of royalty. The random origin of mutation—the fact that it can come out of anywhere—suggests a powerful ethic. It is a solid argument for organizing society around a level playing field. This is not only fair; it's smart. When the track is wide open to the full range of human potential, the baton gets handed off to the leading contenders. If, for example, the most gifted minds are directed to achieving a cure for some disease, we all benefit. With truly equal opportunity, everyone gets to hitch a ride with the winners.

Anchoring our values to the survival instinct and honoring nature's sovereign call for renewal also suggests a kind of guiding moral orthodoxy that is not beholden to particular religious beliefs. Hundreds of thousands of years before we enjoyed the luxury of language, long before the creation of scriptural lore, men and women venerated life. This eternal reverence for revival, and the sexual bond that incubates our future, are rich in moral possibilities and social values. This regenerative essence suggests we honor life, its renewal through pregnancy, and its advancement. We are called upon to support our blood line and make sacrifices for our partner and family.

To Err Is Divine, To Forgive Human

We began this voyage of discovery into men, women, and modern life on the broad shoulders of scientific knowledge. We have been instructed by living creatures and looked for confirmation of our insights in the shared customs of humanity. We have searched inward for validation, drawing upon the design of our own bodies and our intuitive wisdom. It seems only fitting, then, to conclude this journey by attempting to raise our sights from the earth below to the heavens above. We might then see a place on the horizon where nature, knowledge, and faith come together.

It can take millions of years for physical traits to be altered. Without apparent direction, natural selection massages the Earth's creatures over an eternity. The same is not true of an idea. A helpful, adaptive notion can be selected for and nurtured by our will. Imagination is the gift we gained when a thousand generations ago our ancestors had the time and the wit to propel invention. Since then it has been the bright light of powerful ideas that have lit up the human odyssey.

Unlike genes, idea nodules, called "memes" by some, can replicate, mutate, take on direction, and evolve in a hurry. News travels fast these days and intellectual selection can send the evolution of a bold new idea into a sprint. This is a source of hope, because the way humanity is going we need to get smart in a hurry. More than smart, we must also find our way to exalted ground. Spirituality is, in a sense, another way of knowing. Perhaps, the most important way.

"God would not dare to appear to a starving man, except in the form of bread," observed Mahatma Gandhi, mindful of the primacy of survival and the hierarchy of needs. Yet when we conquer the natural obsession with survival, our minds begin to wander. And if not before, religious faith and spirituality often take wing when we catch sight of the angel of death.

Half a century before we succumb to nature's last call, we are provoked into thinking about the meaning of our existence. We are the only animals who must confront the awareness of mortality. This revelation can set in motion a psychological dilemma, a fearful plight that paralyzes many people who get so caught up deflecting death they fail to embrace life.

In 1996, Pope John Paul II drew nature to the church's bosom once again and declared that evolution was more than a theory—that, in effect, the scientific unraveling of the universe's workings revealed God's plan. Despite ambivalence and retrenchment by the church, His Holiness professed to see a divine break in the process of natural selection, the insertion of a soul, as *Homo sapiens* emerged at last in the eternal parade of nature.

Perhaps the pope had uncovered a bridge between faith and science; there is a genetic basis for religiousity. Spiritual yearning and religion are adaptations, accommodations to nature. We live longer, better, and happier lives because we believe in higher powers, congregate in devotion, and celebrate ritual traditions. It is useful, perhaps even necessary, to believe in something. But what?

Whatever our particular religious beliefs, or lack thereof, many of us are inclined to see a spiritual energy at work in the unfolding wonders of the universe. It resides in the awe and humility so many of us feel before nature's grandeur, the stunning ascent of humanity, and the breath of life that is our gift. Taking comfort in religion's embrace, we draw hope from humankind's splendid achievements.

Yet we have not evolved to sainthood. Even as we celebrate our own heroic achievements, humanity has been called upon, time and again, to endure man's works of abomination. When we fail, nature—ever imperial—remains indifferent to our fate. It is people who forgive and forget. We take advantage of nature's fortuitous mutations to move forward and somehow find the grace to pardon human excess. In this sense, the common adage is reversed: to err is divine, to forgive human.

Whether or not it was our old friend Zeus who got the ball rolling fourteen billion years ago, the Big Bang propelled an infinite number of planets into motion. No doubt an evolutionary process of one kind or another is unfolding on some of these celestial embryos as well. With a little heat and light, chemical properties must have propelled some form of natural selection into play on these other planets.

For all we know, living creatures on these planets may have achieved spectacular advances in scientific mastery. Considering how far we have come technologically over just the last few thousand years, what might we expect of evolved societies on distant planets that, for one reason or another, got way out ahead of us? Say, by a measly few million years. To contemplate what that might mean, think of where *we* might be a million years from now. It is unimaginable, of course, which is the point.

Are we alone in the universe? Hardly. The scientific consensus is that there are at least a million planets that support some evolutionary form of life, although some believe it to be far fewer. Are any of them technically more advanced than us? It is a statistical certainty. Are they listening? Maybe. Have they been here before?

Are they here now?

The Chance of a Lifetime

Many of the great religions of man extol the most dignified of human graces; tolerance, generosity, and forgiveness to name but a few. Wisdom, both mystical and practical, often illuminates their scrolls. The gifted prophets who have appeared among us have espoused many things, but they have all beseeched us to embrace an abiding kind of enlightenment—a shining vision of a harmonious village high atop a mountain peak. It is a community in concord with nature and joyous with promise, a family of diverse tribes in peaceable communion.

We are of nature. Drawn from common origins, we are connected to all living things. We share identical strands of DNA with most of the Earth's creatures, and each of us carries a triumphant database of ancestral guidance folded into every one of our living cells. These universal archives, Carl Jung's "collective unconscious," have encoded within us all the traces of the world's accumulated wisdom.

Whether we are here by divine seeding or not—we're here. There may or may not be life after death. Grace is the chance of life we have now and the right to make the most of it. For if there is no evident design to natural selection, neither does it impose any limit.

The perennial chorus of spiritual wisdom implores us to raise our sights. Anchored confidently in nature's legacy, we are free to reach for the wondrous heights of human potential. We can do no more. Yet, if we are to surmount the perils before us, we can do no less.

BEEP

"Are we having a great day?

"Jennifer Cooper-Farina here. Your spanking-new, highly skilled and trained personal advisor? Hoping to kick things off on the right foot.

"So sad, but your former representative is no longer permitted to sell securities. In fact, if he so much as utters the phrase 'exciting investment opportunity' or 'the growth stock of the century', he will be disemboweled on the steps of the SEC.

"On a more uplifting note, we'd be tickled pink to show off some hot new moves designed to firm up that slumping portfolio of yours. Make it stand up and salute!

"May we suggest opening with a 'butterfly spread,' then flipping into a reverse 'straddle.' Short, or long, whichever way you like to go.

"By the way, I double team with another rep? You'll love Amanda. Everyone loves Amanda. Working in tandem, there's always someone here to service our valued clients.

"Check out our site. Then how 'bout lunch?

"It's on us. Well (giggle) not actually, y'know, <u>on us</u>.

"Whaddayasay?"

ACKNOWLEDGMENTS

T HE DISPOSABLE MALE DRAWS UPON THE WORK OF A WIDE ARRAY OF DEDICATED researchers and scientists in a multitude of academic disciplines. I wish to express my gratitude to this army of fine scholars, especially those I was unable to single out due to limitations of one sort or another, including my desire to avoid burdening readers with lengthy references in the text.

At a crucial stage in the book's development, three distinguished professors and authors undertook a summary review of the manuscript, providing me with their general assessment of its underlying scientific assumptions: Lionel Tiger, Charles Darwin Professor of Anthropology at Rutgers University; David P. Barash, Professor of Psychology at the University of Washington; and David M. Buss, Professor of Psychology at the University of Texas. They managed to steer me clear of several lurking pitfalls, and the book profited greatly from their suggestions.

Over the long years that I thought about and worked on the book, friends, colleagues, and helping hands contributed their insights, read drafts, and offered encouragement. In particular, I wish to thank Bob Berman, Doug Childers, Eric Croddy, Tijen Kino, Lee Reynolds, and Larry Shurwitz for their productive provocations and helpful suggestions. Shannon McWeeney, Ph.D., Assistant Professor of Biostatistics and Bioinformatics at the Oregon Health & Science University, reviewed early drafts of the manuscript and guided me through the mysteries of genetic science. Jeremy Tarcher, a treasured friend and distinguished elder in the publishing world, offered sage counsel, pointing me in the right direction at several critical junctures.

Last, and hardly least, I would like to express my deep appreciation for the unstinting efforts of Douglas Wengell, my gifted researcher and editor. When by chance we met, this audacious enterprise took a mighty step forward. Douglas was a constant source of encouragement, even in the darkest hours. He played a crucial role in helping me develop my ideas with no end of trenchant editorial suggestions, always pushing me to do better. Most every page in the book benefits from his diligent research, nearly every paragraph is better for his deft editorial comments.

Like many authors who take this space to account for the errors and omissions in their work, I assume full responsibility for the book's conclusions and wish to relieve my contributors from any blame for the text's inaccuracies. This exculpation is especially necessary with *The Disposable Male*, which was written with the help of people who were not called upon to confirm its details and who do not necessarily share its opinions.

FURTHER READING

A complete bibliography, containing more than four hundred entries, can be found at www.thedisposablemale.com. Readers inclined to further explore the themes in this book may find the following references a good place to start.

On Human Nature by **Edward O. Wilson**
The distinguished Harvard naturalist, a Pulitzer Prize winner, and scientific titan drew together evolutionary thinking when he introduced sociobiology in the 1970s. In this modern classic, he explores the biological roots of human behavior with typical clarity and elegance. Three decades on, however, readers may discover that Dr. Wilson, a towering figure among secular humanists, let the gentleman get the better of the scientist in his pivotal chapter on sex. His artful equivocations over the nature/nurture divide between the human sexes and the issue of homosexuality did not, in the end, spare him the wrath of the era's angry placard carriers. Nor is it sufficient to diminish an otherwise brilliant book that brims with lucid insights.

The Selfish Gene by **Richard Dawkins**
A zoologist and professor of the public understanding of science at Oxford draws an unrelenting, albeit entertaining picture of life from a gene's point of view, a perspective that reminds us that there are genetic forces lurking behind nearly all of our human motives. Some readers may find this a bit daunting and prefer Dr. Dawkins's other more accessible and smartly crafted books, including *The Blind Watchmaker*, *River Out of Eden*, and *The Ancestor's Tale*.

Genome: The Autobiography of a Species in 23 Chapters by **Matt Ridley**
In this casual exploration, journalist Matt Ridley uses a newly discovered gene—the complete human genome was mapped at the millennium—from each of our twenty-three chromosomes to ponder the meaning and future application of genetics.

The Blank Slate: The Modern Denial of Human Nature by **Steven Pinker**
A Harvard psychology professor refutes the notion that we arrive in the world an empty vessel, suggesting instead that human behavior has long been shaped by the survival instinct. Avoiding rigid determinism, he argues with wit and

clarity that a world view grounded in our evolutionary past can "complement insights about the human condition."

Why We Love: The Nature and Chemistry of Romantic Love by **Helen Fisher**

In this accessible and fun read, Rutgers anthropologist Helen Fisher delves deeply into the evolutionary origins of love and romance.

What Our Mothers Didn't Tell Us: Why Happiness Eludes the Modern Woman by **Danielle Crittenden**

How does a modern woman balance independence and traditional feminine desires? In this thoughtful and relevant book, the vital differences between the sexes are deemed not only worthy of celebration but essential to women's fulfillment.

The War Against Boys: How Misguided Feminism Is Harming Our Young Men by **Christina Hoff Sommers**

"It's a bad time to be a boy in America," begins an account by American Enterprise Institute scholar Christina Hoff Sommers of how it became fashionable to label normal boy behavior as pathological. Her methodical criticism amounts to a casebook example of what happens when we substitute voguish philosophies for common sense.

The Moral Animal: The New Science of Evolutionary Psychology by **Robert Wright**

More than a decade after its debut, Robert Wright's book remains a lively and readable introduction to the burgeoning science of evolutionary psychology, which the author interweaves with the life story of Charles Darwin. Toward the book's end, he departs from his journalistic roots to contemplate evolution's ethical implications.

Readers may also find books of interest by the following authors: David M. Buss, Ann Crittenden, Daniel C. Dennett, Frans de Waal, Jared Diamond, Warren Farrell, Stephen Jay Gould, Sylvia Ann Hewlett, Desmond Morris, Lionel Tiger, and George Gilder (author of *Men and Marriage*).

Michael Gilbert
Douglas Wengell

INDEX

sowing wild oats strategy 44
Sexual interest
  high among males 241
Sexual parity
  diminishing women and
    demeaning men 260–61
Sexual selection 38, 54–55, 73
  amplifying specialties 79
  and gossip 85
  choosing intelligent partners 36
  development of 30–33
  qualities of the provider in past and
    present 37
Sexuality
  as sin 107
  celebrating 281–82
  double standards 96–98
Shelter
  introduction of 39
Single parenthood
  cost of 140
  electing 180–81
  rise in 138, 260
Single sex schooling
  benefits to both boys and girls 191
Single-minded concentration
  in men 74
Slavery 112
Snowe, Olympia 218
Social capital
  decline of 135
Social cohesion
  fortified by gossip 85
Social engineering 162–63, 168
Social isolation
  effects of disconnection from
    family 137
  hazards of 25
Social issues
  in early societies 83
Social structure
  of early agrarian societies 85

Socialism 121
  and scientific achievement 126
  going up against natural instinct
    124
Specialization xiv, 79, 270
  advent of 24
  encouraging 279
  gender 26
  leads to social contracts 46
  the despecializing of the sexes 194
Species
  development of new species 9
  number of 19
Speech
  development of 40–42
Spirituality 284
  increase in 132
Sports
  and proportionality in schools
    204–7, 254
  and racial differences 203
  compensating role for males 203
  confusion about natural place of
    athletics 207
  filling male competitive needs 201
  importance in men's lives 201–3
  leads to less crime and violence
    202
  physical disparities between the
    genders 206
  professional women's teams 206
  value of fan projection 202
  women in 202–6
Sports injuries
  increasing in women 206
Stalking
  rise in 265
Stanton, Elizabeth Cady 167
Status 85
  in early civilizations 103
Stress
  in America 134